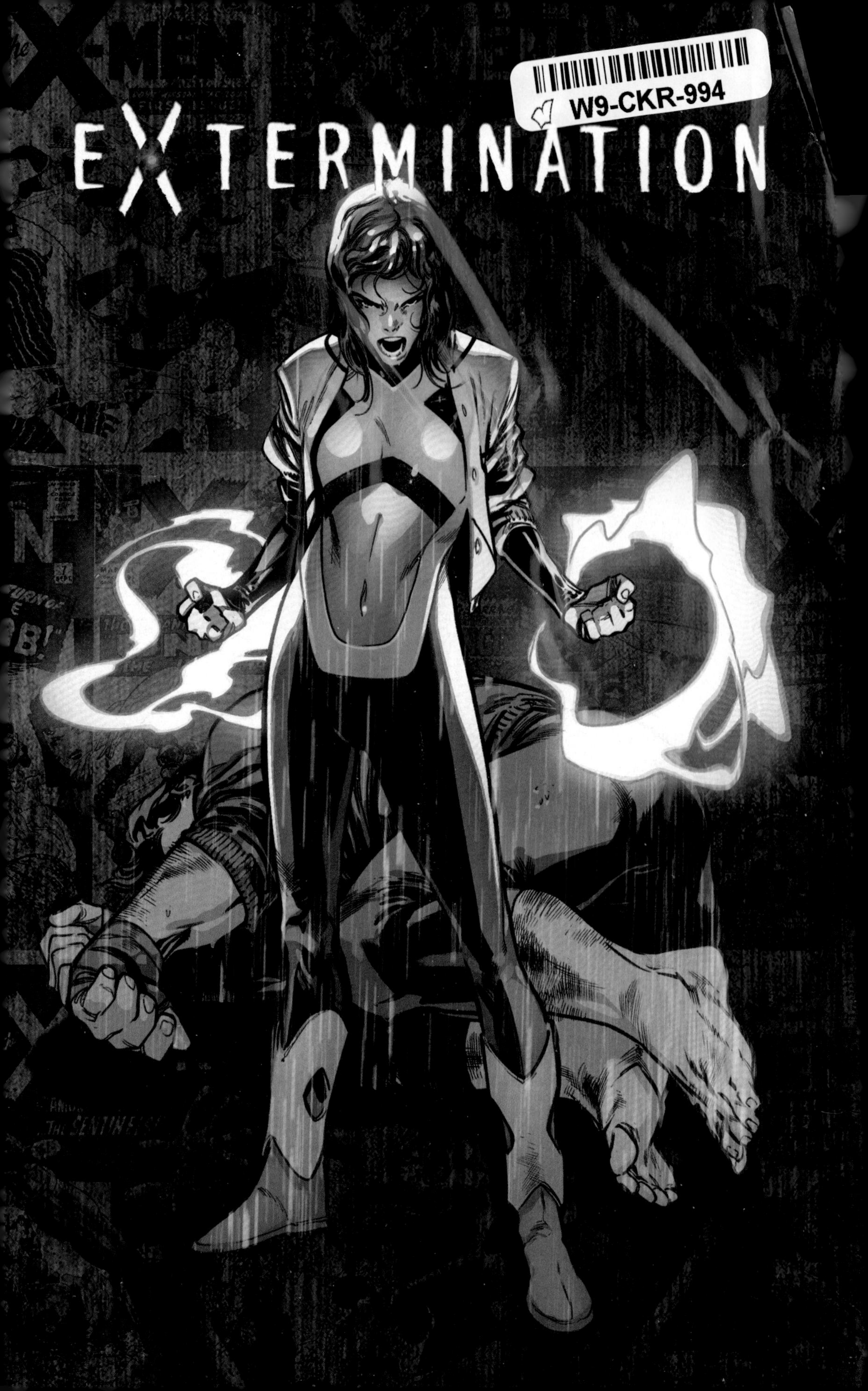
X-MEN
EXTERMINATION

**EXTERMINATION.** Contains material originally published in magazine form as EXTERMINATION #1-5. First printing 2018. ISBN 978-1-302-91357-1. Published by MARVEL WORLDWIDE, INC., a subsidiary of MARVEL ENTERTAINMENT, LLC. OFFICE OF PUBLICATION: 135 West 50th Street, New York, NY 10020. Copyright © 2018 MARVEL No similarity between any of the names, characters, persons, and/or institutions in this magazine with those of any living or dead person or institution is intended, and any such similarity which may exist is purely coincidental. **Printed in Canada.** DAN BUCKLEY, President, Marvel Entertainment; JOHN NEE, Publisher; JOE QUESADA, Chief Creative Officer; TOM BREVOORT, SVP of Publishing; DAVID BOGART, SVP of Business Affairs & Operations, Publishing & Partnership; DAVID GABRIEL, SVP of Sales & Marketing, Publishing; JEFF YOUNGQUIST, VP of Production & Special Projects; DAN CARR, Executive Director of Publishing Technology; ALEX MORALES, Director of Publishing Operations; DAN EDINGTON, Managing Editor; SUSAN CRESPI, Production Manager; STAN LEE, Chairman Emeritus. For information regarding advertising in Marvel Comics or on Marvel.com, please contact Vit DeBellis, Custom Solutions & Integrated Advertising Manager, at vdebellis@marvel.com. For Marvel subscription inquiries, please call 888-511-5480. **Manufactured between 11/29/2018 and 12/31/2018 by SOLISCO PRINTERS, SCOTT, QC, CANADA.**

1 0 9 8 7 6 5 4 3 2 1

GENETICALLY GIFTED WITH UNCANNY ABILITIES, MUTANTS ARE BELIEVED TO BE THE NEXT STAGE OF HUMAN EVOLUTION. WHILE THE WORLD HATES AND FEARS THEM, TEAMS OF MUTANT HEROES KNOWN AS X-MEN USE THEIR POWERS FOR GOOD AND TO SPREAD A POSITIVE IMAGE OF MUTANTKIND.

# EXTERMINATION

BELIEVING THE X-MEN HAD LOST THEIR WAY, BEAST (A.K.A. HANK McCOY) USED TIME-TRAVEL TECHNOLOGY TO BRING HIS YOUNGER SELF AND THE OTHER FIRST FIVE STUDENTS OF CHARLES XAVIER (CYCLOPS, A.K.A. SCOTT SUMMERS; MARVEL GIRL, A.K.A. JEAN GREY; ICEMAN, A.K.A. BOBBY DRAKE; AND ANGEL, A.K.A. WARREN WORTHINGTON III) TO THE PRESENT TO INSPIRE THE X-MEN AND SET THE FUTURE RIGHT.

SINCE THEN, ALTHOUGH THEIR MISSION OF HOPE AND MUTANT AID REMAINS THE SAME, THE ORIGINAL FIVE X-MEN'S ADVENTURES IN THE PRESENT HAVE LEFT THEM IRREVOCABLY CHANGED.

## Ed Brisson
WRITER

ISSUES #1-3 & #5

## Pepe Larraz
ARTIST

## Marte Gracia
COLOR ARTIST

ISSUE #4

## Pepe Larraz
LAYOUTS

## Ario Anindito
PENCILER

## Dexter Vines
INKER

## Erick Arciniega
COLOR ARTIST

## VC's Joe Sabino
LETTERER

## Mark Brooks
COVER ART

## Chris Robinson & Danny Khazem
ASSISTANT EDITORS

## Darren Shan
EDITOR

## Jordan D. White
X-MEN GROUP EDITOR

SPECIAL THANKS TO MARK PANICCIA

X-MEN CREATED BY STAN LEE & JACK KIRBY

COLLECTION EDITOR JENNIFER GRÜNWALD    ASSISTANT EDITOR CAITLIN O'CONNELL
ASSOCIATE MANAGING EDITOR KATERI WOODY    EDITOR, SPECIAL PROJECTS MARK D. BEAZLEY
VP PRODUCTION & SPECIAL PROJECTS JEFF YOUNGQUIST    SVP PRINT, SALES & MARKETING DAVID GABRIEL
BOOK DESIGNER JAY BOWEN

EDITOR IN CHIEF C.B. CEBULSKI    CHIEF CREATIVE OFFICER JOE QUESADA
PRESIDENT DAN BUCKLEY    EXECUTIVE PRODUCER ALAN FINE

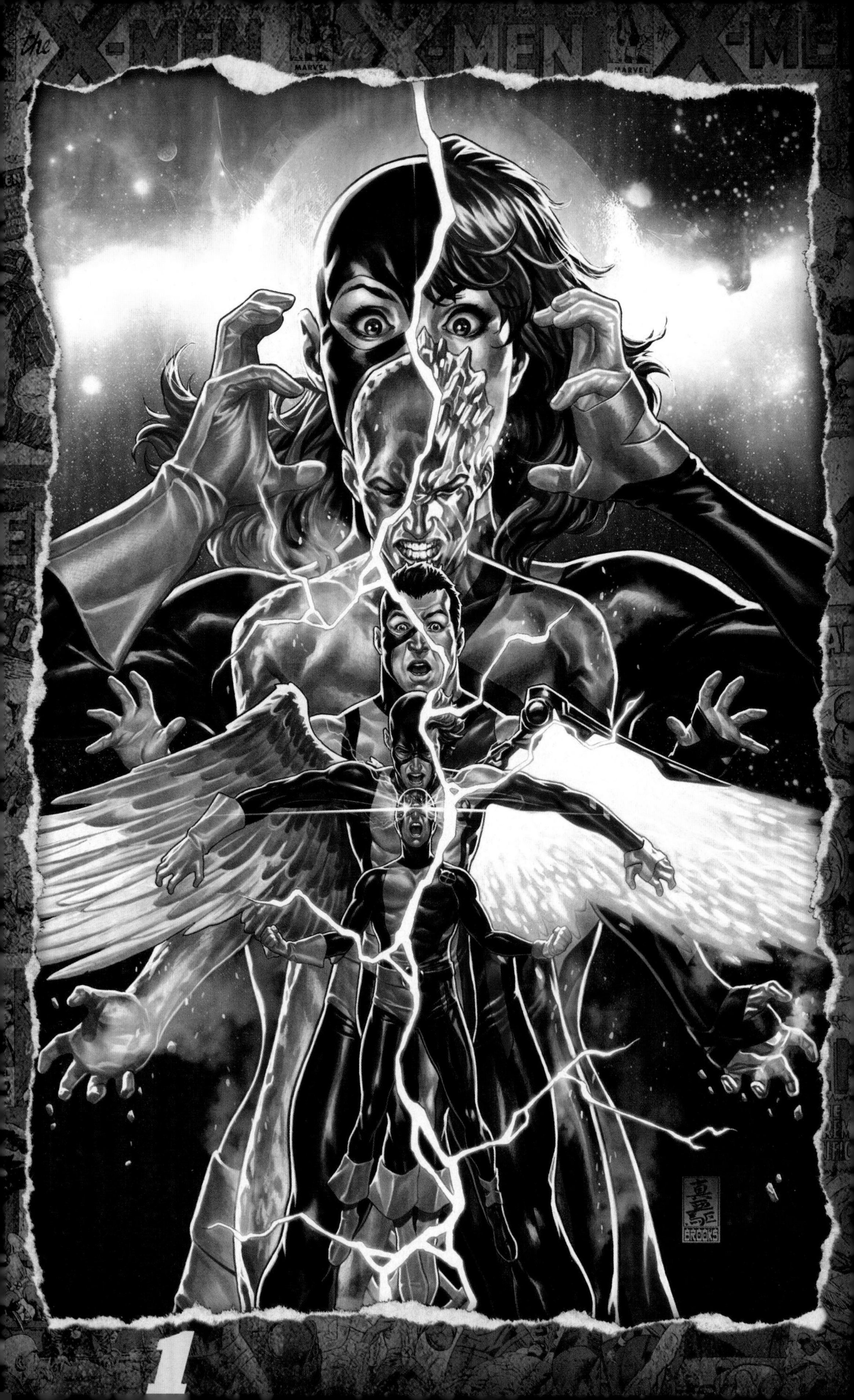
the X-MEN
X-MEN
BROOKS
1

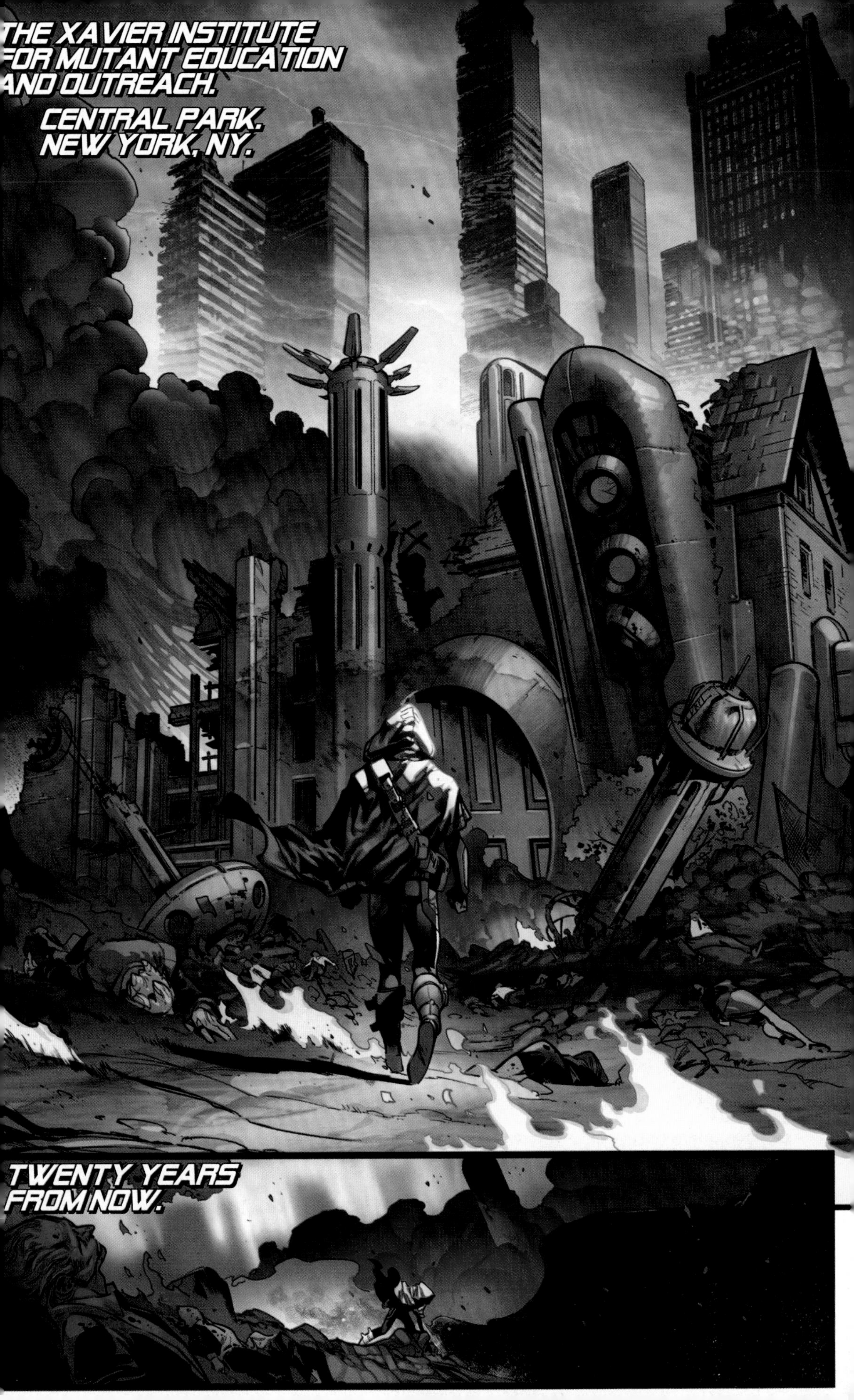
THE XAVIER INSTITUTE FOR MUTANT EDUCATION AND OUTREACH.
CENTRAL PARK. NEW YORK, NY.
TWENTY YEARS FROM NOW.

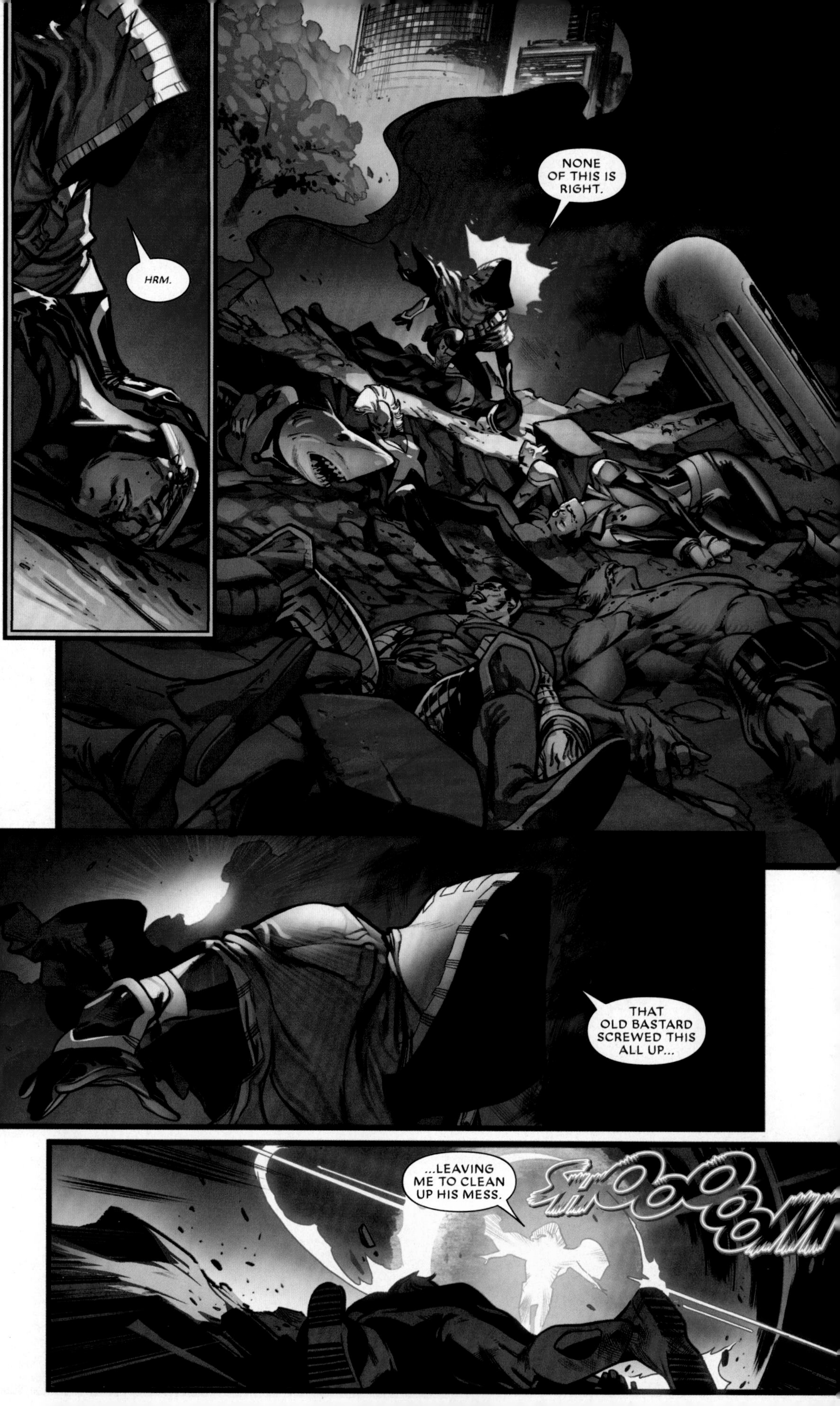
HRM.
NONE OF THIS IS RIGHT.
THAT OLD BASTARD SCREWED THIS ALL UP...
...LEAVING ME TO CLEAN UP HIS MESS.
SHROOOOOM!!

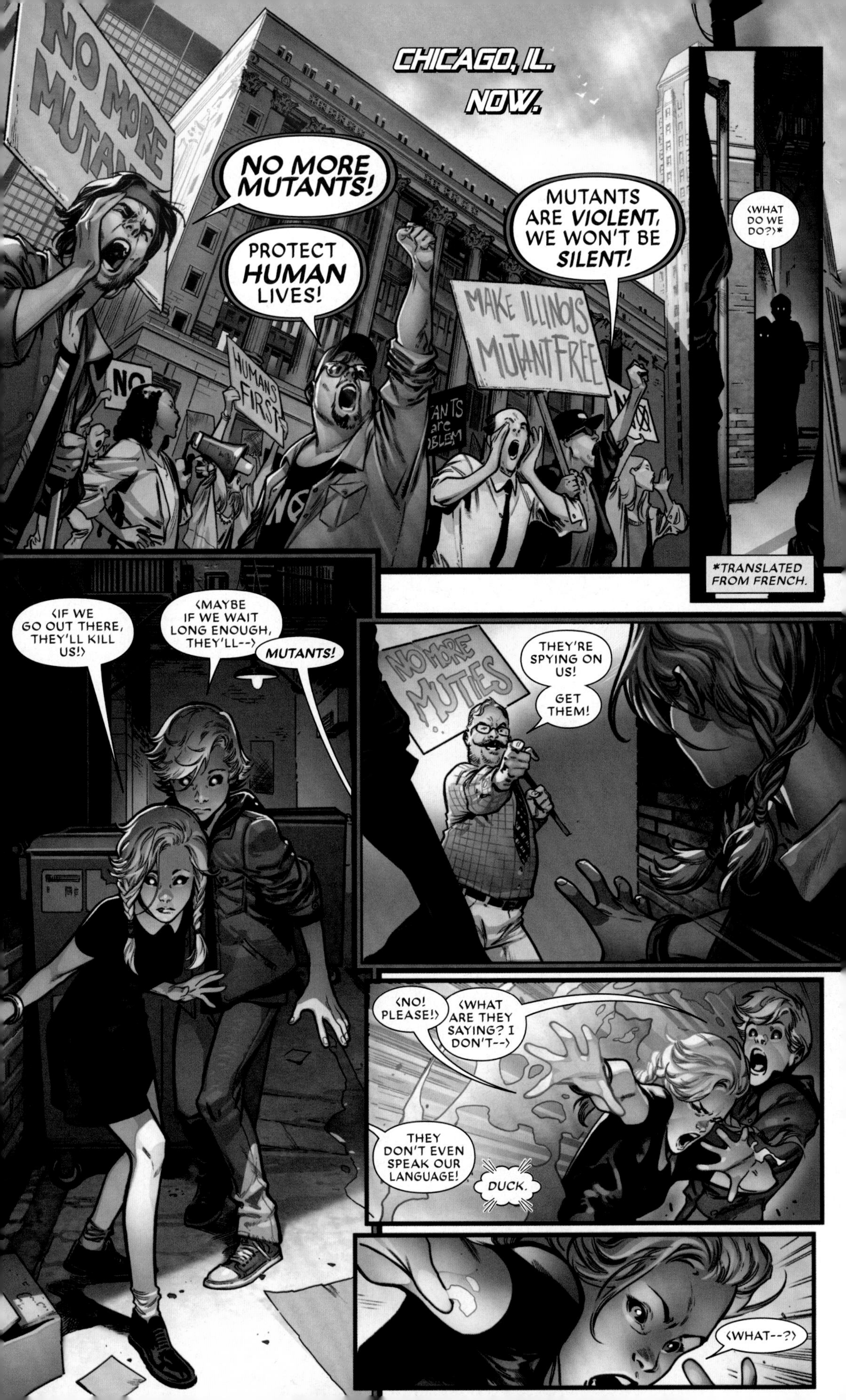
CHICAGO, IL.
NOW.
NO MORE MUTANTS!
NO MORE MUTANTS!
PROTECT HUMAN LIVES!
MUTANTS ARE VIOLENT, WE WON'T BE SILENT!
MAKE ILLINOIS MUTANT FREE
HUMANS FIRST
‹WHAT DO WE DO?›*
*TRANSLATED FROM FRENCH.
‹IF WE GO OUT THERE, THEY'LL KILL US!›
‹MAYBE IF WE WAIT LONG ENOUGH, THEY'LL--›
MUTANTS!
NO MORE MUTIES
THEY'RE SPYING ON US!
GET THEM!
‹NO! PLEASE!›
‹WHAT ARE THEY SAYING? I DON'T--›
THEY DON'T EVEN SPEAK OUR LANGUAGE!
DUCK.
‹WHAT--?›

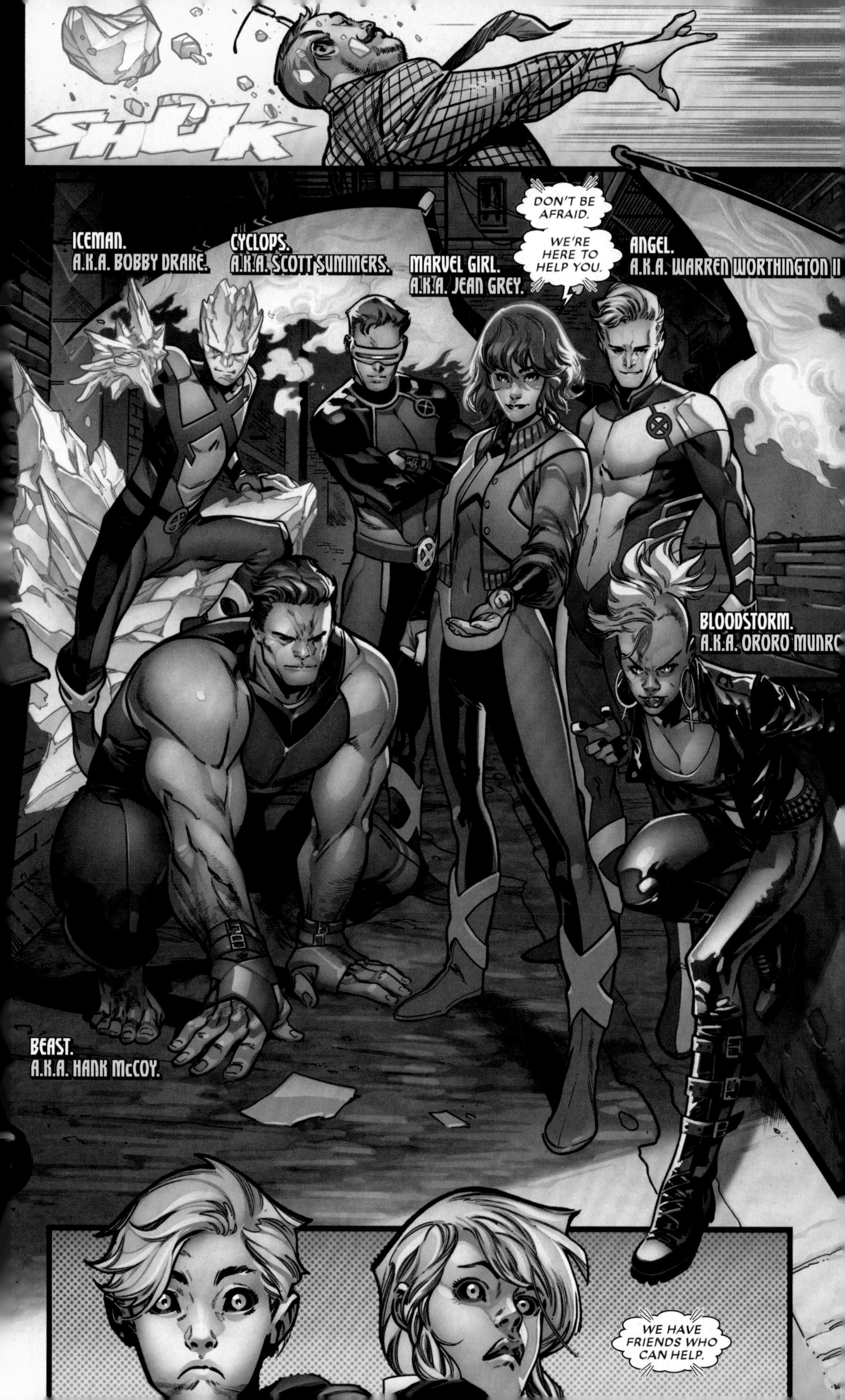
SHUK
ICEMAN.
A.K.A. BOBBY DRAKE.
CYCLOPS.
A.K.A. SCOTT SUMMERS.
MARVEL GIRL.
A.K.A. JEAN GREY.
DON'T BE AFRAID.
WE'RE HERE TO HELP YOU.
ANGEL.
A.K.A. WARREN WORTHINGTON II
BLOODSTORM.
A.K.A. ORORO MUNRO
BEAST.
A.K.A. HANK McCOY.
WE HAVE FRIENDS WHO CAN HELP.

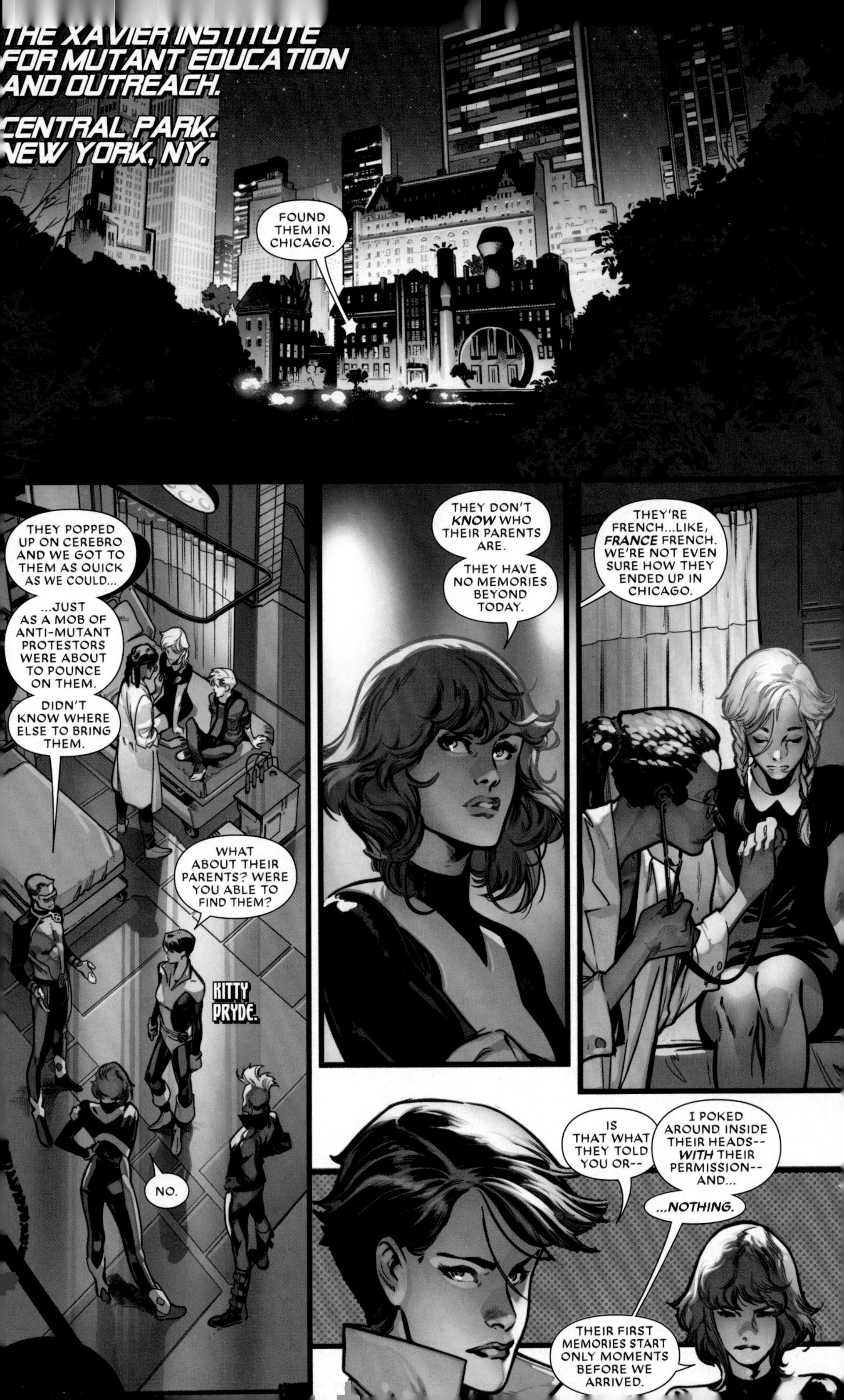
THE XAVIER INSTITUTE FOR MUTANT EDUCATION AND OUTREACH.
CENTRAL PARK. NEW YORK, NY.
FOUND THEM IN CHICAGO.
THEY POPPED UP ON CEREBRO AND WE GOT TO THEM AS QUICK AS WE COULD...
...JUST AS A MOB OF ANTI-MUTANT PROTESTORS WERE ABOUT TO POUNCE ON THEM.
DIDN'T KNOW WHERE ELSE TO BRING THEM.
WHAT ABOUT THEIR PARENTS? WERE YOU ABLE TO FIND THEM?
KITTY PRYDE.
NO.
THEY DON'T *KNOW* WHO THEIR PARENTS ARE.
THEY HAVE NO MEMORIES BEYOND TODAY.
THEY'RE FRENCH...LIKE, *FRANCE* FRENCH. WE'RE NOT EVEN SURE HOW THEY ENDED UP IN CHICAGO.
IS THAT WHAT THEY TOLD YOU OR--
I POKED AROUND INSIDE THEIR HEADS-- *WITH* THEIR PERMISSION-- AND...
*...NOTHING.*
THEIR FIRST MEMORIES START ONLY MOMENTS BEFORE WE ARRIVED.

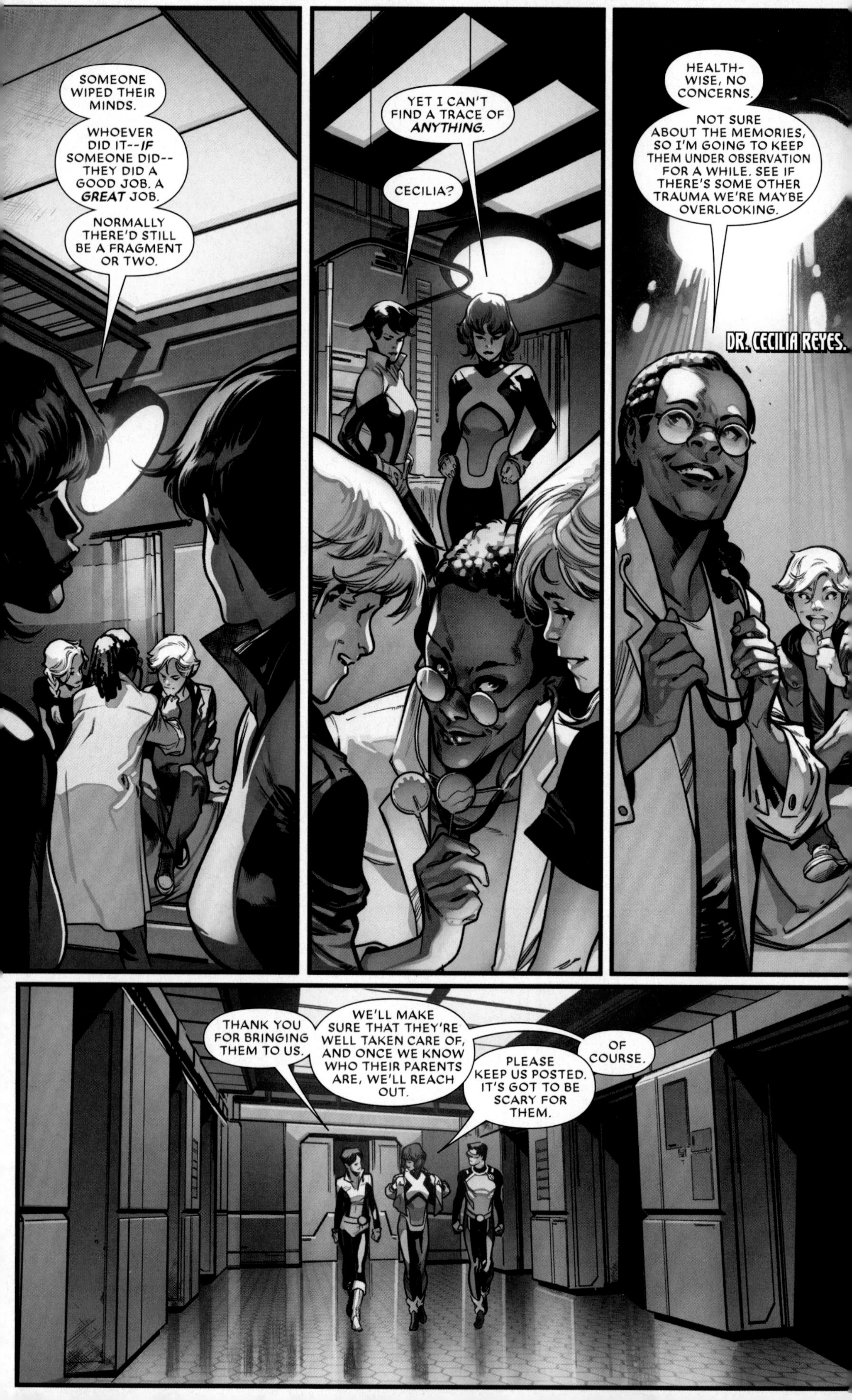
SOMEONE WIPED THEIR MINDS.
WHOEVER DID IT--*IF* SOMEONE DID--THEY DID A GOOD JOB. A *GREAT* JOB.
NORMALLY THERE'D STILL BE A FRAGMENT OR TWO.
YET I CAN'T FIND A TRACE OF *ANYTHING*.
CECILIA?
HEALTH-WISE, NO CONCERNS.
NOT SURE ABOUT THE MEMORIES, SO I'M GOING TO KEEP THEM UNDER OBSERVATION FOR A WHILE. SEE IF THERE'S SOME OTHER TRAUMA WE'RE MAYBE OVERLOOKING.
DR. CECILIA REYES.
THANK YOU FOR BRINGING THEM TO US.
WE'LL MAKE SURE THAT THEY'RE WELL TAKEN CARE OF, AND ONCE WE KNOW WHO THEIR PARENTS ARE, WE'LL REACH OUT.
OF COURSE.
PLEASE KEEP US POSTED. IT'S GOT TO BE SCARY FOR THEM.

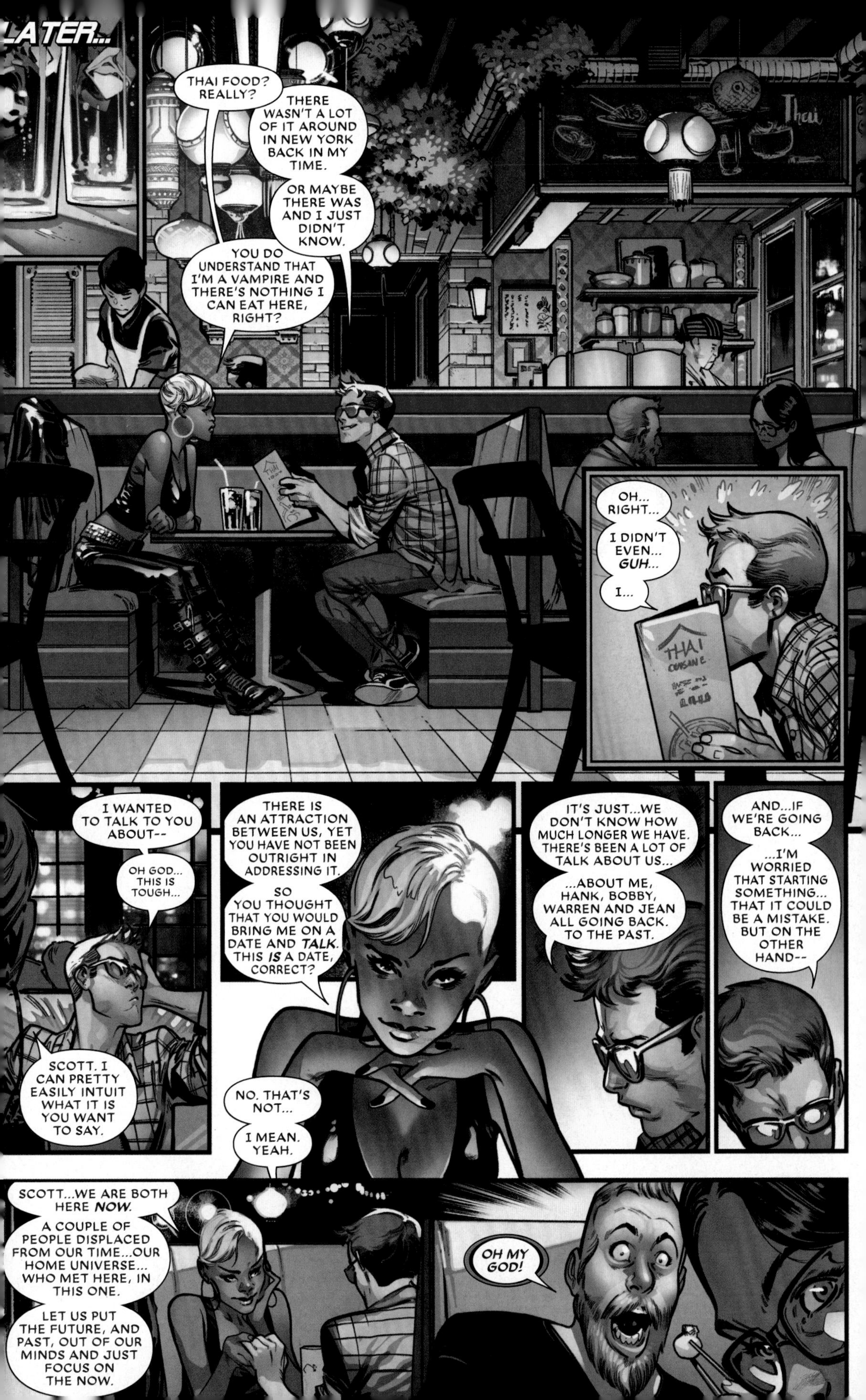
LATER...
THAI FOOD? REALLY?
THERE WASN'T A LOT OF IT AROUND IN NEW YORK BACK IN MY TIME.
OR MAYBE THERE WAS AND I JUST DIDN'T KNOW.
YOU DO UNDERSTAND THAT I'M A VAMPIRE AND THERE'S NOTHING I CAN EAT HERE, RIGHT?
OH... RIGHT...
I DIDN'T EVEN... GUH...
I...
I WANTED TO TALK TO YOU ABOUT--
OH GOD... THIS IS TOUGH...
SCOTT. I CAN PRETTY EASILY INTUIT WHAT IT IS YOU WANT TO SAY.
THERE IS AN ATTRACTION BETWEEN US, YET YOU HAVE NOT BEEN OUTRIGHT IN ADDRESSING IT.
SO YOU THOUGHT THAT YOU WOULD BRING ME ON A DATE AND TALK. THIS IS A DATE, CORRECT?
NO. THAT'S NOT...
I MEAN. YEAH.
IT'S JUST...WE DON'T KNOW HOW MUCH LONGER WE HAVE. THERE'S BEEN A LOT OF TALK ABOUT US...
...ABOUT ME, HANK, BOBBY, WARREN AND JEAN ALL GOING BACK. TO THE PAST.
AND...IF WE'RE GOING BACK...
...I'M WORRIED THAT STARTING SOMETHING... THAT IT COULD BE A MISTAKE. BUT ON THE OTHER HAND--
SCOTT...WE ARE BOTH HERE NOW.
A COUPLE OF PEOPLE DISPLACED FROM OUR TIME...OUR HOME UNIVERSE... WHO MET HERE, IN THIS ONE.
LET US PUT THE FUTURE, AND PAST, OUT OF OUR MINDS AND JUST FOCUS ON THE NOW.
OH MY GOD!

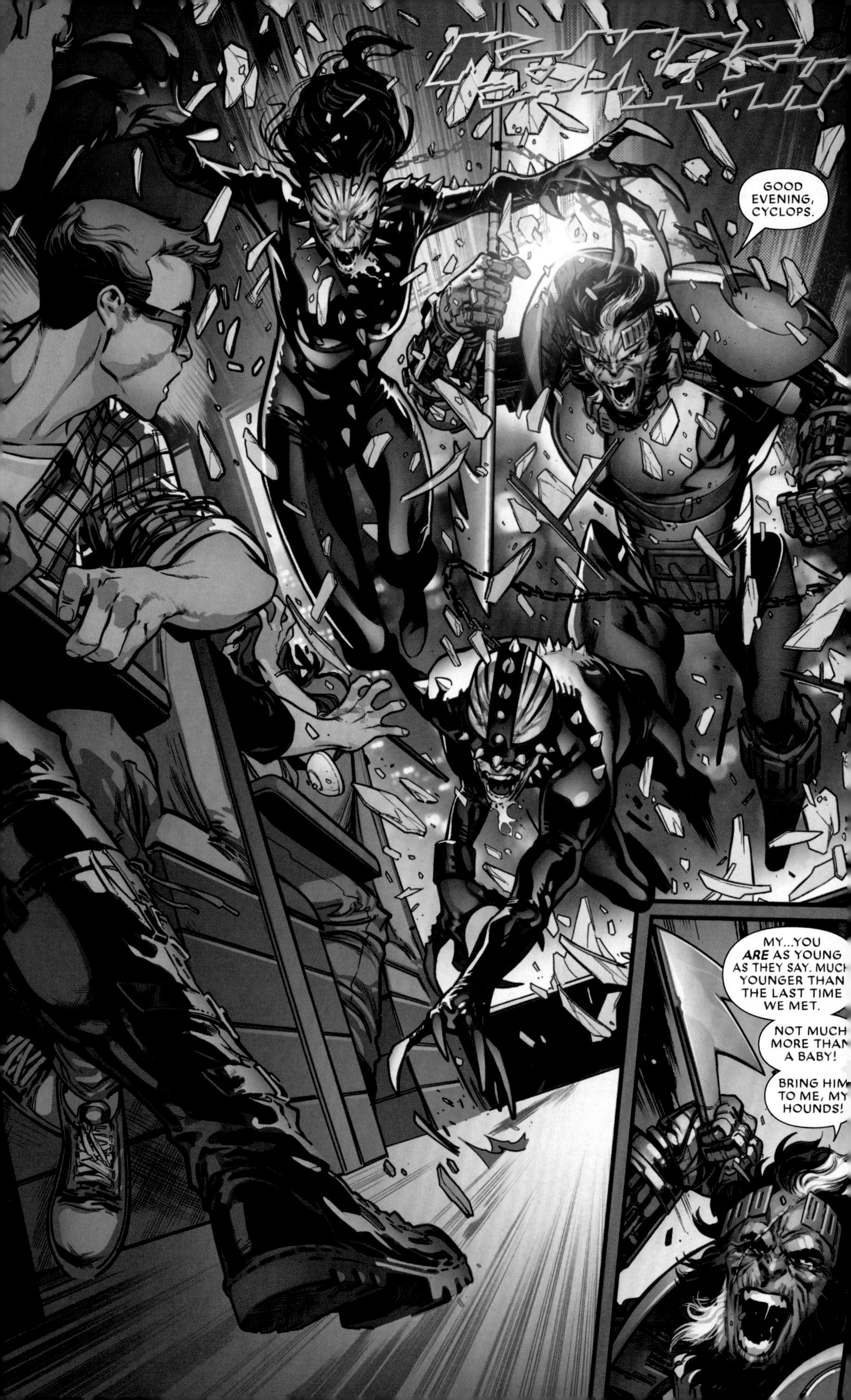
GOOD EVENING, CYCLOPS.
MY...YOU ARE AS YOUNG AS THEY SAY. MUCH YOUNGER THAN THE LAST TIME WE MET.
NOT MUCH MORE THAN A BABY!
BRING HIM TO ME, MY HOUNDS!

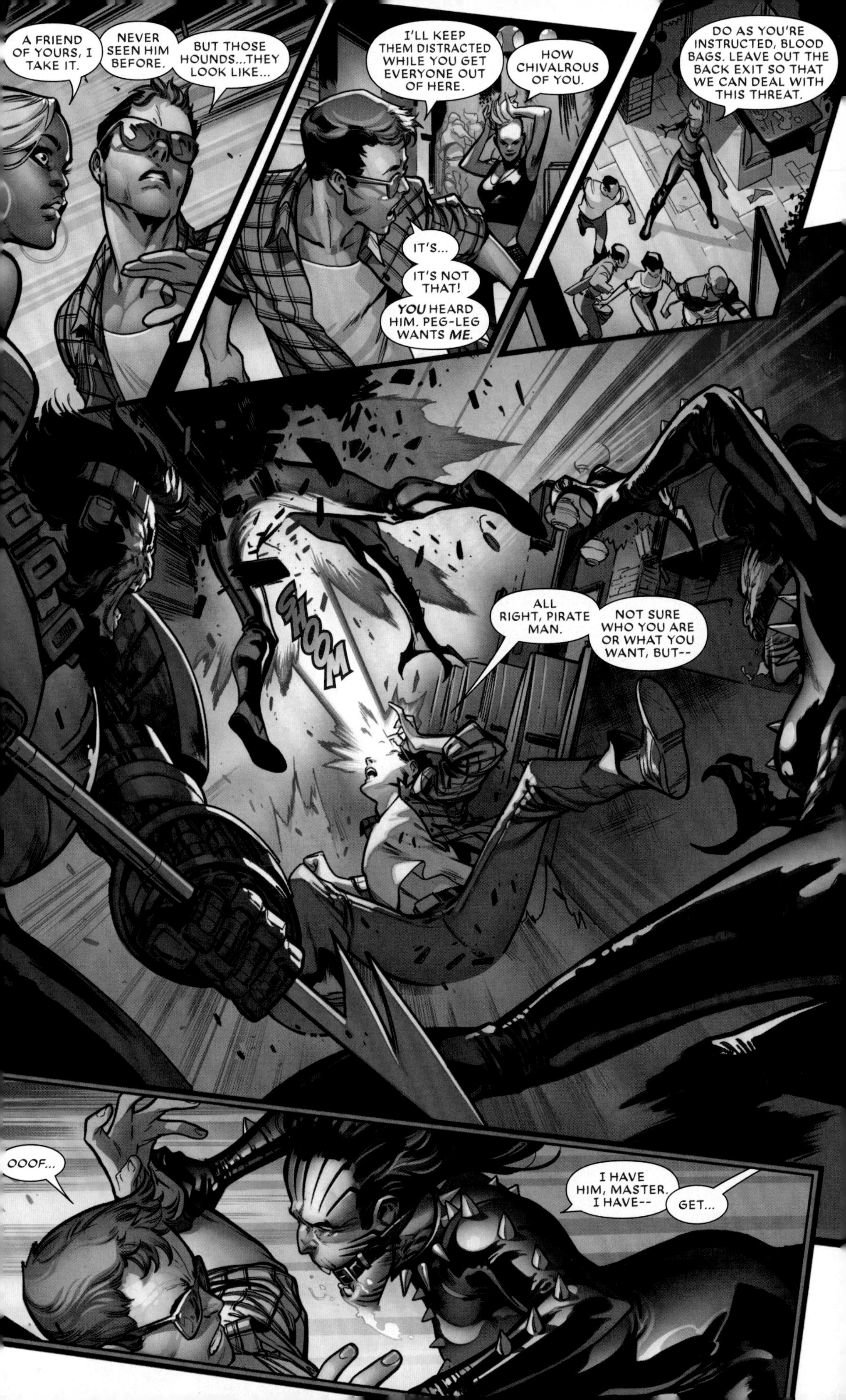
A FRIEND OF YOURS, I TAKE IT.
NEVER SEEN HIM BEFORE.
BUT THOSE HOUNDS...THEY LOOK LIKE...
I'LL KEEP THEM DISTRACTED WHILE YOU GET EVERYONE OUT OF HERE.
HOW CHIVALROUS OF YOU.
IT'S...
IT'S NOT THAT!
*YOU* HEARD HIM. PEG-LEG WANTS *ME*.
DO AS YOU'RE INSTRUCTED, BLOOD BAGS. LEAVE OUT THE BACK EXIT SO THAT WE CAN DEAL WITH THIS THREAT.
GHOOM
ALL RIGHT, PIRATE MAN.
NOT SURE WHO YOU ARE OR WHAT YOU WANT, BUT--
OOOF...
I HAVE HIM, MASTER. I HAVE--
GET...

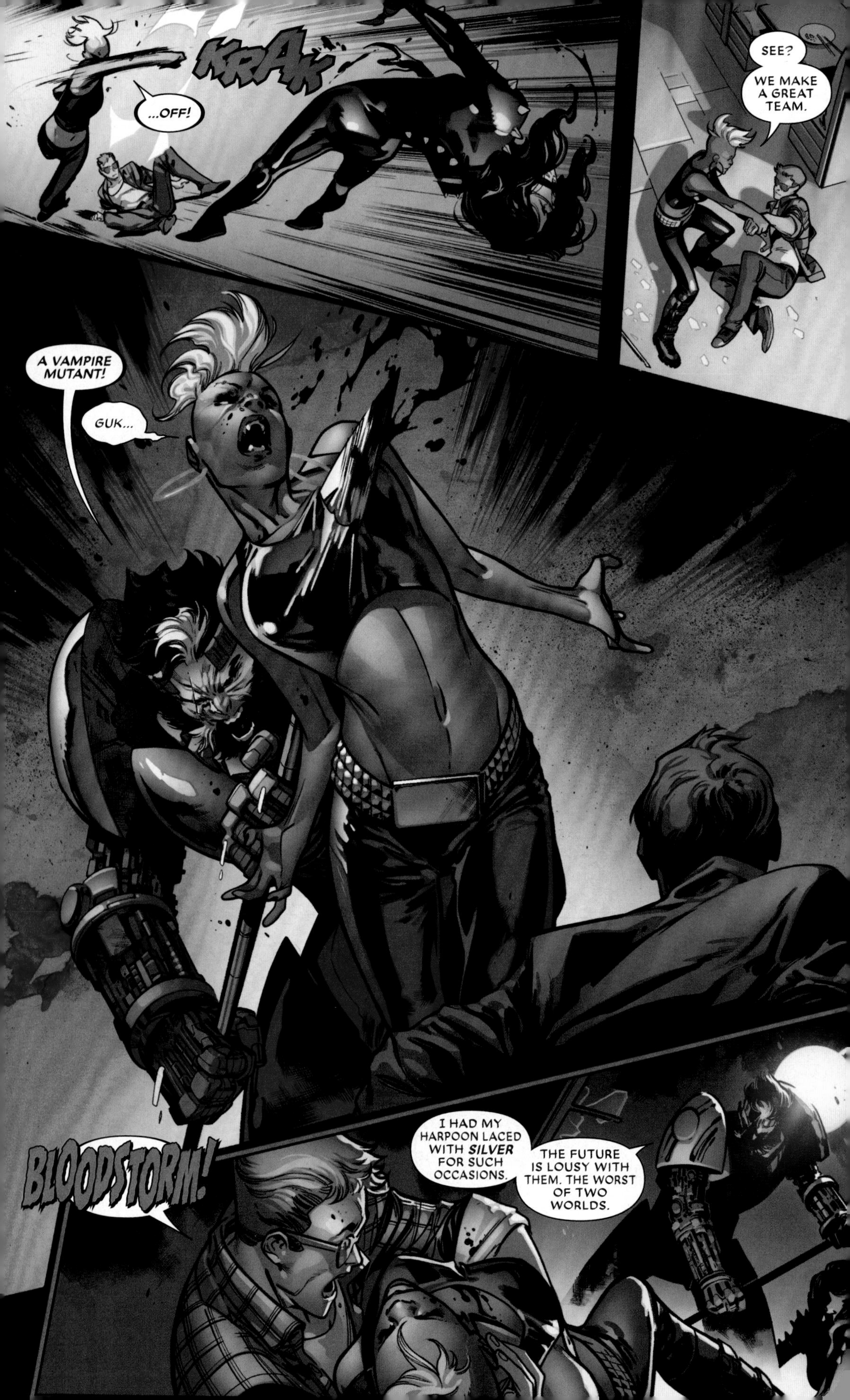
KRAK
...OFF!
SEE?
WE MAKE A GREAT TEAM.
A VAMPIRE MUTANT!
GUK...
BLOODSTORM!
I HAD MY HARPOON LACED WITH SILVER FOR SUCH OCCASIONS.
THE FUTURE IS LOUSY WITH THEM. THE WORST OF TWO WORLDS.

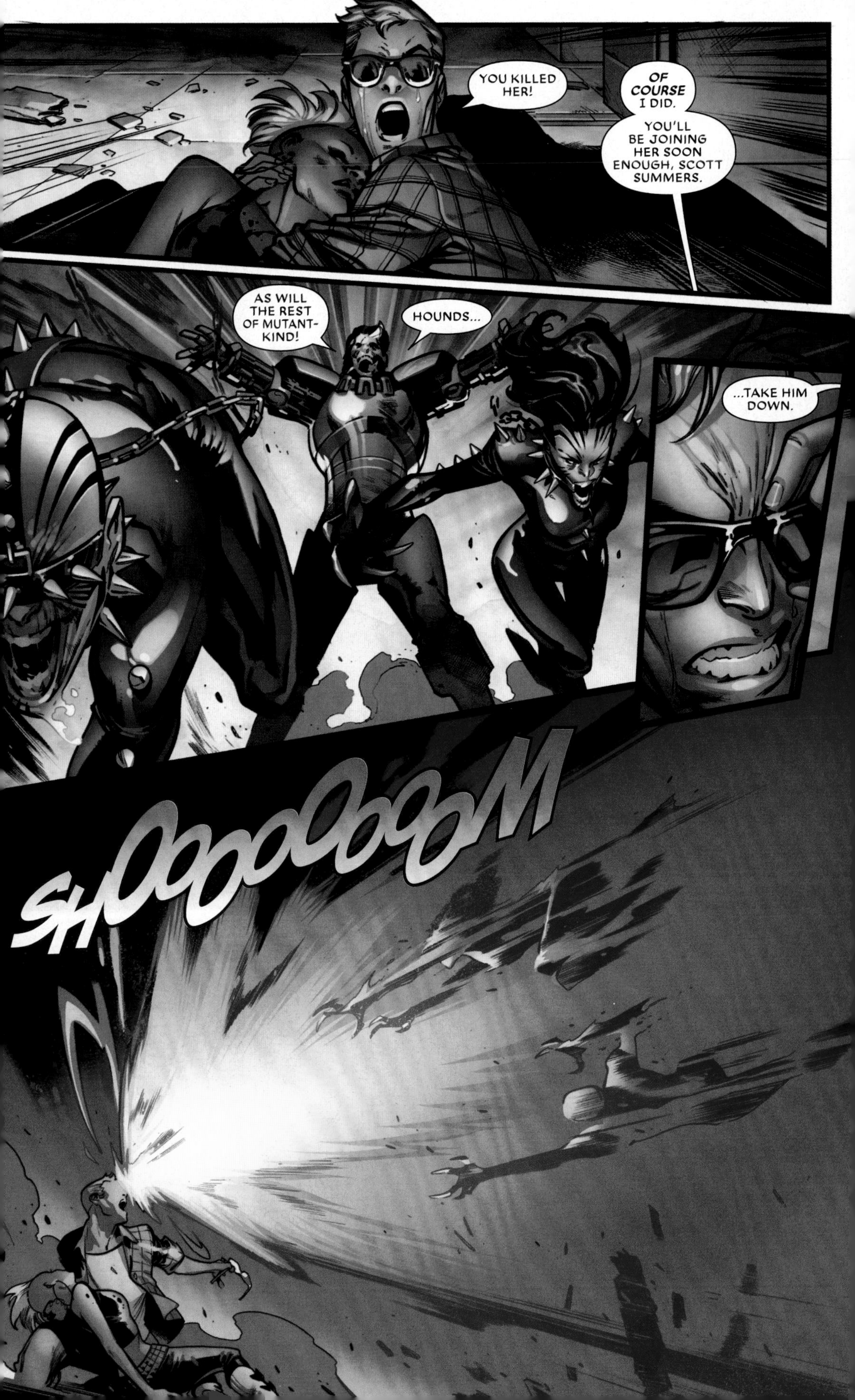
YOU KILLED HER!
OF COURSE I DID.
YOU'LL BE JOINING HER SOON ENOUGH, SCOTT SUMMERS.
AS WILL THE REST OF MUTANT-KIND!
HOUNDS...
...TAKE HIM DOWN.
SHOOOOOOOOM

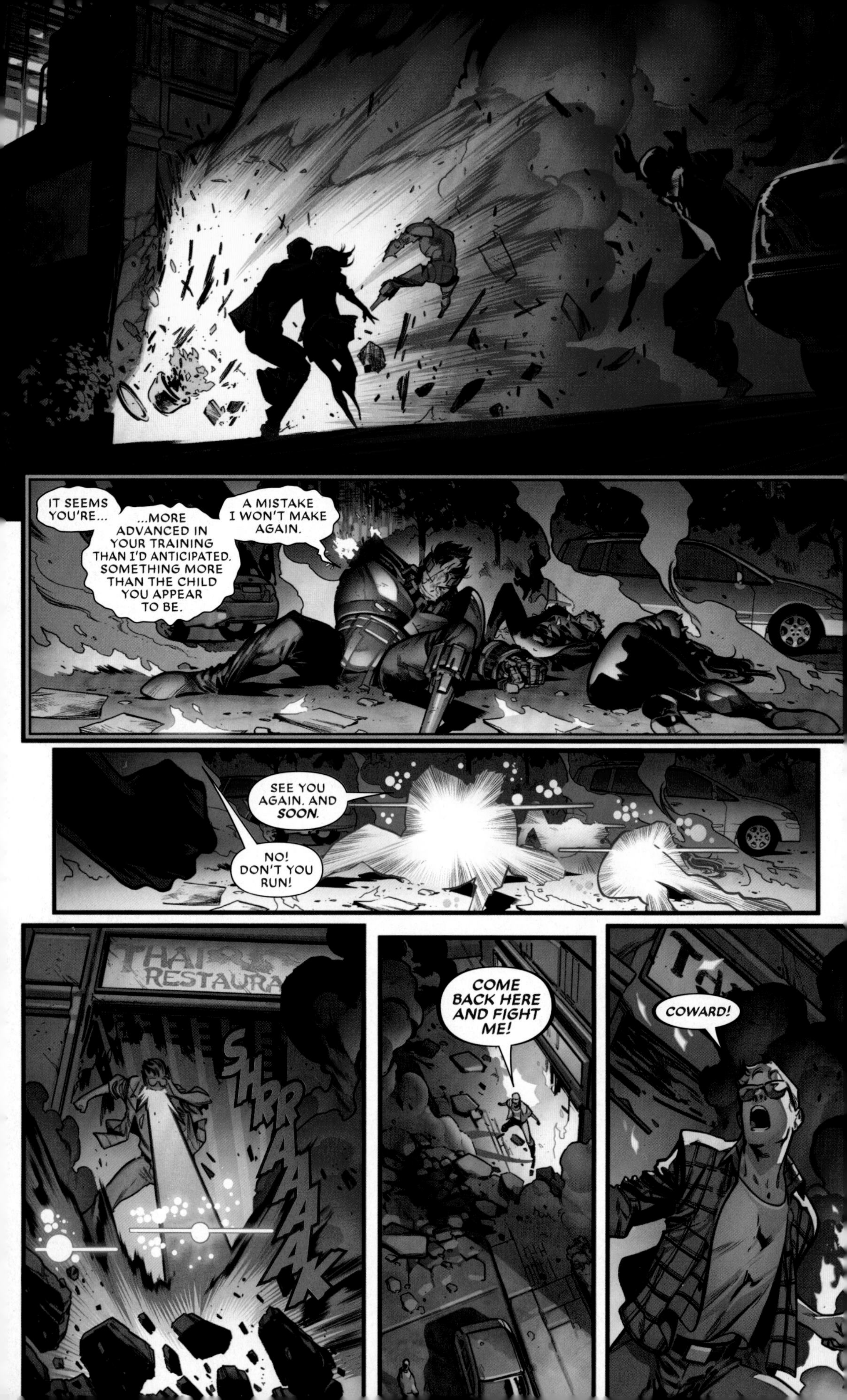
IT SEEMS YOU'RE...
...MORE ADVANCED IN YOUR TRAINING THAN I'D ANTICIPATED. SOMETHING MORE THAN THE CHILD YOU APPEAR TO BE.
A MISTAKE I WON'T MAKE AGAIN.
SEE YOU AGAIN. AND *SOON.*
NO! DON'T YOU RUN!
THAI RESTAURA
SHRRAAAK
COME BACK HERE AND FIGHT ME!
COWARD!

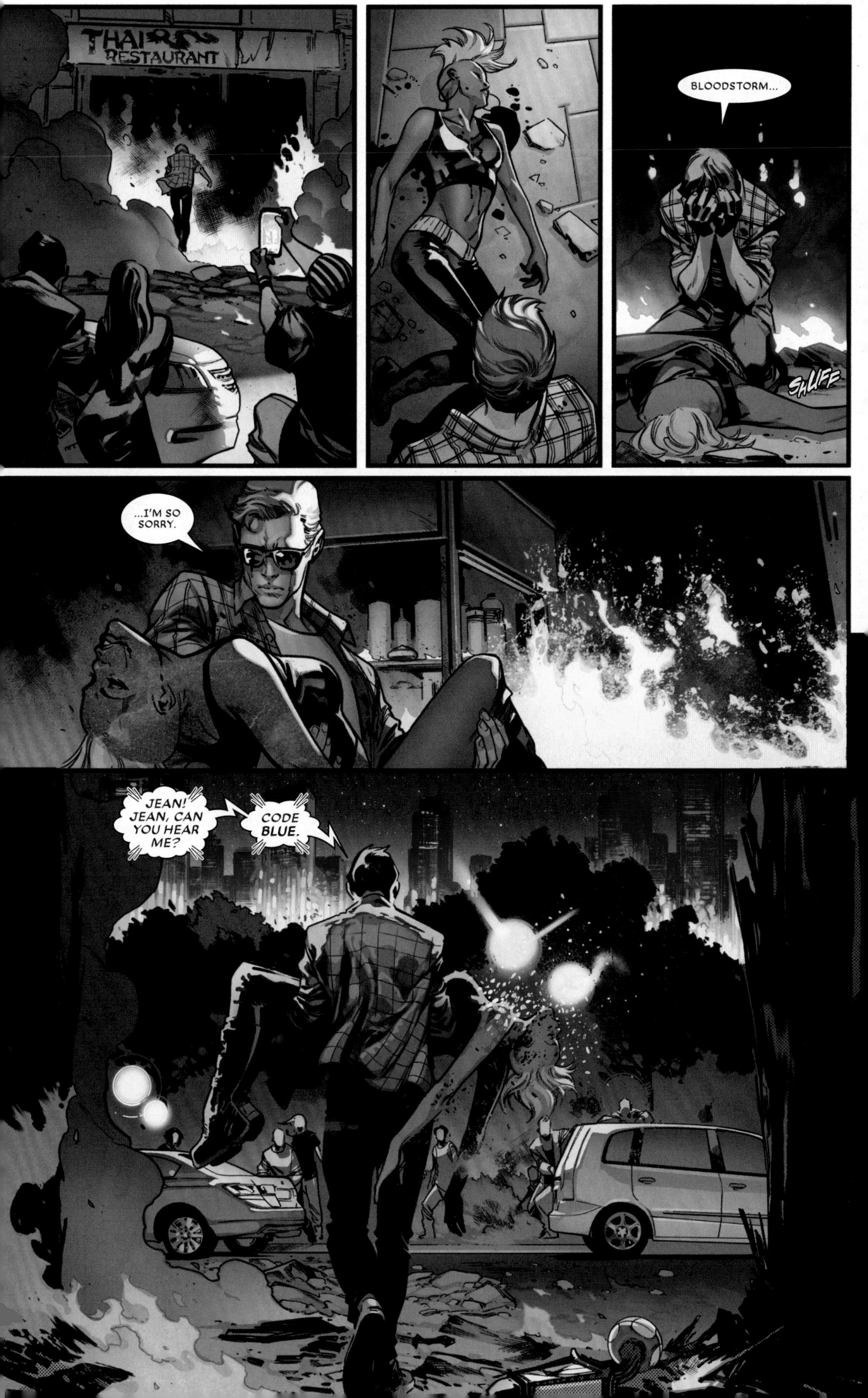
THAI RESTAURANT
BLOODSTORM...
SHUFF
...I'M SO SORRY.
JEAN! JEAN, CAN YOU HEAR ME?
CODE BLUE.

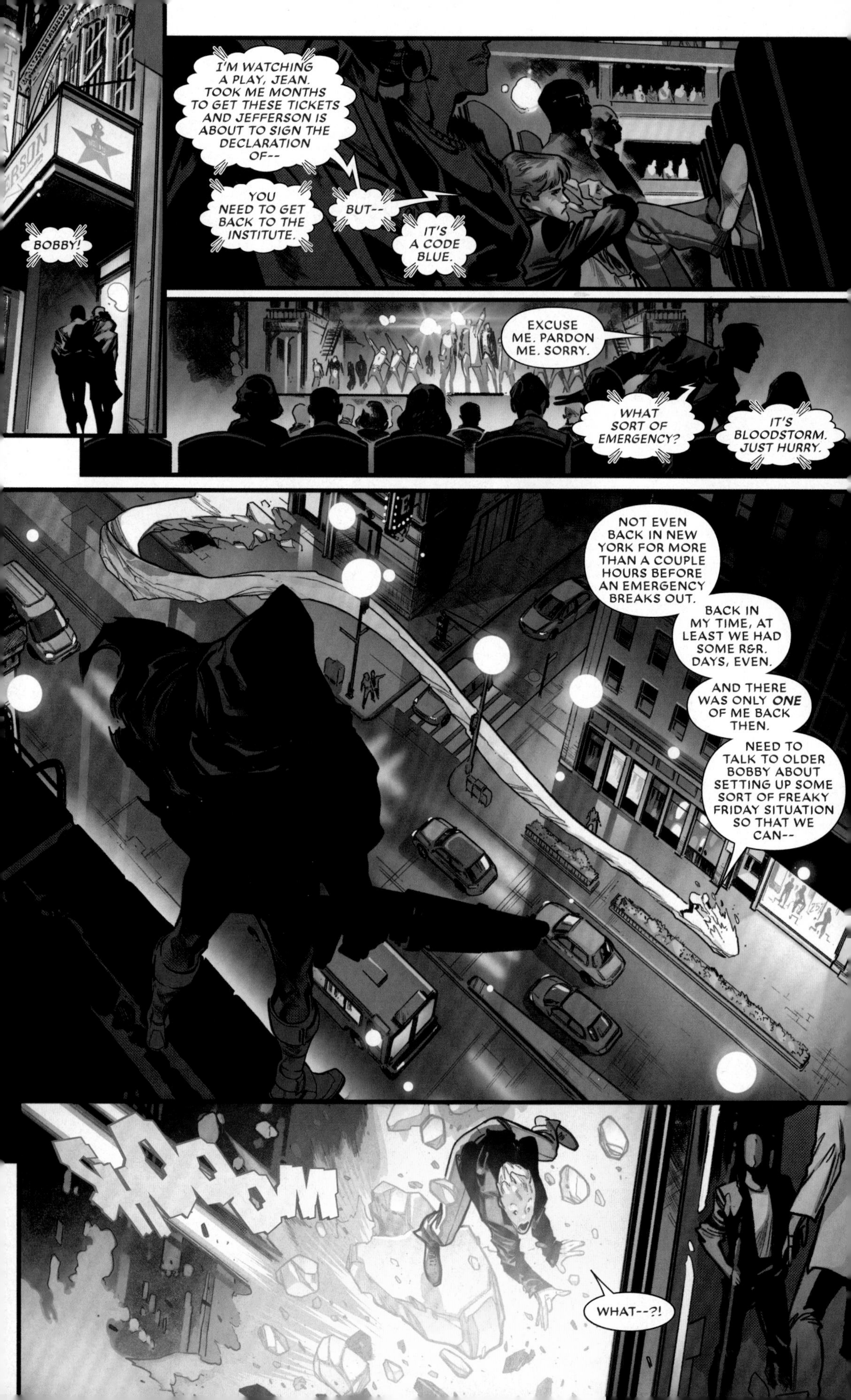
I'M WATCHING A PLAY, JEAN. TOOK ME MONTHS TO GET THESE TICKETS AND JEFFERSON IS ABOUT TO SIGN THE DECLARATION OF--
YOU NEED TO GET BACK TO THE INSTITUTE.
BUT--
IT'S A CODE BLUE.
BOBBY!
EXCUSE ME. PARDON ME. SORRY.
WHAT SORT OF EMERGENCY?
IT'S BLOODSTORM. JUST HURRY.
NOT EVEN BACK IN NEW YORK FOR MORE THAN A COUPLE HOURS BEFORE AN EMERGENCY BREAKS OUT.
BACK IN MY TIME, AT LEAST WE HAD SOME R&R DAYS, EVEN.
AND THERE WAS ONLY ONE OF ME BACK THEN.
NEED TO TALK TO OLDER BOBBY ABOUT SETTING UP SOME SORT OF FREAKY FRIDAY SITUATION SO THAT WE CAN--
SKOOM
WHAT--?!

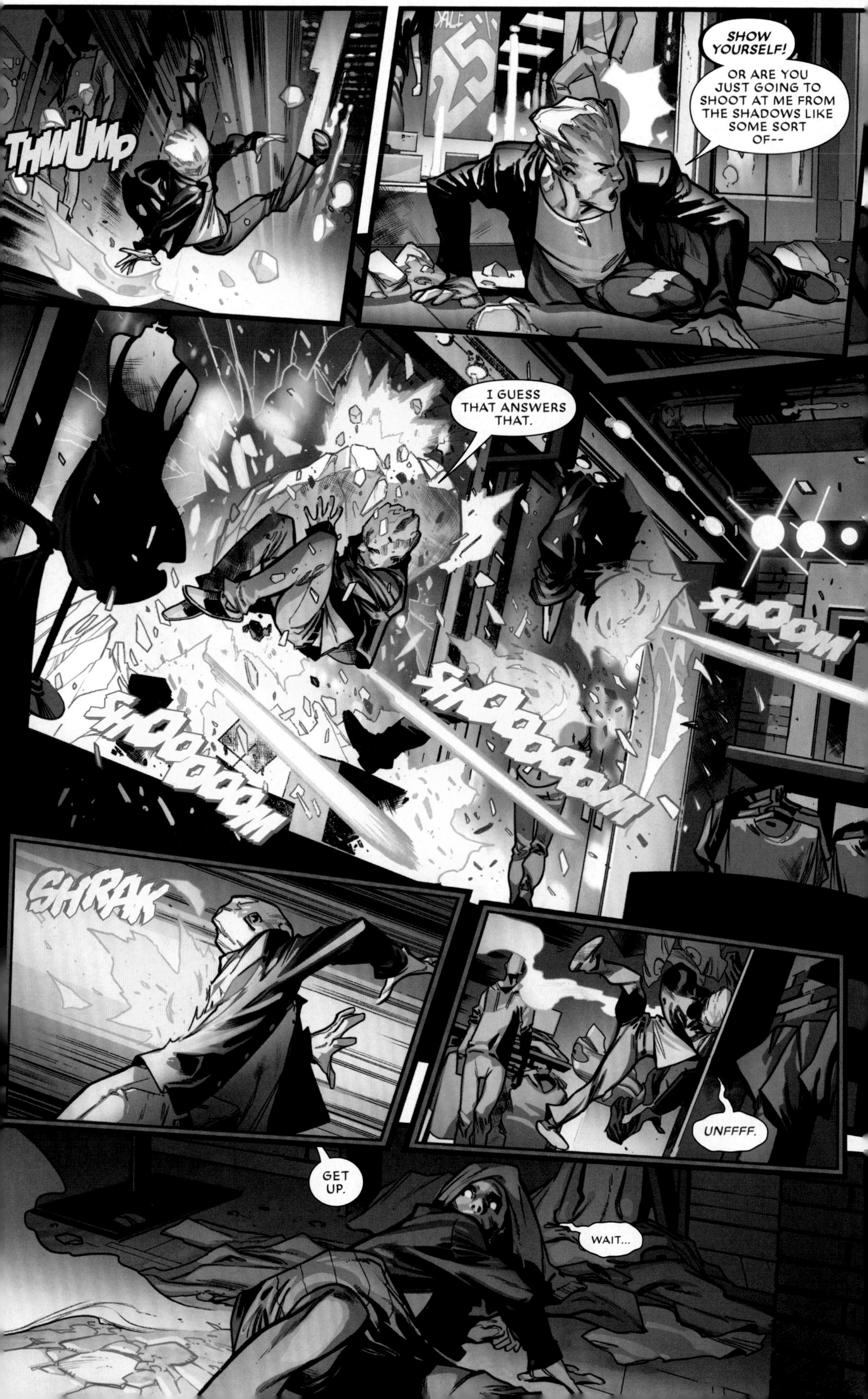
THWUMP
SHOW YOURSELF!
OR ARE YOU JUST GOING TO SHOOT AT ME FROM THE SHADOWS LIKE SOME SORT OF--
I GUESS THAT ANSWERS THAT.
SHOOM
SHOOOOOM
SHOOOOOM
SHRAK
UNFFFF.
GET UP.
WAIT...

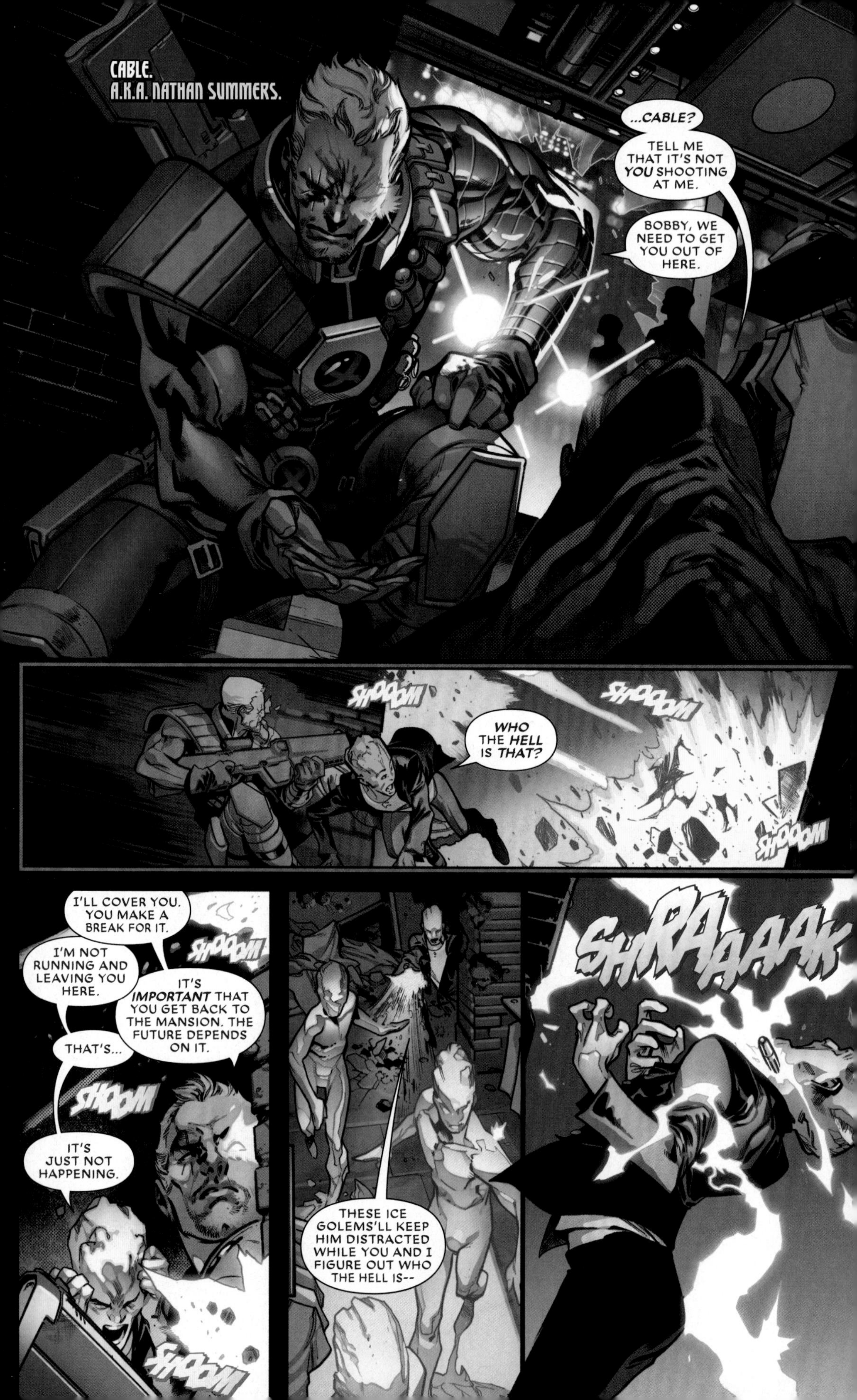
CABLE.
A.K.A. NATHAN SUMMERS.
...CABLE?
TELL ME THAT IT'S NOT YOU SHOOTING AT ME.
BOBBY, WE NEED TO GET YOU OUT OF HERE.
SHOOOM
SHOOOM
WHO THE HELL IS THAT?
SHOOOM
I'LL COVER YOU. YOU MAKE A BREAK FOR IT.
SHOOOM
I'M NOT RUNNING AND LEAVING YOU HERE.
IT'S IMPORTANT THAT YOU GET BACK TO THE MANSION. THE FUTURE DEPENDS ON IT.
THAT'S...
SHOOOM
IT'S JUST NOT HAPPENING.
SHOOOM
THESE ICE GOLEMS'LL KEEP HIM DISTRACTED WHILE YOU AND I FIGURE OUT WHO THE HELL IS--
SHRAAAAK

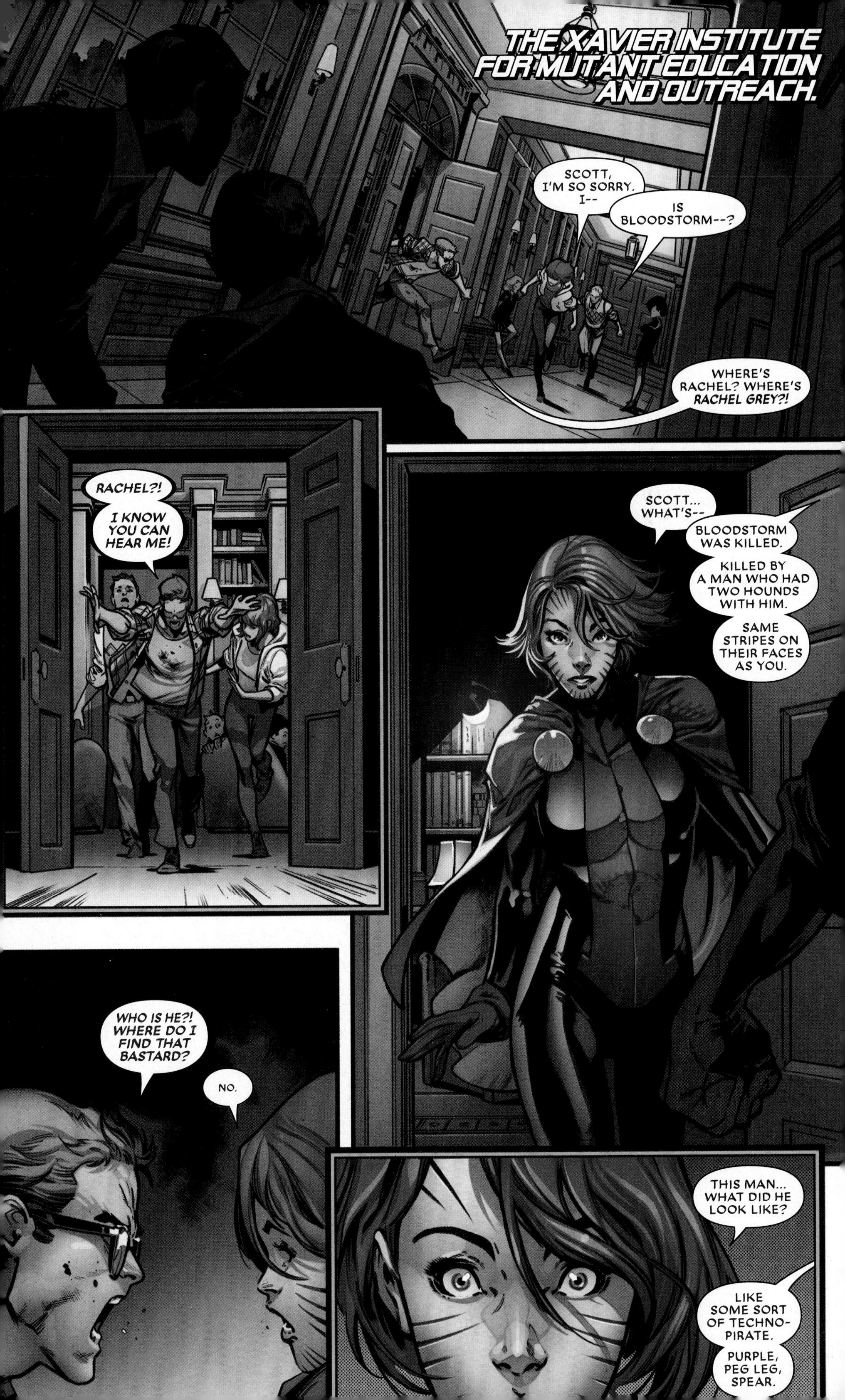
THE XAVIER INSTITUTE FOR MUTANT EDUCATION AND OUTREACH.
SCOTT, I'M SO SORRY. I--
IS BLOODSTORM--?
WHERE'S RACHEL? WHERE'S RACHEL GREY?!
RACHEL?!
I KNOW YOU CAN HEAR ME!
SCOTT... WHAT'S--
BLOODSTORM WAS KILLED.
KILLED BY A MAN WHO HAD TWO HOUNDS WITH HIM.
SAME STRIPES ON THEIR FACES AS YOU.
WHO IS HE?! WHERE DO I FIND THAT BASTARD?
NO.
THIS MAN... WHAT DID HE LOOK LIKE?
LIKE SOME SORT OF TECHNO-PIRATE.
PURPLE, PEG LEG, SPEAR.

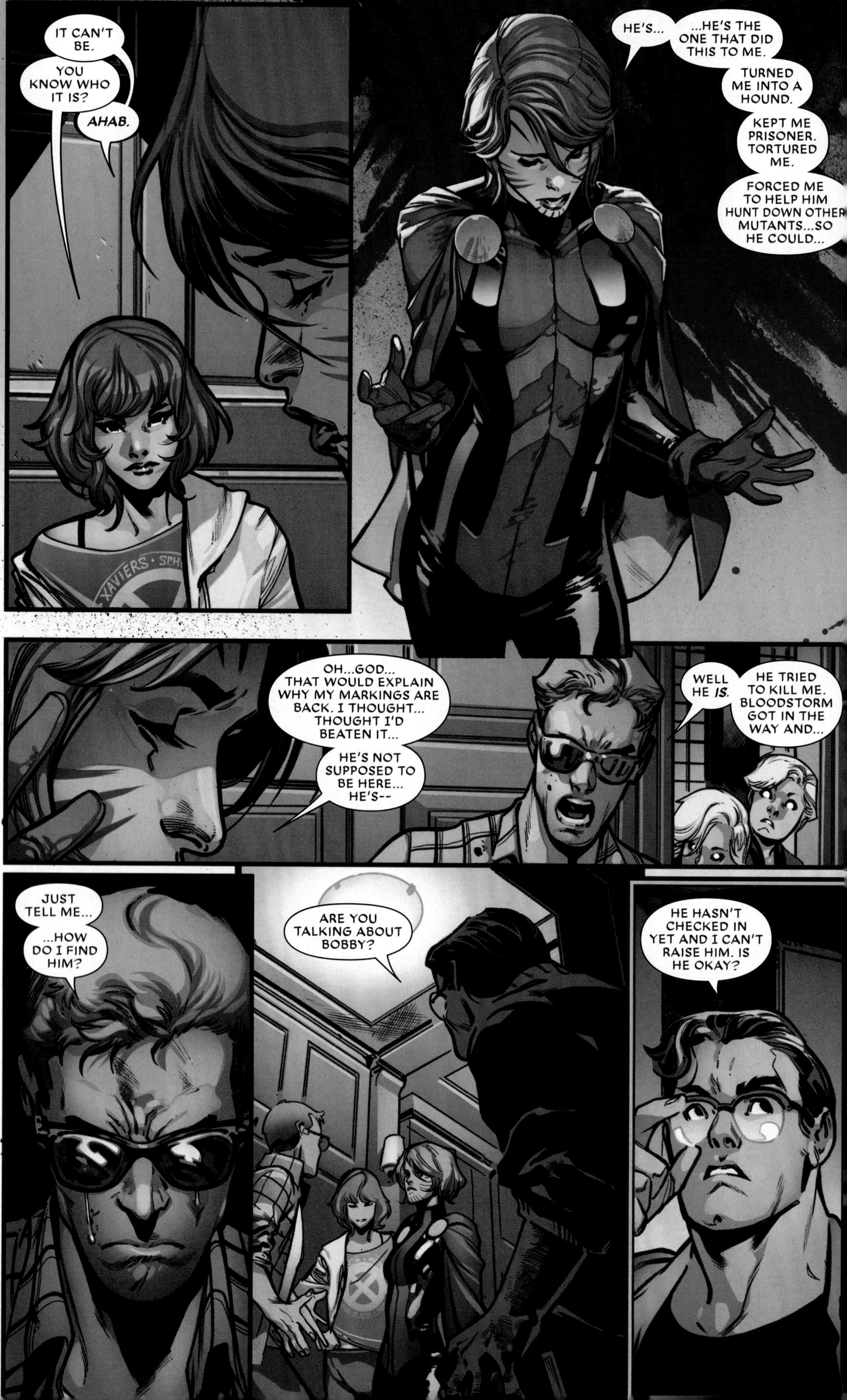
IT CAN'T BE.
YOU KNOW WHO IT IS?
AHAB.
HE'S...
...HE'S THE ONE THAT DID THIS TO ME.
TURNED ME INTO A HOUND.
KEPT ME PRISONER. TORTURED ME.
FORCED ME TO HELP HIM HUNT DOWN OTHER MUTANTS...SO HE COULD...
OH...GOD... THAT WOULD EXPLAIN WHY MY MARKINGS ARE BACK. I THOUGHT... THOUGHT I'D BEATEN IT...
HE'S NOT SUPPOSED TO BE HERE... HE'S--
WELL HE *IS*.
HE TRIED TO KILL ME. BLOODSTORM GOT IN THE WAY AND...
JUST TELL ME...
...HOW DO I FIND HIM?
ARE YOU TALKING ABOUT BOBBY?
HE HASN'T CHECKED IN YET AND I CAN'T RAISE HIM. IS HE OKAY?

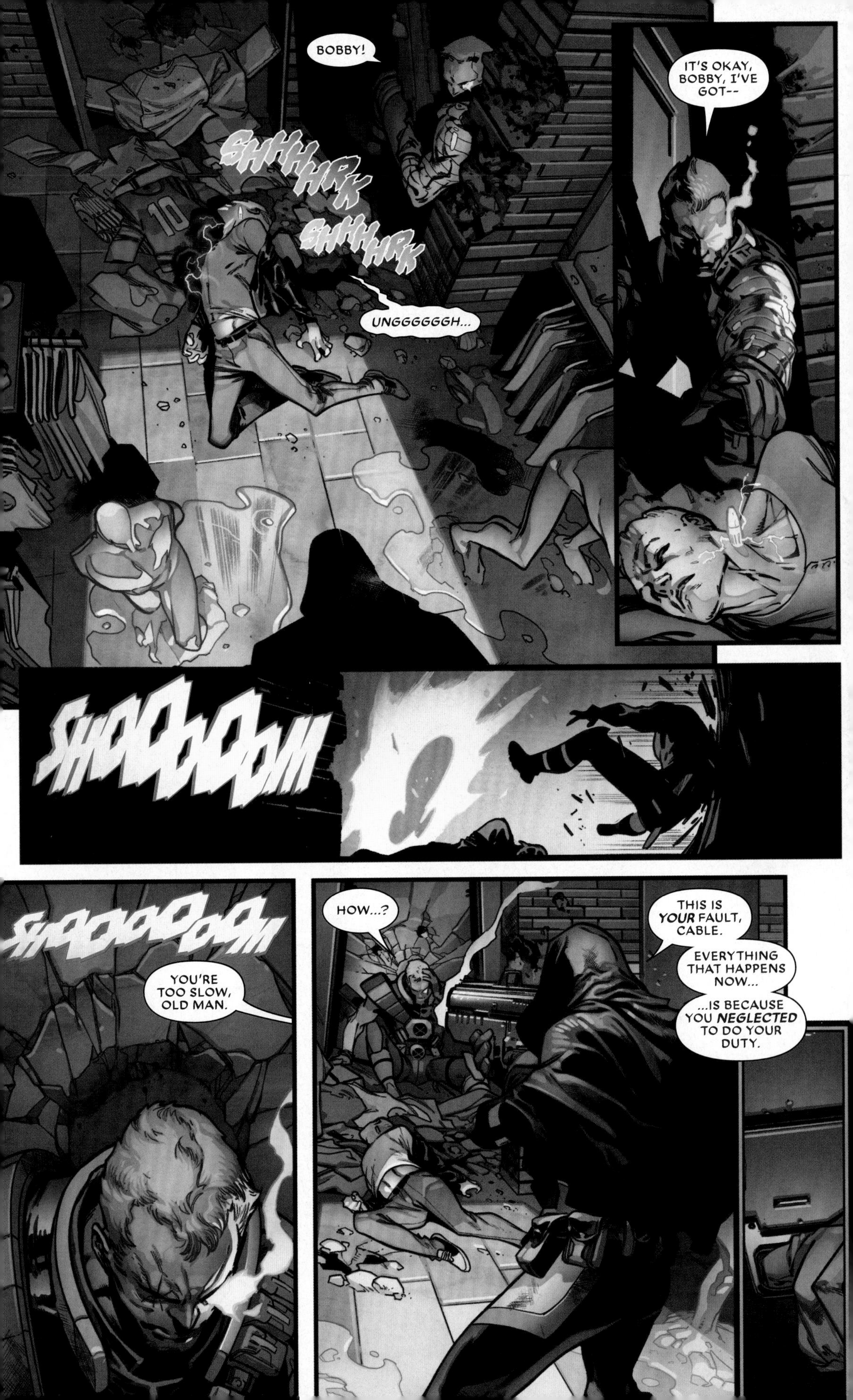
BOBBY!
SHHHHRK
SHHHHRK
UNGGGGGGH...
IT'S OKAY, BOBBY, I'VE GOT--
SHOOOOOM
SHOOOOOOM
YOU'RE TOO SLOW, OLD MAN.
HOW...?
THIS IS *YOUR* FAULT, CABLE.
EVERYTHING THAT HAPPENS NOW...
...IS BECAUSE YOU *NEGLECTED* TO DO YOUR DUTY.

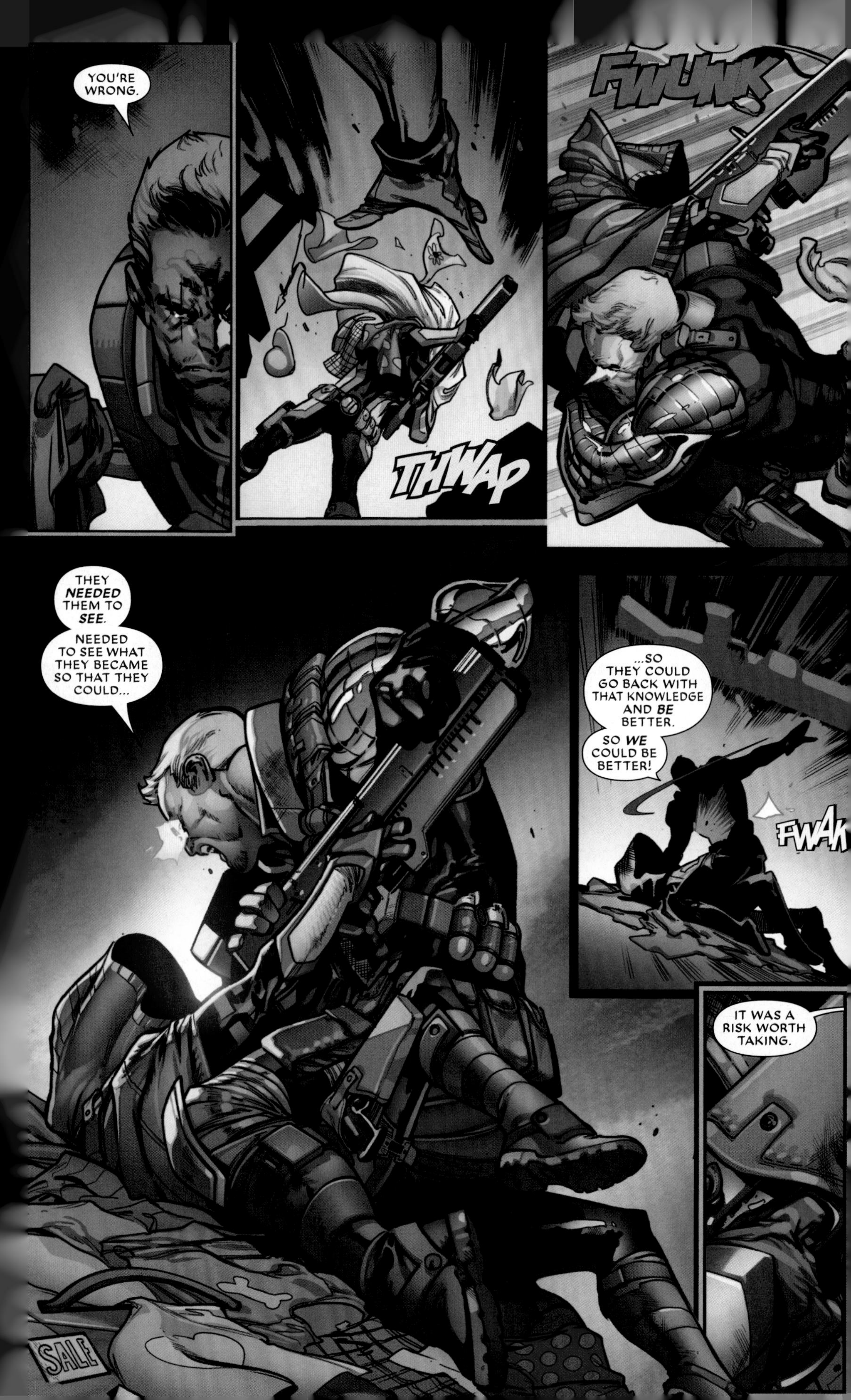
YOU'RE WRONG.
FWUNK
THWAP
THEY NEEDED THEM TO SEE.
NEEDED TO SEE WHAT THEY BECAME SO THAT THEY COULD...
...SO THEY COULD GO BACK WITH THAT KNOWLEDGE AND BE BETTER.
SO WE COULD BE BETTER!
FWAK
IT WAS A RISK WORTH TAKING.
SALE

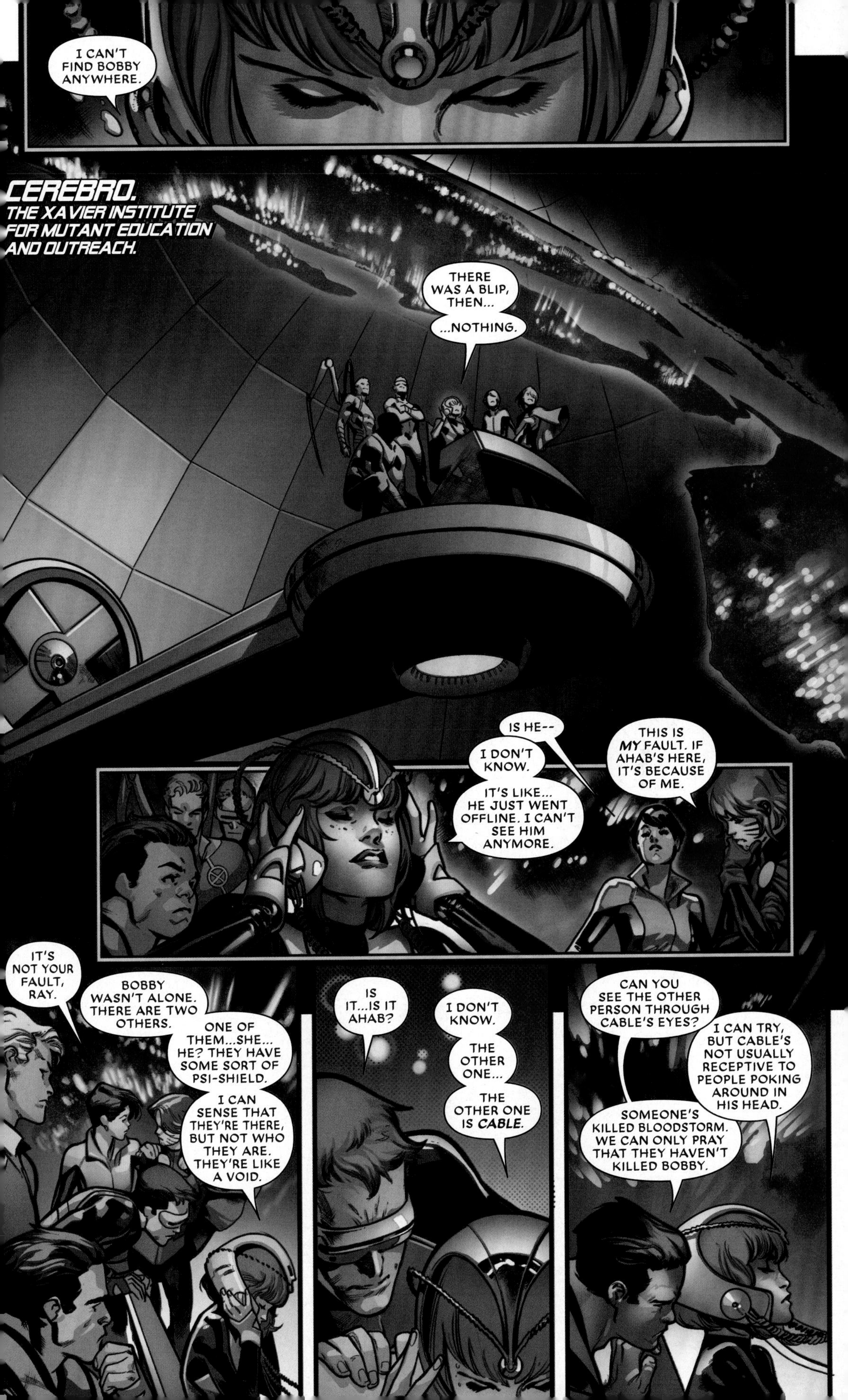
I CAN'T FIND BOBBY ANYWHERE.
CEREBRO. THE XAVIER INSTITUTE FOR MUTANT EDUCATION AND OUTREACH.
THERE WAS A BLIP, THEN...
...NOTHING.
IS HE--
I DON'T KNOW.
IT'S LIKE... HE JUST WENT OFFLINE. I CAN'T SEE HIM ANYMORE.
THIS IS MY FAULT. IF AHAB'S HERE, IT'S BECAUSE OF ME.
IT'S NOT YOUR FAULT, RAY.
BOBBY WASN'T ALONE. THERE ARE TWO OTHERS.
ONE OF THEM...SHE... HE? THEY HAVE SOME SORT OF PSI-SHIELD.
I CAN SENSE THAT THEY'RE THERE, BUT NOT WHO THEY ARE. THEY'RE LIKE A VOID.
IS IT...IS IT AHAB?
I DON'T KNOW.
THE OTHER ONE...
THE OTHER ONE IS CABLE.
CAN YOU SEE THE OTHER PERSON THROUGH CABLE'S EYES?
I CAN TRY, BUT CABLE'S NOT USUALLY RECEPTIVE TO PEOPLE POKING AROUND IN HIS HEAD.
SOMEONE'S KILLED BLOODSTORM. WE CAN ONLY PRAY THAT THEY HAVEN'T KILLED BOBBY.

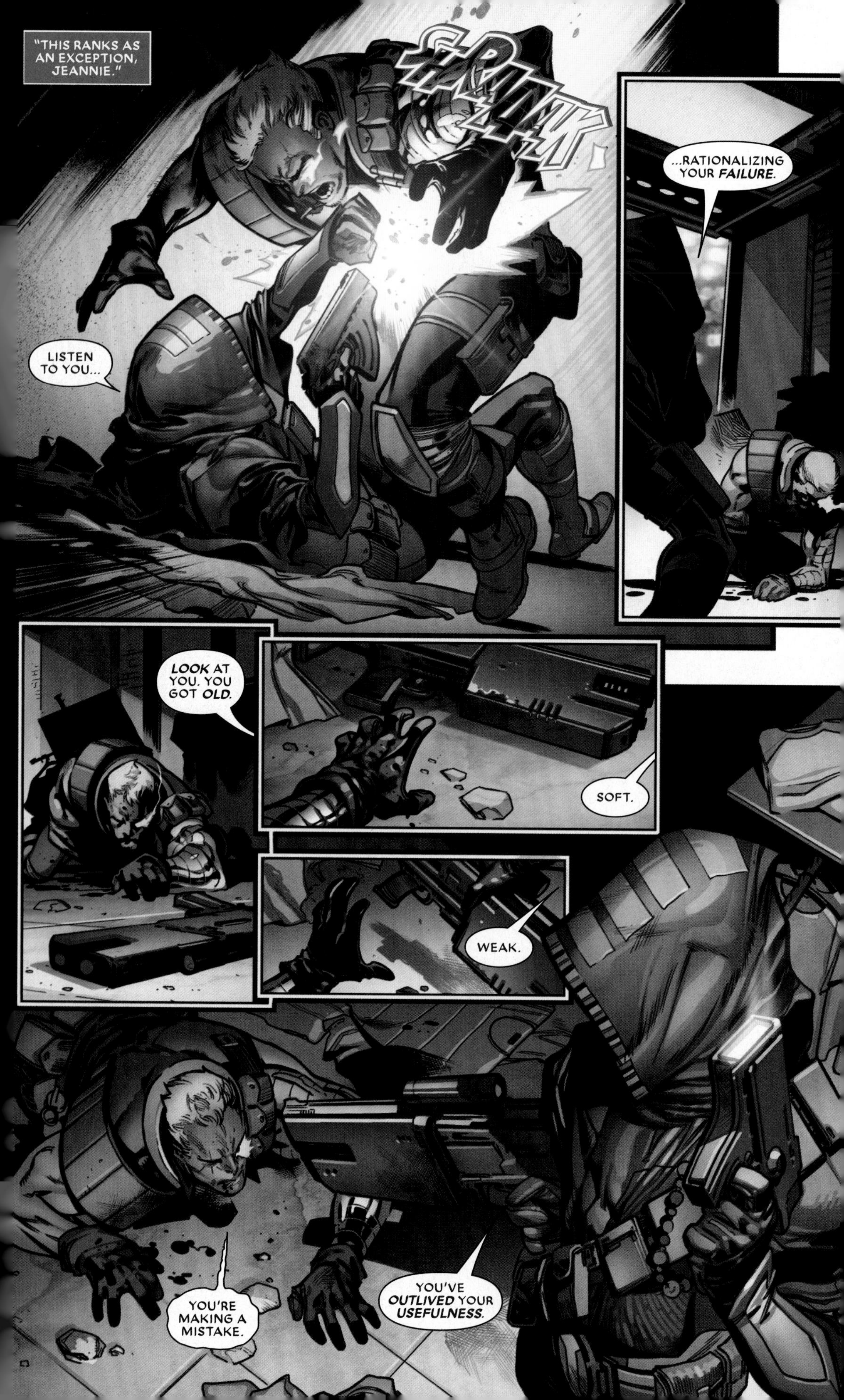
"THIS RANKS AS AN EXCEPTION, JEANNIE."
LISTEN TO YOU...
...RATIONALIZING YOUR FAILURE.
LOOK AT YOU. YOU GOT OLD.
SOFT.
WEAK.
YOU'RE MAKING A MISTAKE.
YOU'VE OUTLIVED YOUR USEFULNESS.

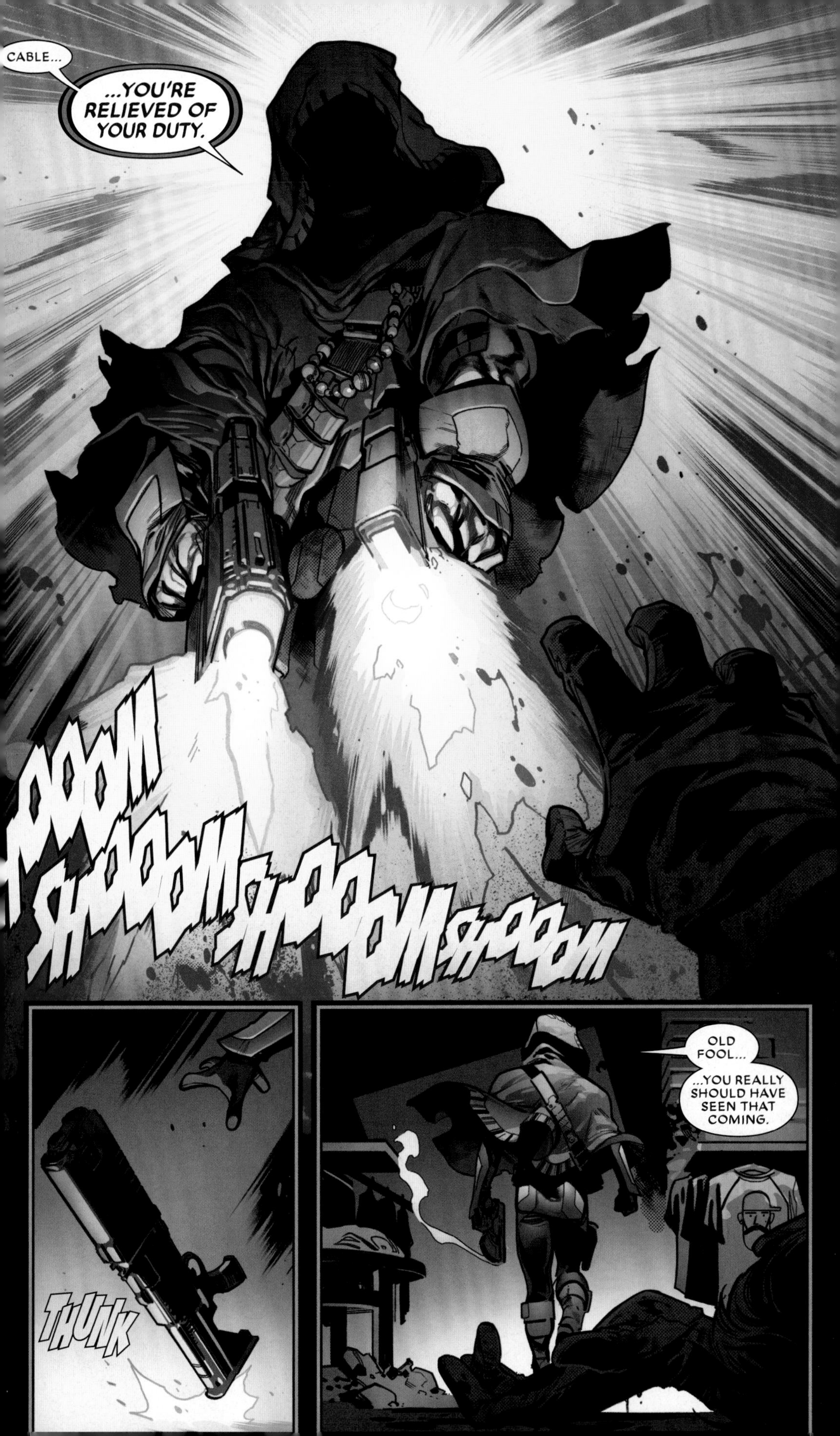
CABLE...
...YOU'RE RELIEVED OF YOUR DUTY.
OOOM
SHOOOM SHOOOM SHOOOM
THUNK
OLD FOOL...
...YOU REALLY SHOULD HAVE SEEN THAT COMING.

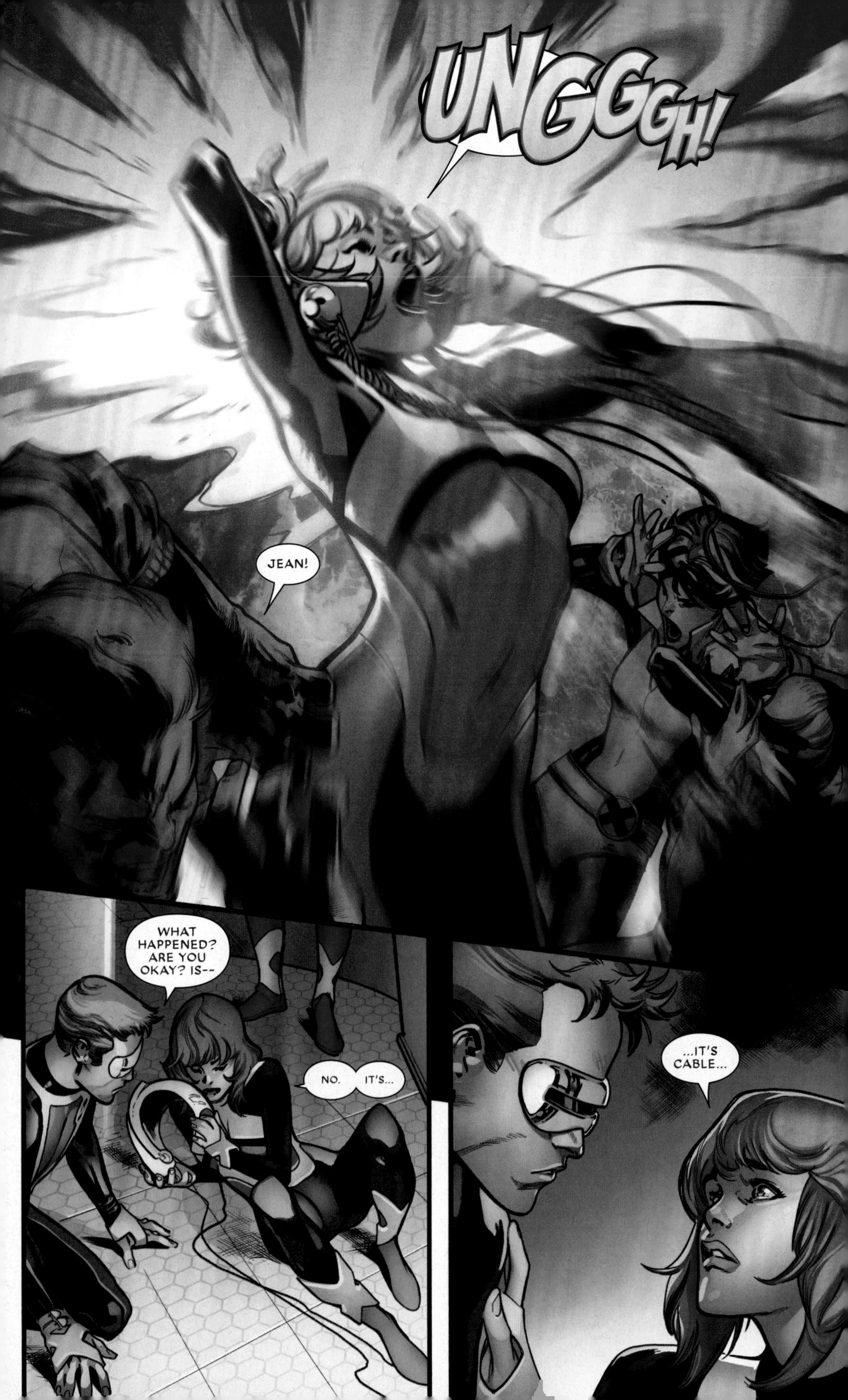
UNGGGH!
JEAN!
WHAT HAPPENED? ARE YOU OKAY? IS--
NO.
IT'S...
...IT'S CABLE...

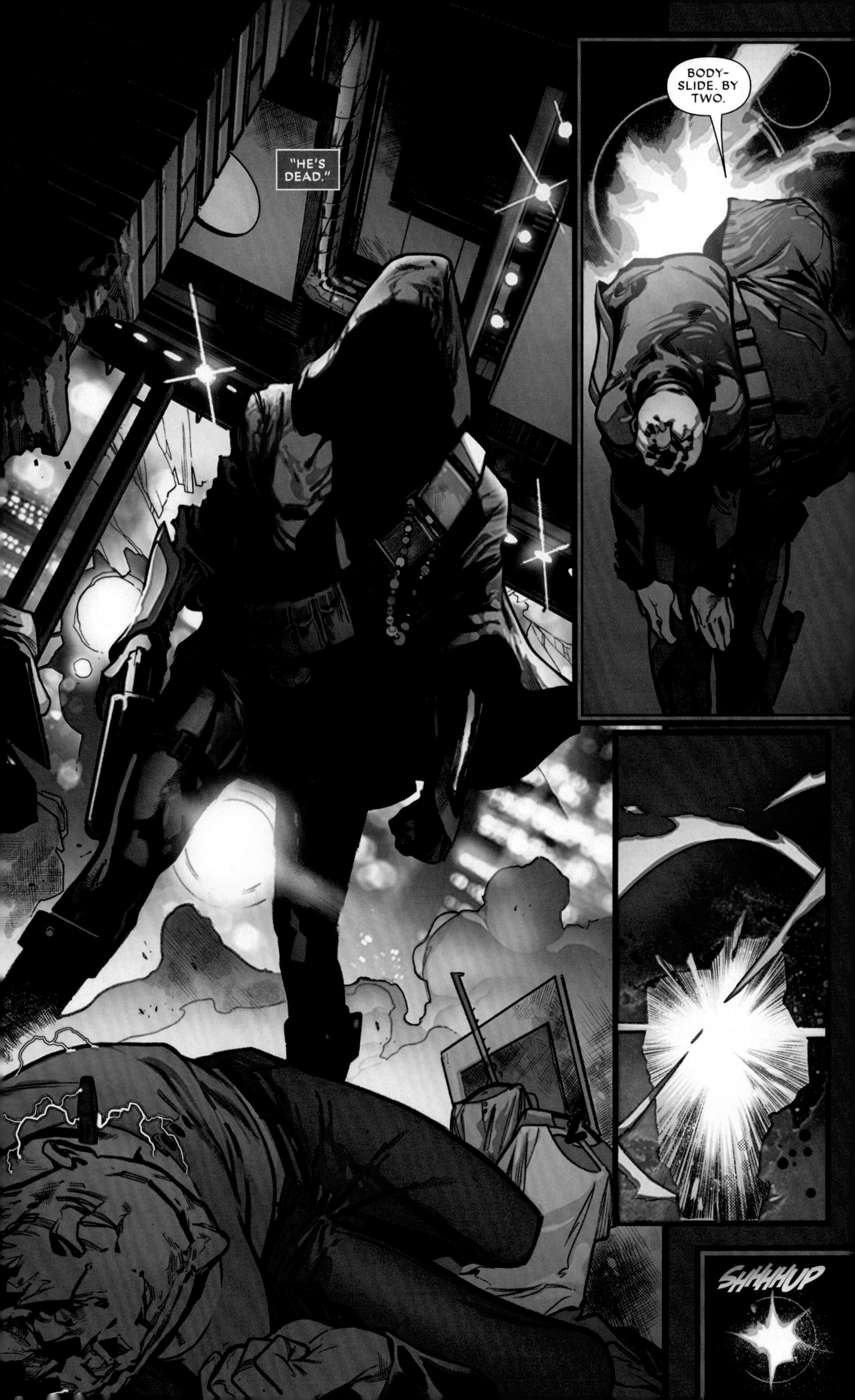
"HE'S DEAD."
BODY-SLIDE. BY TWO.
SHHHUP

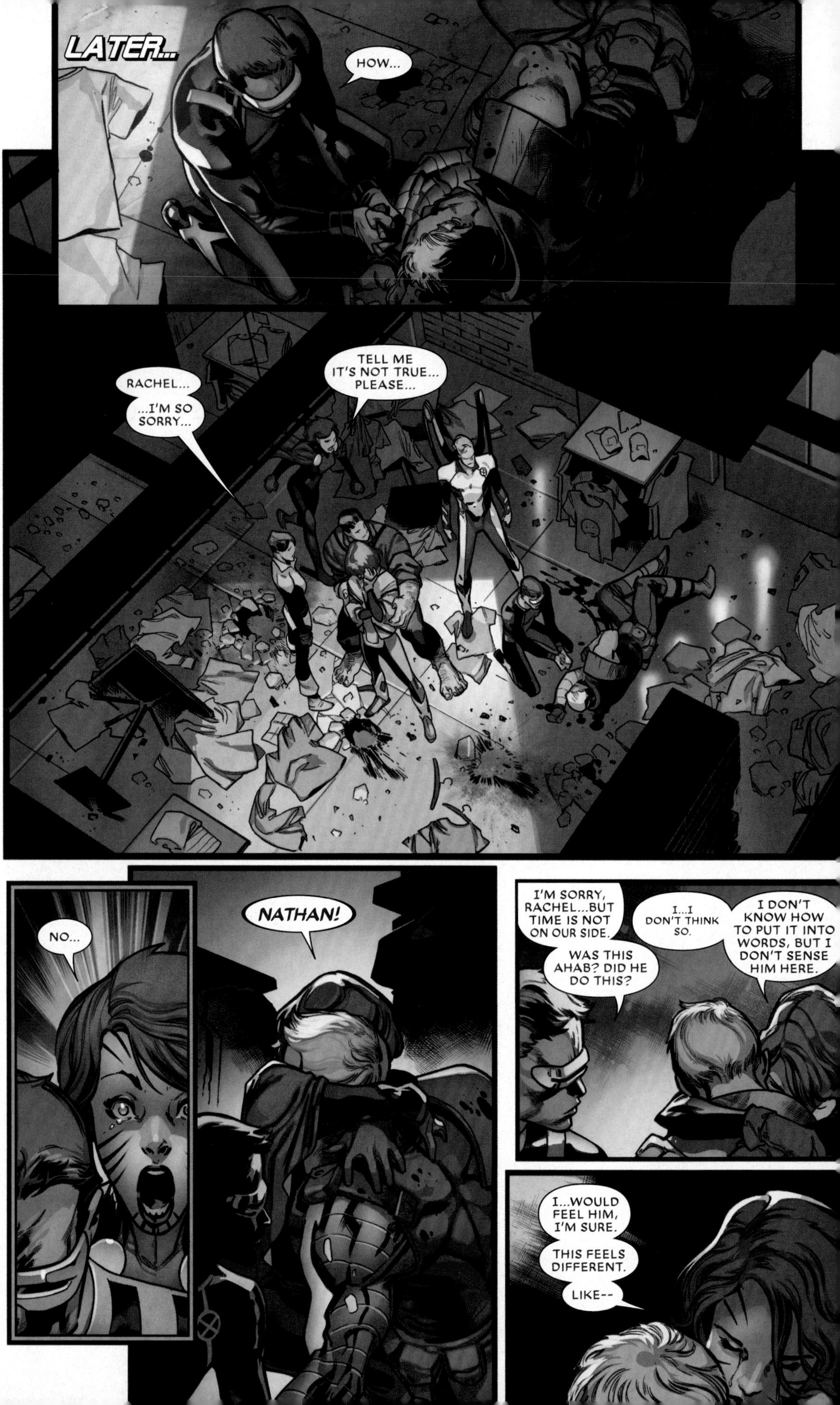
LATER...
HOW...
RACHEL...
...I'M SO SORRY...
TELL ME IT'S NOT TRUE... PLEASE...
NO...
NATHAN!
I'M SORRY, RACHEL...BUT TIME IS NOT ON OUR SIDE.
WAS THIS AHAB? DID HE DO THIS?
I...I DON'T THINK SO.
I DON'T KNOW HOW TO PUT IT INTO WORDS, BUT I DON'T SENSE HIM HERE.
I...WOULD FEEL HIM, I'M SURE.
THIS FEELS DIFFERENT.
LIKE--

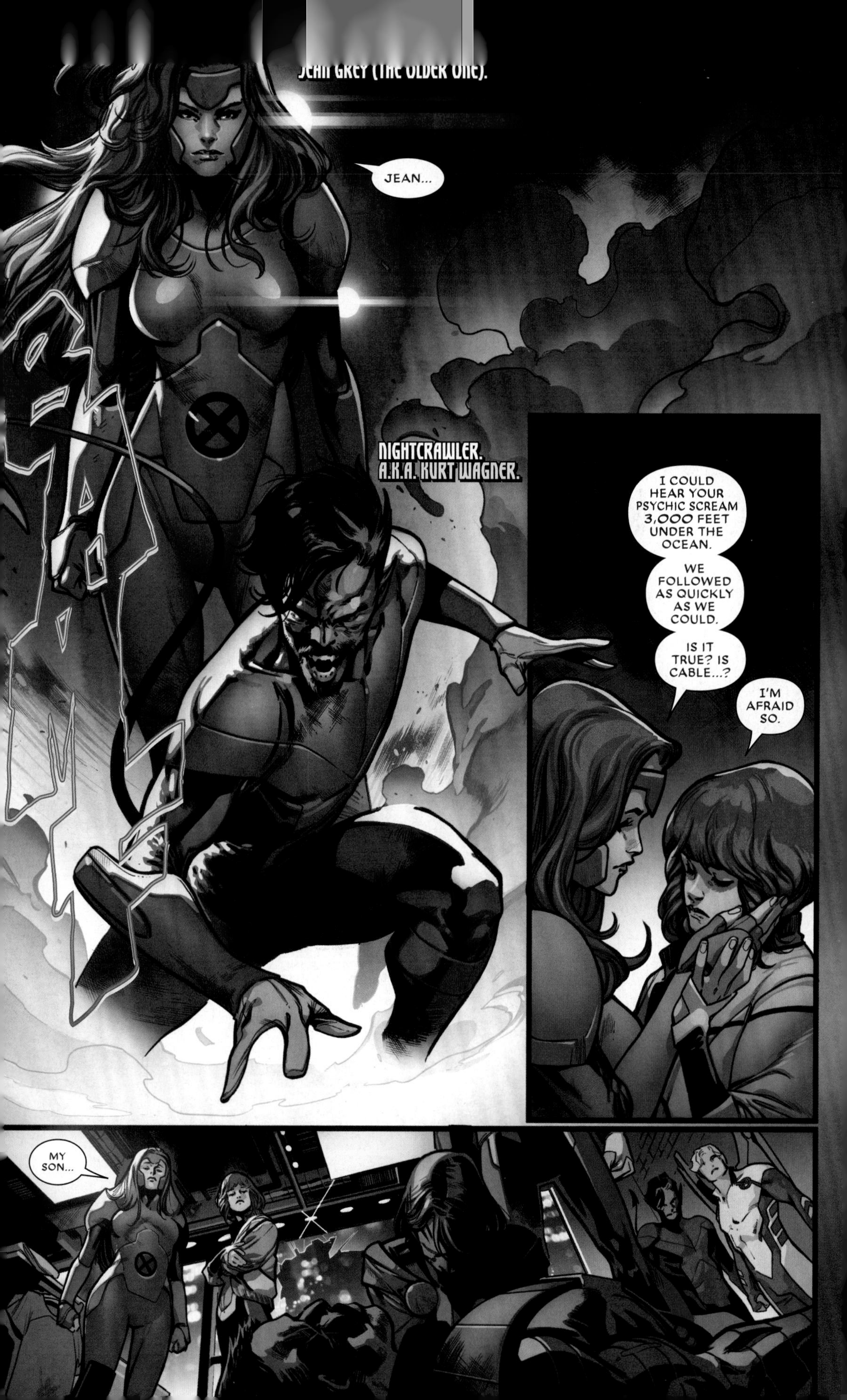

JEAN GREY (THE OLDER ONE).
JEAN...
NIGHTCRAWLER. A.K.A. KURT WAGNER.
I COULD HEAR YOUR PSYCHIC SCREAM 3,000 FEET UNDER THE OCEAN.
WE FOLLOWED AS QUICKLY AS WE COULD.
IS IT TRUE? IS CABLE...?
I'M AFRAID SO.
MY SON...

MEIN GOTT. THEY... THEY GOT BLOODSTORM... I WAS THERE...I COULDN'T--

DON'T WORRY, THIS WILL NOT GO UNANSWERED.

AND NOW BOBBY'S GONE. GOD, WHAT'S GOING ON?!

I DON'T KNOW...

...BUT WHOEVER DID THIS...WHOEVER KILLED *MY SON*...WILL PAY FOR IT.

THEY...HE...WAS USING A PSI-SHIELD, SO THEY'RE SMART ENOUGH TO KNOW TO PROTECT THEMSELVES FROM US. BUT THAT DOESN'T MEAN WE WON'T FIND THEM.

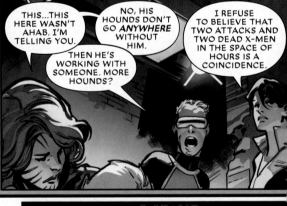

I CAN TRACK BOBBY TO THIS SPOT, BUT HIS TRAIL ENDS HERE.

WE'RE LOOKING FOR A TELEPORTER.

AHAB DID THE SAME EARLIER.

AS SOON AS I GOT THE UPPER HAND, HE TELEPORTED AWAY.

IT WON'T HAPPEN AGAIN! HE'S GOING TO PAY FOR WHAT HE'S DONE HERE!

THIS...THIS HERE WASN'T AHAB. I'M TELLING YOU.

NO, HIS HOUNDS DON'T GO *ANYWHERE* WITHOUT HIM.

THEN HE'S WORKING WITH SOMEONE. MORE HOUNDS?

I REFUSE TO BELIEVE THAT TWO ATTACKS AND TWO DEAD X-MEN IN THE SPACE OF HOURS IS A COINCIDENCE.

IF IT'S NOT AHAB...

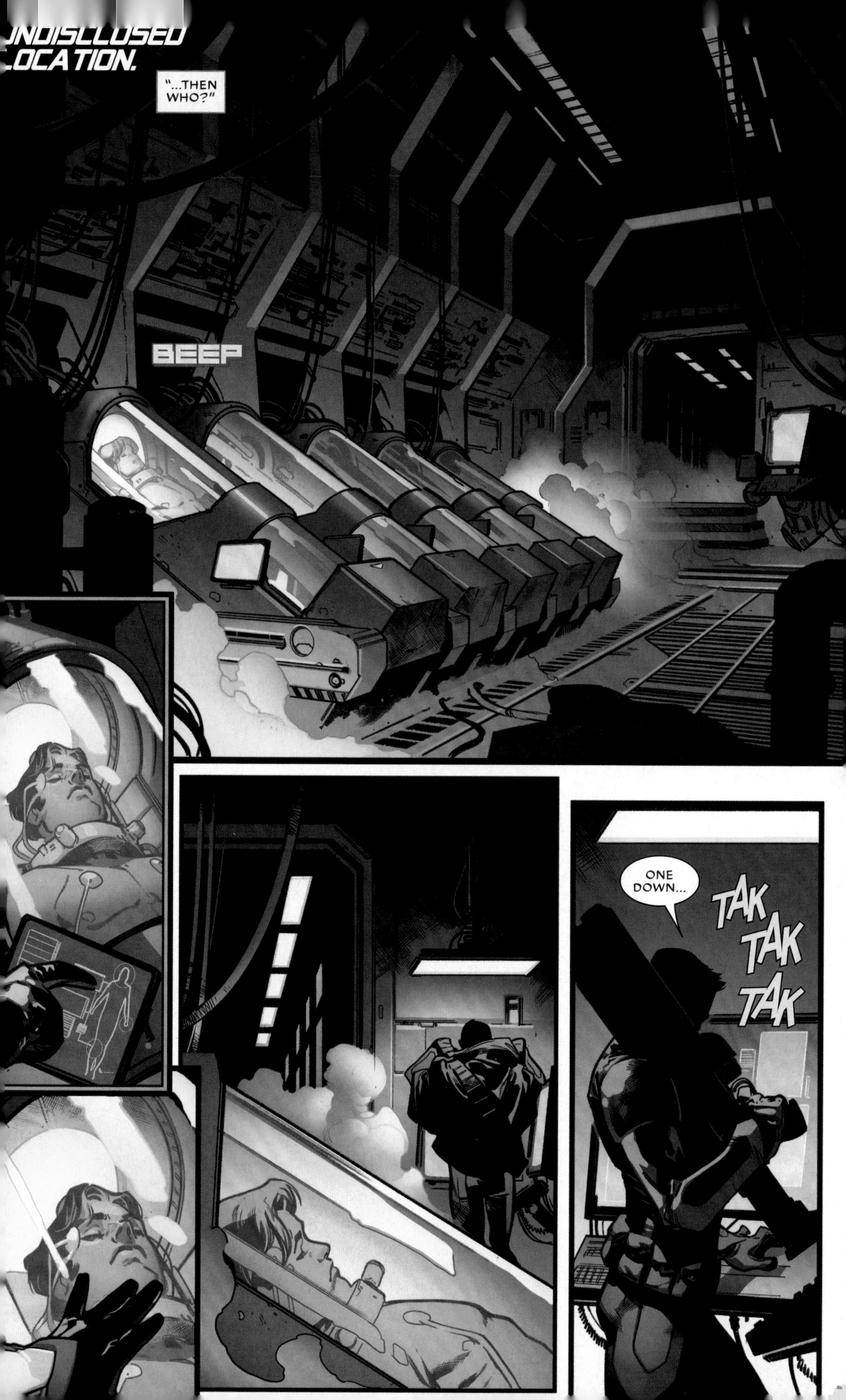
UNDISCLOSED
LOCATION.
"...THEN WHO?"
BEEP
ONE DOWN...
TAK
TAK
TAK

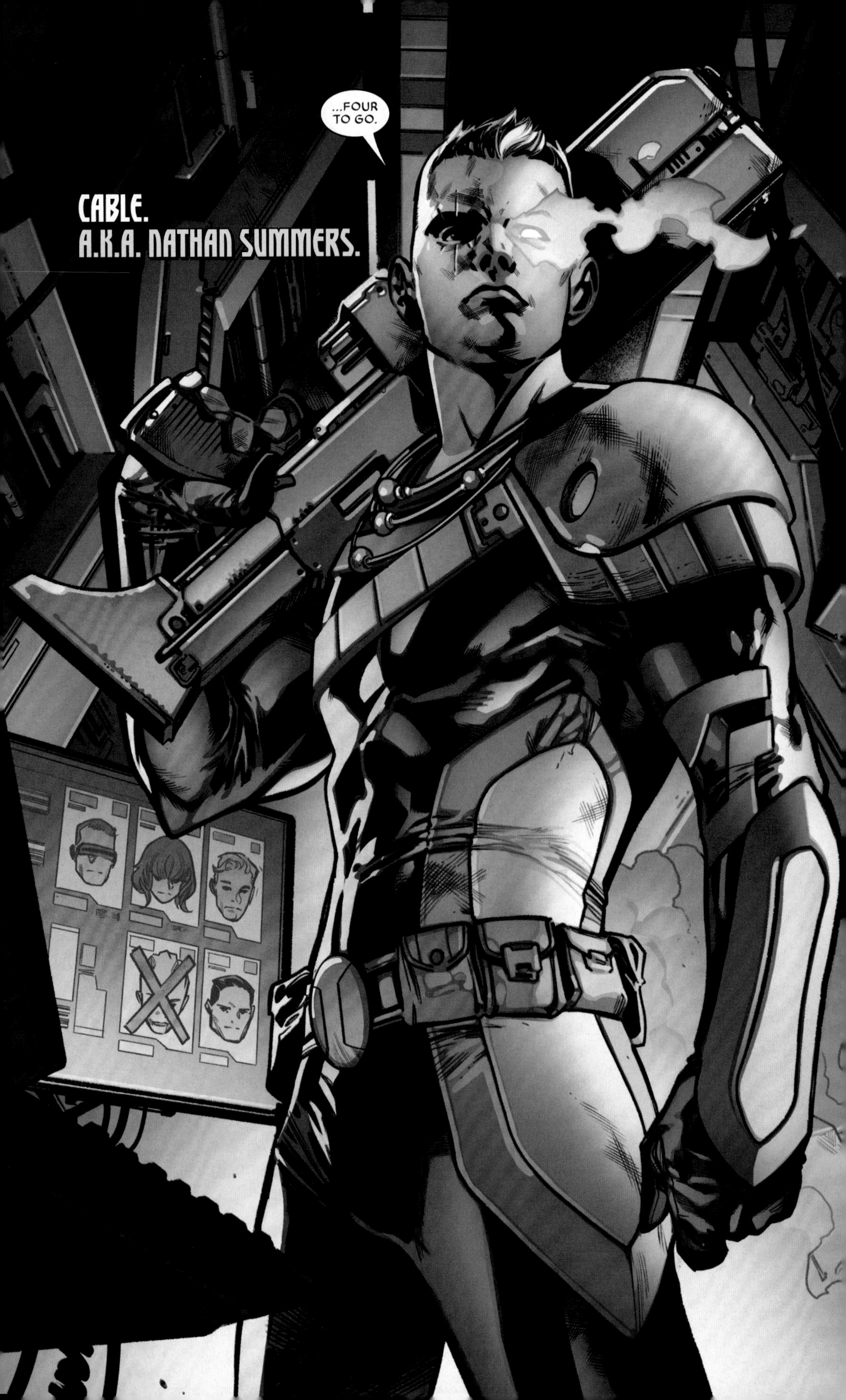
CABLE.
A.K.A. NATHAN SUMMERS.
...FOUR TO GO.

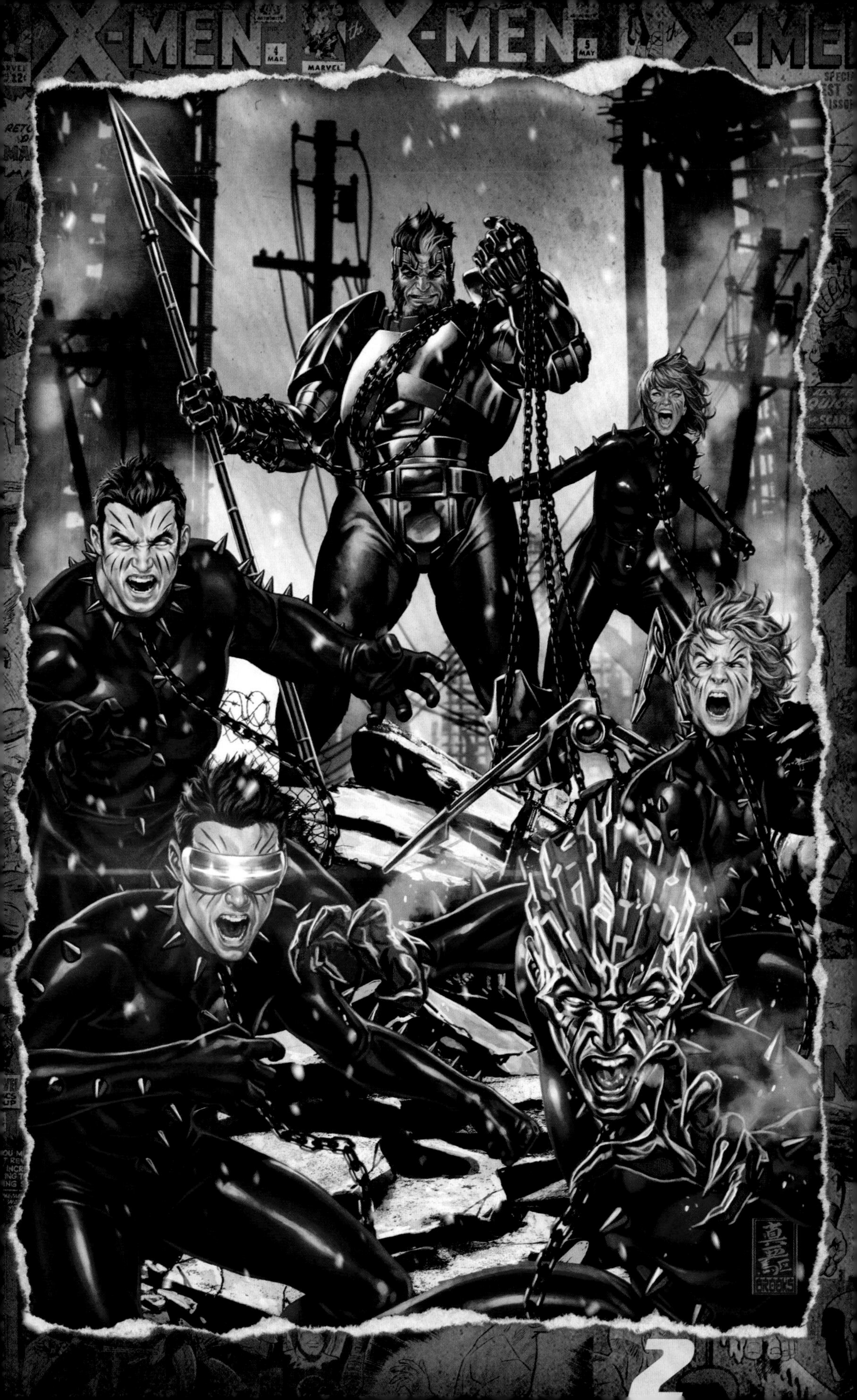

X-MEN
4 MAR.
MARVEL
X-MEN
5 MAY
BROOKS
2

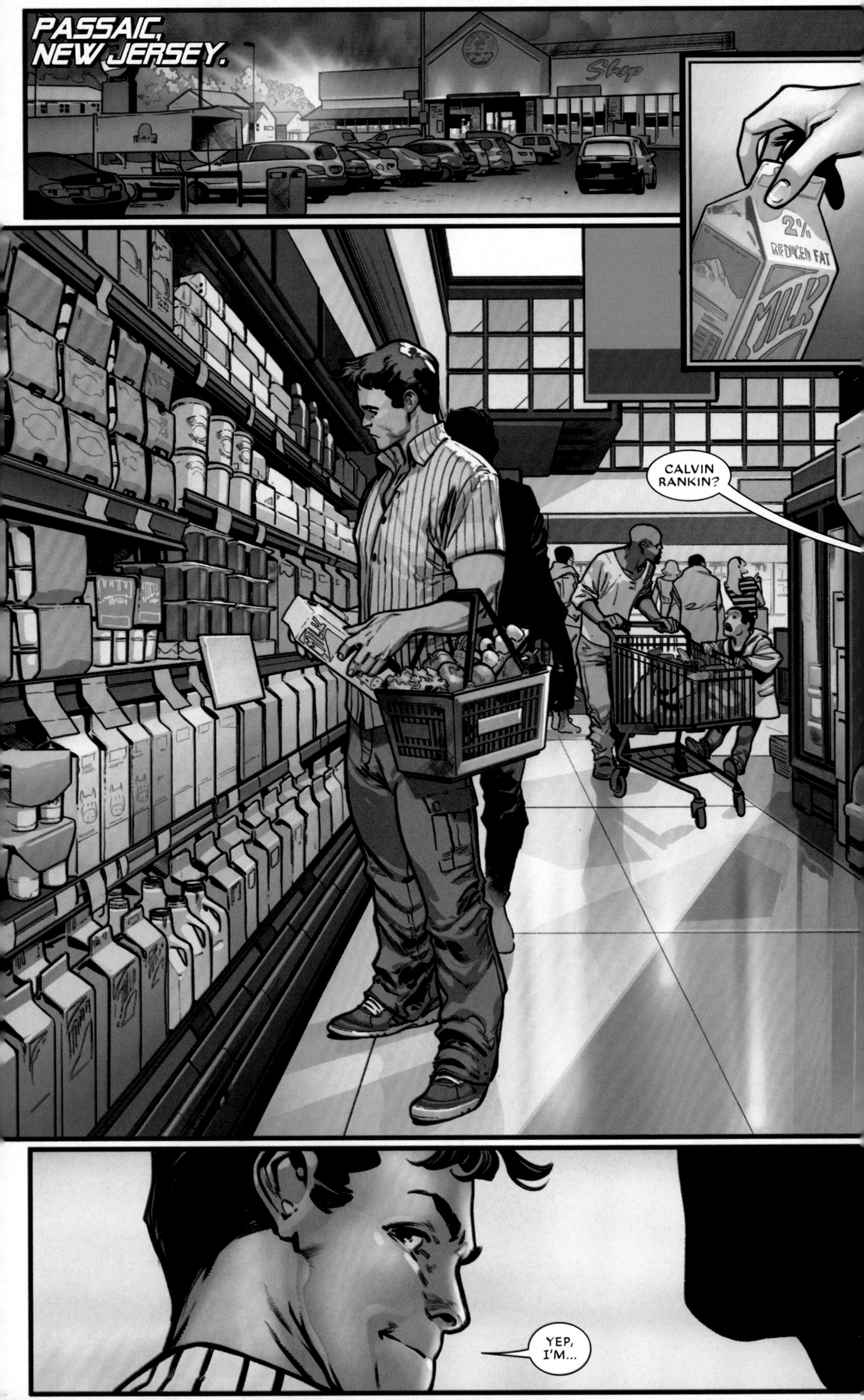
PASSAIC, NEW JERSEY.
Shop
2%
REDUCED FAT
MILK
CALVIN RANKIN?
YEP, I'M...

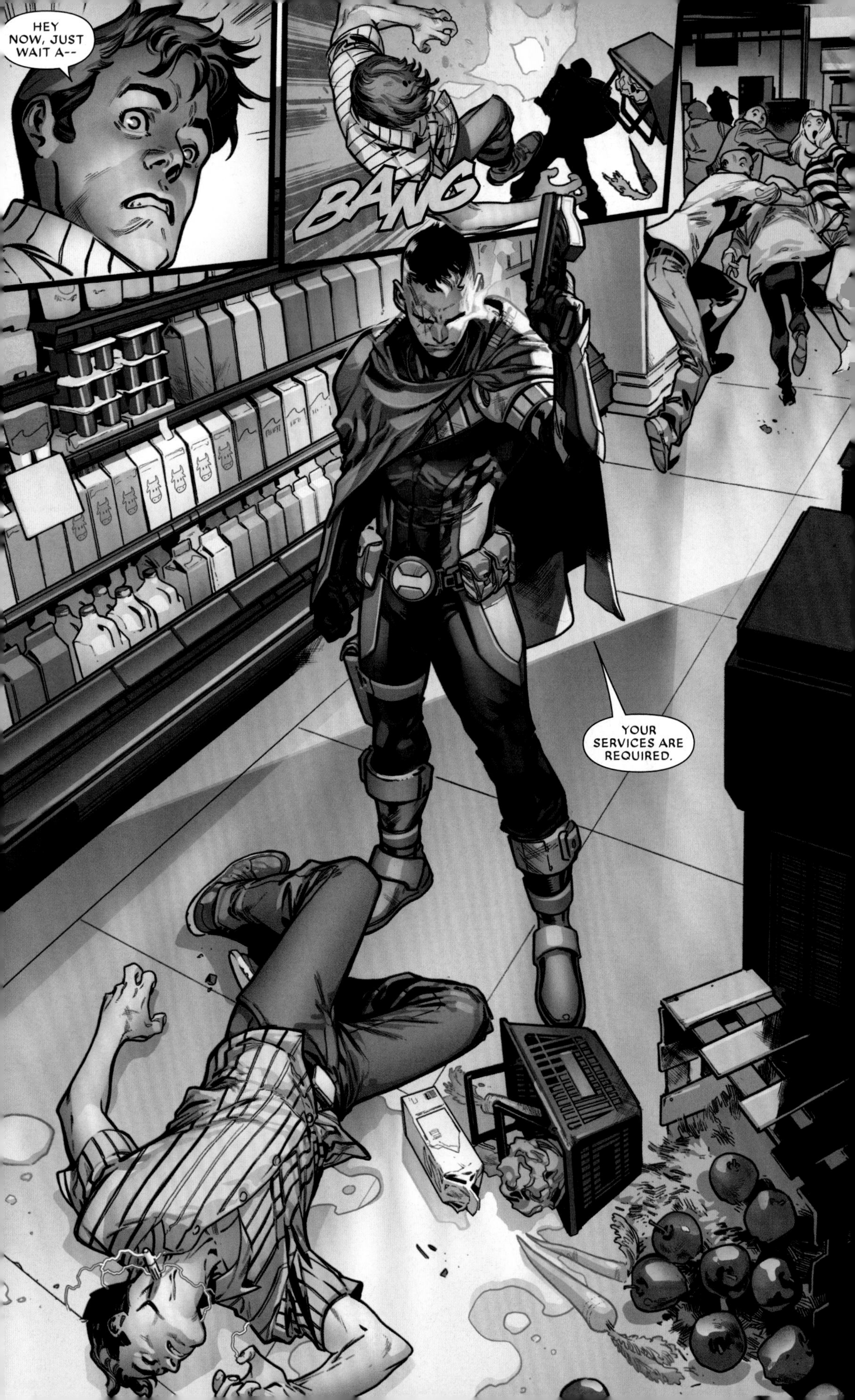

HEY NOW, JUST WAIT A--
BANG
YOUR SERVICES ARE REQUIRED.

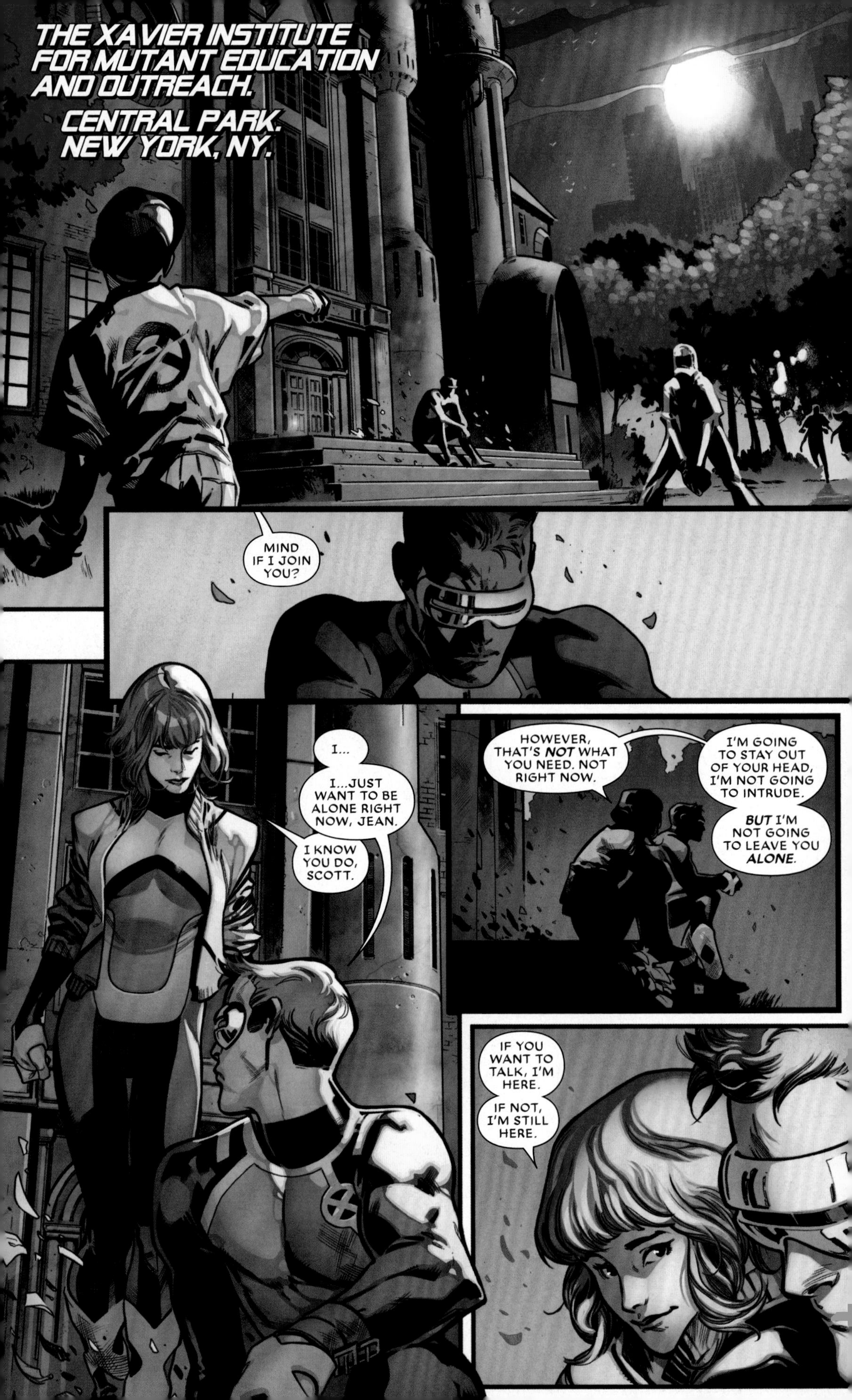
THE XAVIER INSTITUTE FOR MUTANT EDUCATION AND OUTREACH.
CENTRAL PARK. NEW YORK, NY.
MIND IF I JOIN YOU?
I...
I...JUST WANT TO BE ALONE RIGHT NOW, JEAN.
I KNOW YOU DO, SCOTT.
I'M GOING TO STAY OUT OF YOUR HEAD, I'M NOT GOING TO INTRUDE.
HOWEVER, THAT'S NOT WHAT YOU NEED. NOT RIGHT NOW.
BUT I'M NOT GOING TO LEAVE YOU ALONE.
IF YOU WANT TO TALK, I'M HERE.
IF NOT, I'M STILL HERE.

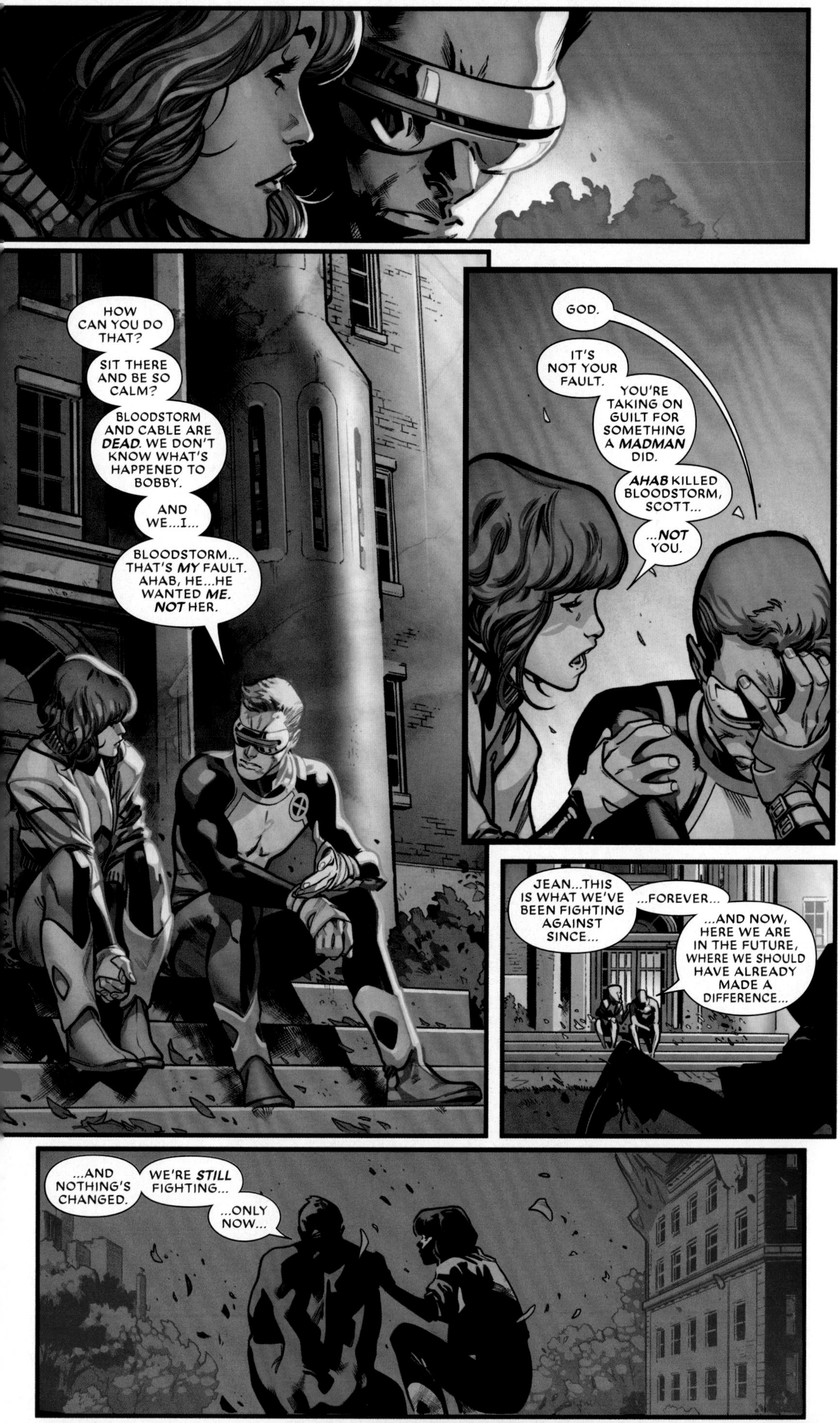
HOW CAN YOU DO THAT?
SIT THERE AND BE SO CALM?
BLOODSTORM AND CABLE ARE *DEAD.* WE DON'T KNOW WHAT'S HAPPENED TO BOBBY.
AND WE...I...
BLOODSTORM... THAT'S *MY* FAULT. AHAB, HE...HE WANTED *ME. NOT* HER.
GOD.
IT'S NOT YOUR FAULT.
YOU'RE TAKING ON GUILT FOR SOMETHING A *MADMAN* DID.
*AHAB* KILLED BLOODSTORM, SCOTT...
...*NOT* YOU.
JEAN...THIS IS WHAT WE'VE BEEN FIGHTING AGAINST SINCE...
...FOREVER...
...AND NOW, HERE WE ARE IN THE FUTURE, WHERE WE SHOULD HAVE ALREADY MADE A DIFFERENCE...
...AND NOTHING'S CHANGED.
WE'RE *STILL* FIGHTING...
...ONLY NOW...

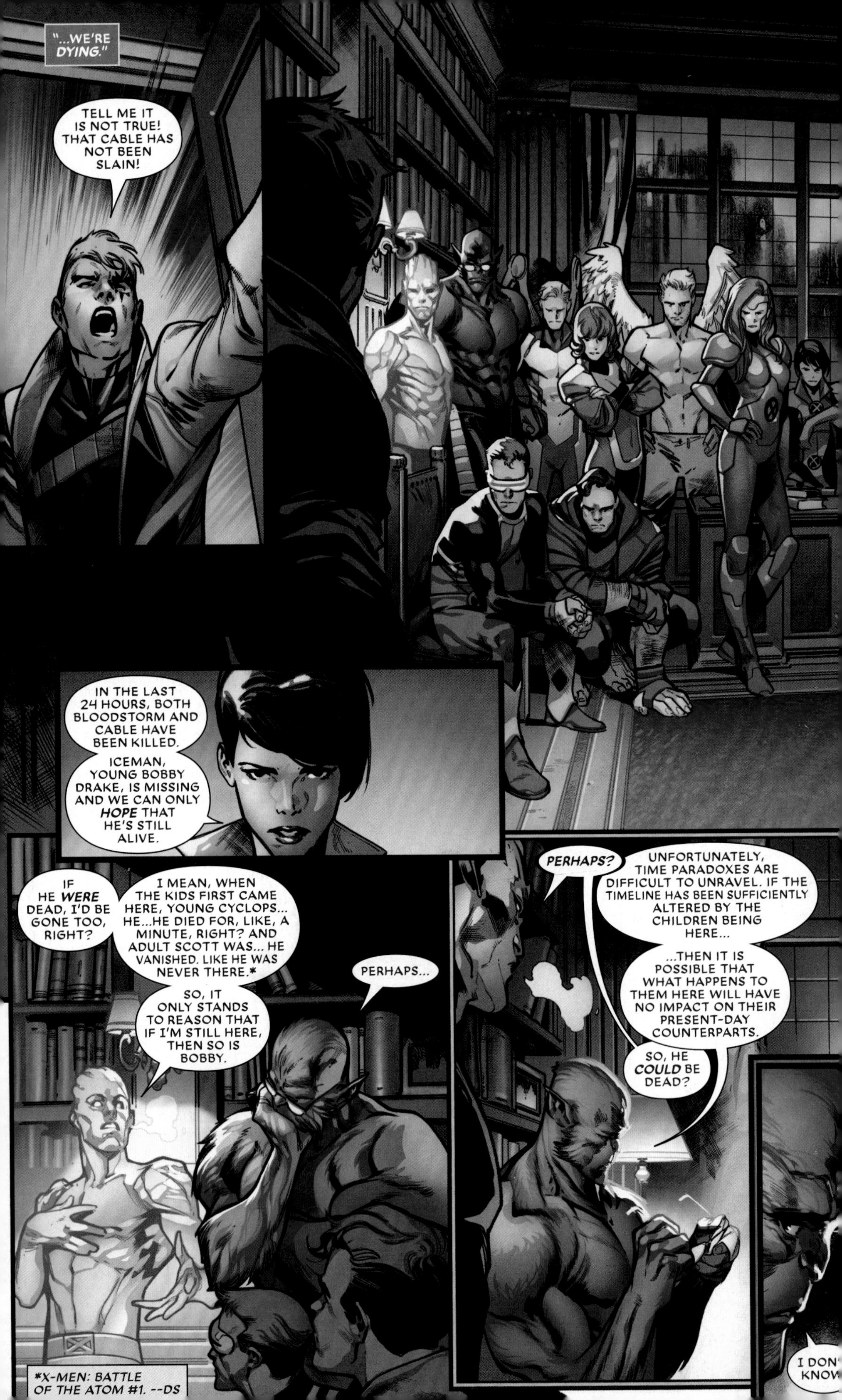
"...WE'RE DYING."
TELL ME IT IS NOT TRUE! THAT CABLE HAS NOT BEEN SLAIN!
IN THE LAST 24 HOURS, BOTH BLOODSTORM AND CABLE HAVE BEEN KILLED.
ICEMAN, YOUNG BOBBY DRAKE, IS MISSING AND WE CAN ONLY HOPE THAT HE'S STILL ALIVE.
IF HE WERE DEAD, I'D BE GONE TOO, RIGHT?
I MEAN, WHEN THE KIDS FIRST CAME HERE, YOUNG CYCLOPS... HE...HE DIED FOR, LIKE, A MINUTE, RIGHT? AND ADULT SCOTT WAS... HE VANISHED. LIKE HE WAS NEVER THERE.*
SO, IT ONLY STANDS TO REASON THAT IF I'M STILL HERE, THEN SO IS BOBBY.
PERHAPS...
PERHAPS?
UNFORTUNATELY, TIME PARADOXES ARE DIFFICULT TO UNRAVEL. IF THE TIMELINE HAS BEEN SUFFICIENTLY ALTERED BY THE CHILDREN BEING HERE...
...THEN IT IS POSSIBLE THAT WHAT HAPPENS TO THEM HERE WILL HAVE NO IMPACT ON THEIR PRESENT-DAY COUNTERPARTS.
SO, HE COULD BE DEAD?
I DON KNOW
*X-MEN: BATTLE OF THE ATOM #1. --DS

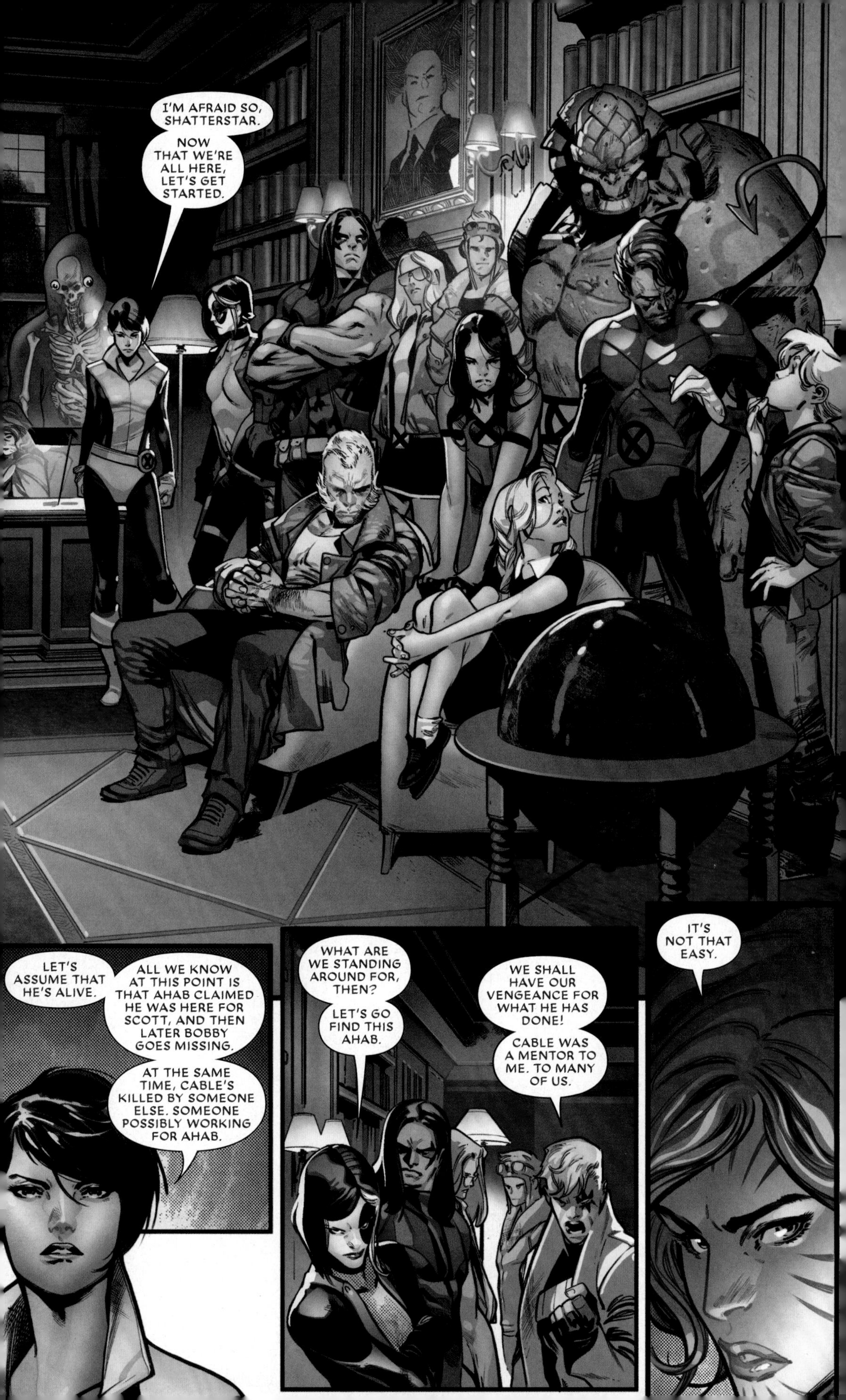
I'M AFRAID SO, SHATTERSTAR.
NOW THAT WE'RE ALL HERE, LET'S GET STARTED.
LET'S ASSUME THAT HE'S ALIVE.
ALL WE KNOW AT THIS POINT IS THAT AHAB CLAIMED HE WAS HERE FOR SCOTT, AND THEN LATER BOBBY GOES MISSING.
AT THE SAME TIME, CABLE'S KILLED BY SOMEONE ELSE. SOMEONE POSSIBLY WORKING FOR AHAB.
WHAT ARE WE STANDING AROUND FOR, THEN?
LET'S GO FIND THIS AHAB.
WE SHALL HAVE OUR VENGEANCE FOR WHAT HE HAS DONE!
CABLE WAS A MENTOR TO ME. TO MANY OF US.
IT'S NOT THAT EASY.

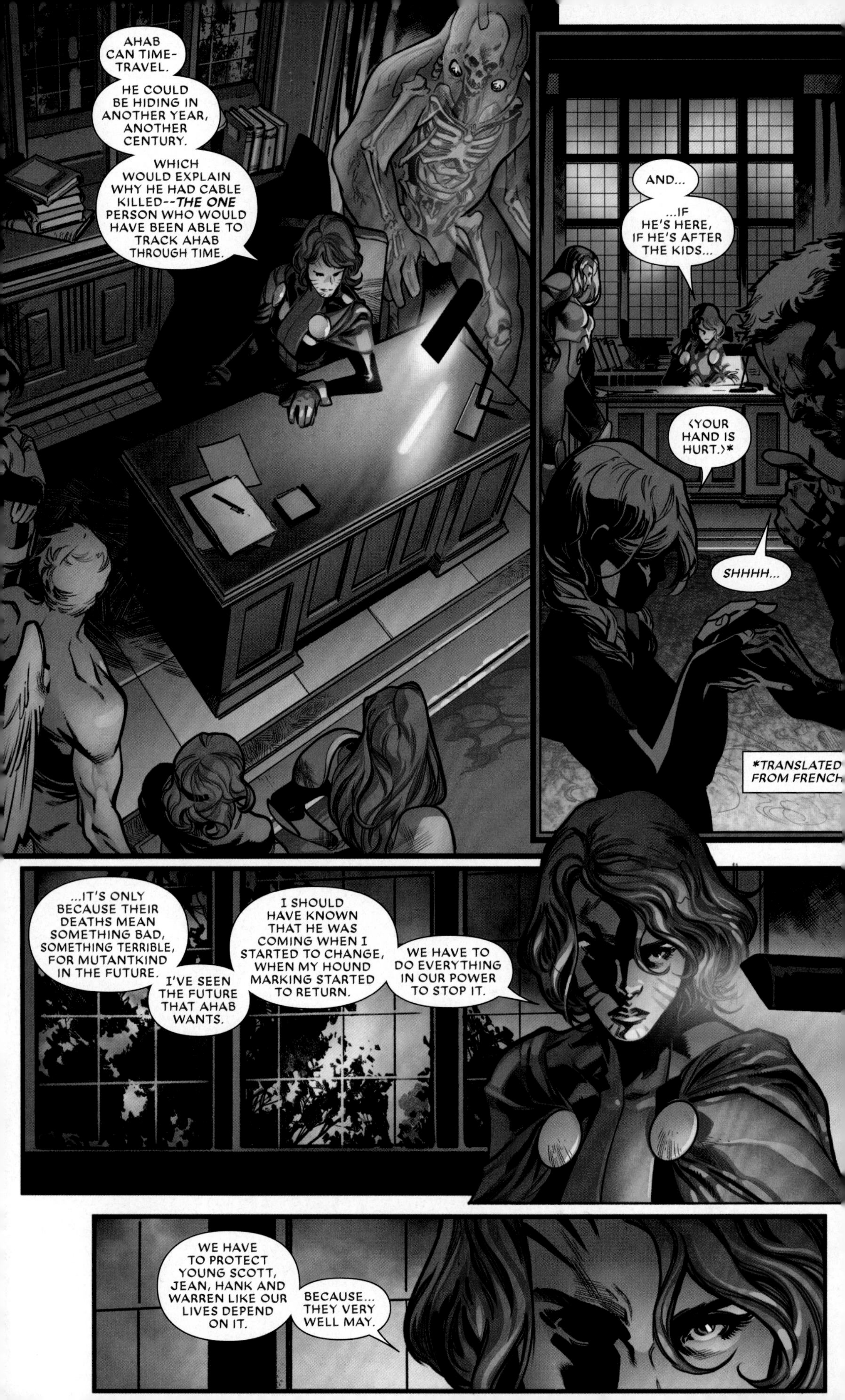
AHAB CAN TIME-TRAVEL.
HE COULD BE HIDING IN ANOTHER YEAR, ANOTHER CENTURY.
WHICH WOULD EXPLAIN WHY HE HAD CABLE KILLED--*THE ONE* PERSON WHO WOULD HAVE BEEN ABLE TO TRACK AHAB THROUGH TIME.
AND...
...IF HE'S HERE, IF HE'S AFTER THE KIDS...
‹YOUR HAND IS HURT.›*
*SHHHH...*
*TRANSLATED FROM FRENCH
...IT'S ONLY BECAUSE THEIR DEATHS MEAN SOMETHING BAD, SOMETHING TERRIBLE, FOR MUTANTKIND IN THE FUTURE.
I'VE SEEN THE FUTURE THAT AHAB WANTS.
I SHOULD HAVE KNOWN THAT HE WAS COMING WHEN I STARTED TO CHANGE, WHEN MY HOUND MARKING STARTED TO RETURN.
WE HAVE TO DO EVERYTHING IN OUR POWER TO STOP IT.
WE HAVE TO PROTECT YOUNG SCOTT, JEAN, HANK AND WARREN LIKE OUR LIVES DEPEND ON IT.
BECAUSE... THEY VERY WELL MAY.

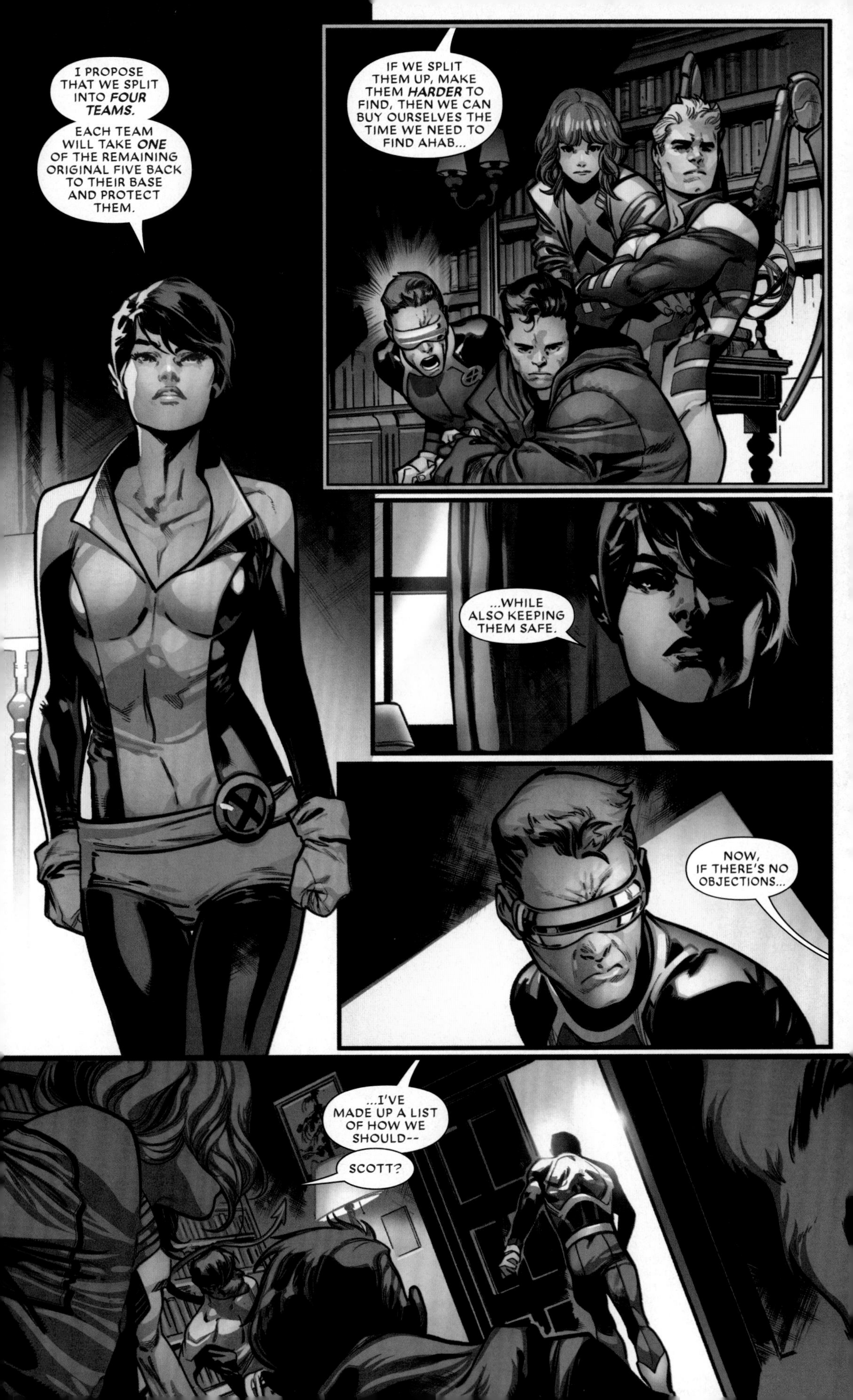
I PROPOSE THAT WE SPLIT INTO *FOUR TEAMS.*
EACH TEAM WILL TAKE *ONE* OF THE REMAINING ORIGINAL FIVE BACK TO THEIR BASE AND PROTECT THEM.
IF WE SPLIT THEM UP, MAKE THEM *HARDER* TO FIND, THEN WE CAN BUY OURSELVES THE TIME WE NEED TO FIND AHAB...
...WHILE ALSO KEEPING THEM SAFE.
NOW, IF THERE'S NO OBJECTIONS...
...I'VE MADE UP A LIST OF HOW WE SHOULD--
SCOTT?

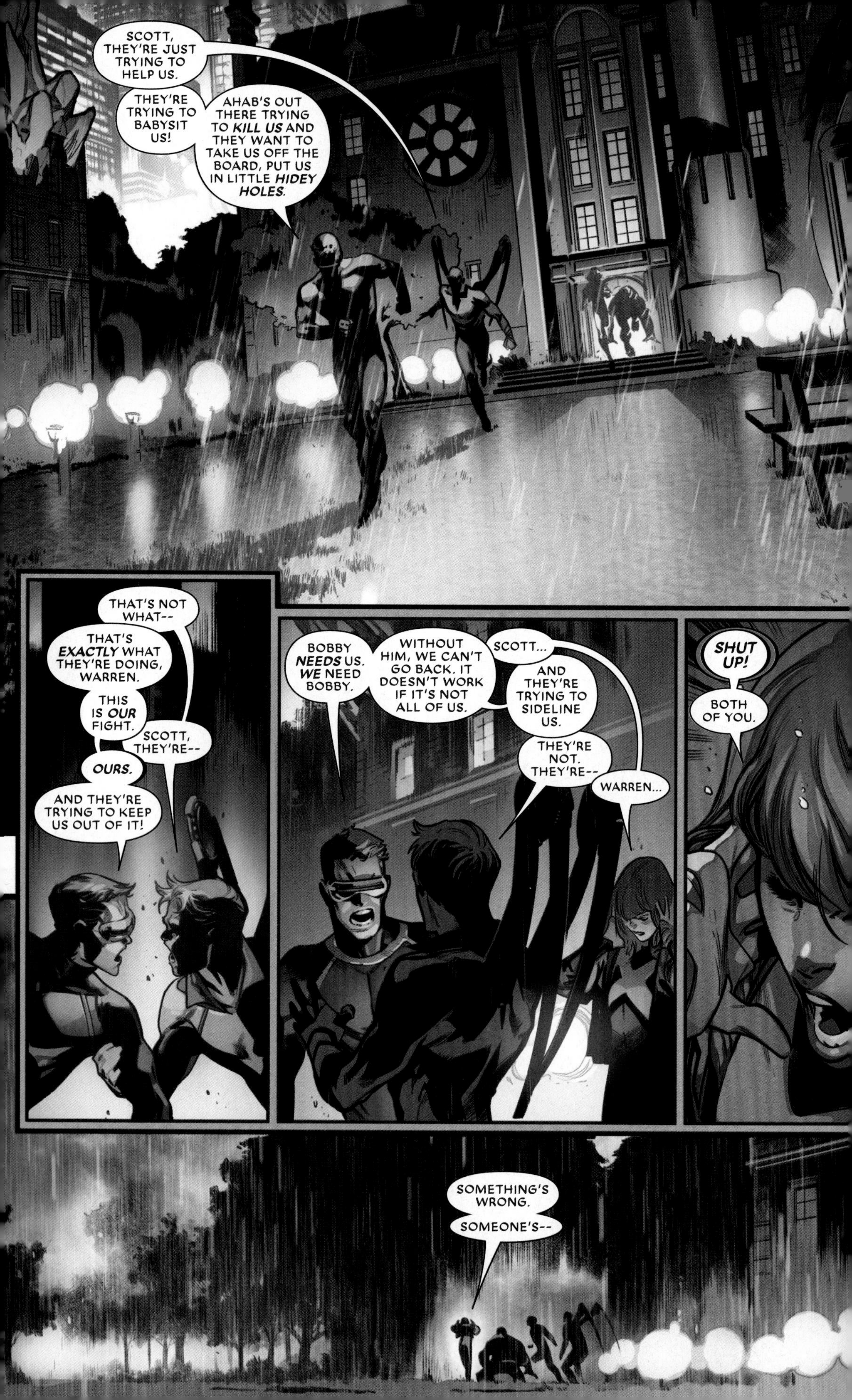

SCOTT, THEY'RE JUST TRYING TO HELP US.
THEY'RE TRYING TO BABYSIT US!
AHAB'S OUT THERE TRYING TO KILL US AND THEY WANT TO TAKE US OFF THE BOARD, PUT US IN LITTLE HIDEY HOLES.
THAT'S NOT WHAT--
THAT'S EXACTLY WHAT THEY'RE DOING, WARREN.
THIS IS OUR FIGHT.
SCOTT, THEY'RE--
OURS.
AND THEY'RE TRYING TO KEEP US OUT OF IT!
BOBBY NEEDS US. WE NEED BOBBY.
WITHOUT HIM, WE CAN'T GO BACK. IT DOESN'T WORK IF IT'S NOT ALL OF US.
SCOTT...
AND THEY'RE TRYING TO SIDELINE US.
THEY'RE NOT. THEY'RE--
WARREN...
SHUT UP!
BOTH OF YOU.
SOMETHING'S WRONG.
SOMEONE'S--

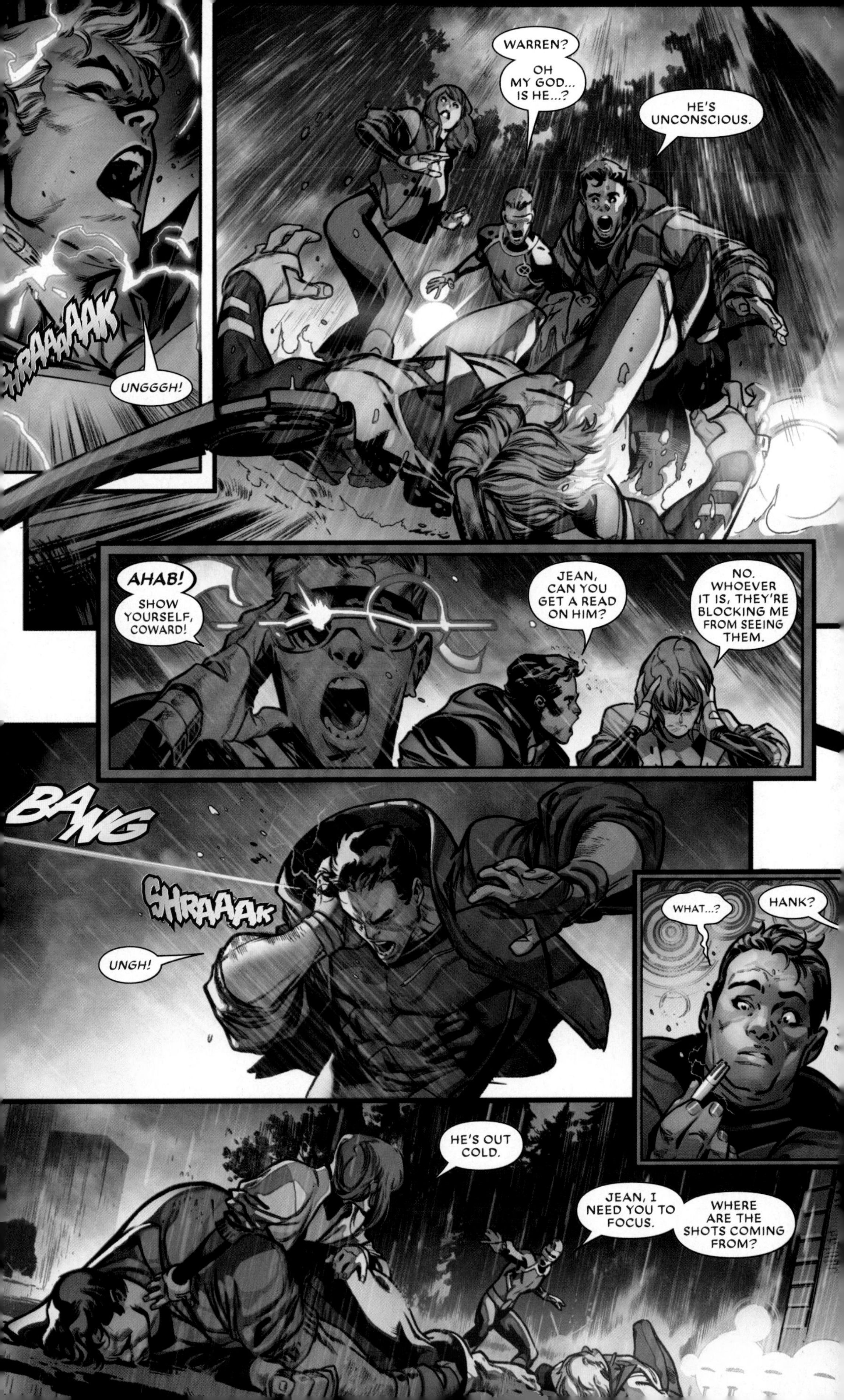
SHRAAAAK
UNGGGH!
WARREN?
OH MY GOD... IS HE...?
HE'S UNCONSCIOUS.
AHAB! SHOW YOURSELF, COWARD!
JEAN, CAN YOU GET A READ ON HIM?
NO. WHOEVER IT IS, THEY'RE BLOCKING ME FROM SEEING THEM.
BANG
SHRAAAK
UNGH!
WHAT...?
HANK?
HE'S OUT COLD.
JEAN, I NEED YOU TO FOCUS.
WHERE ARE THE SHOTS COMING FROM?

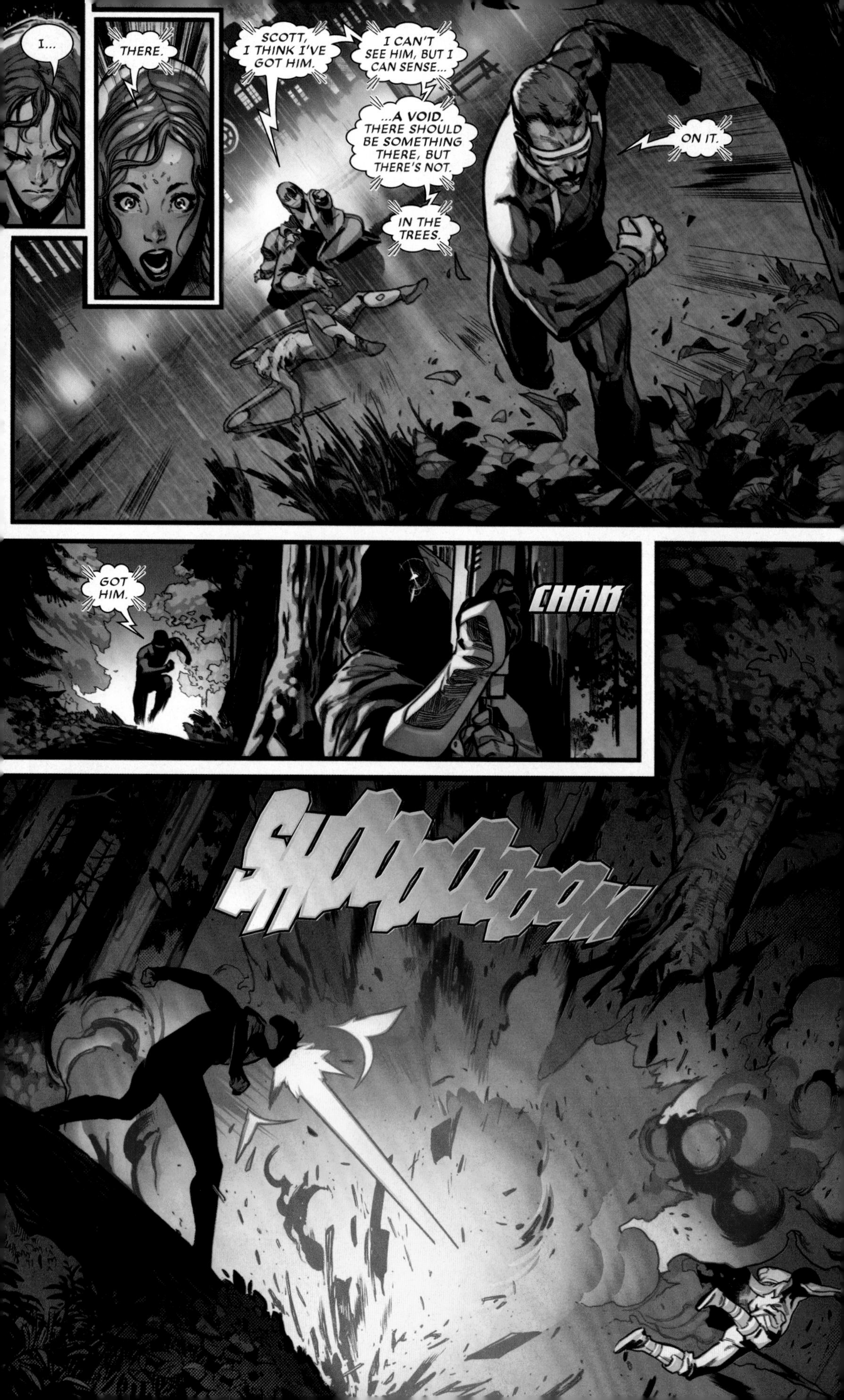
I...
THERE.
SCOTT, I THINK I'VE GOT HIM.
I CAN'T SEE HIM, BUT I CAN SENSE...
...A VOID. THERE SHOULD BE SOMETHING THERE, BUT THERE'S NOT.
IN THE TREES.
ON IT.
GOT HIM.
CHAK
SHOOOOOOM

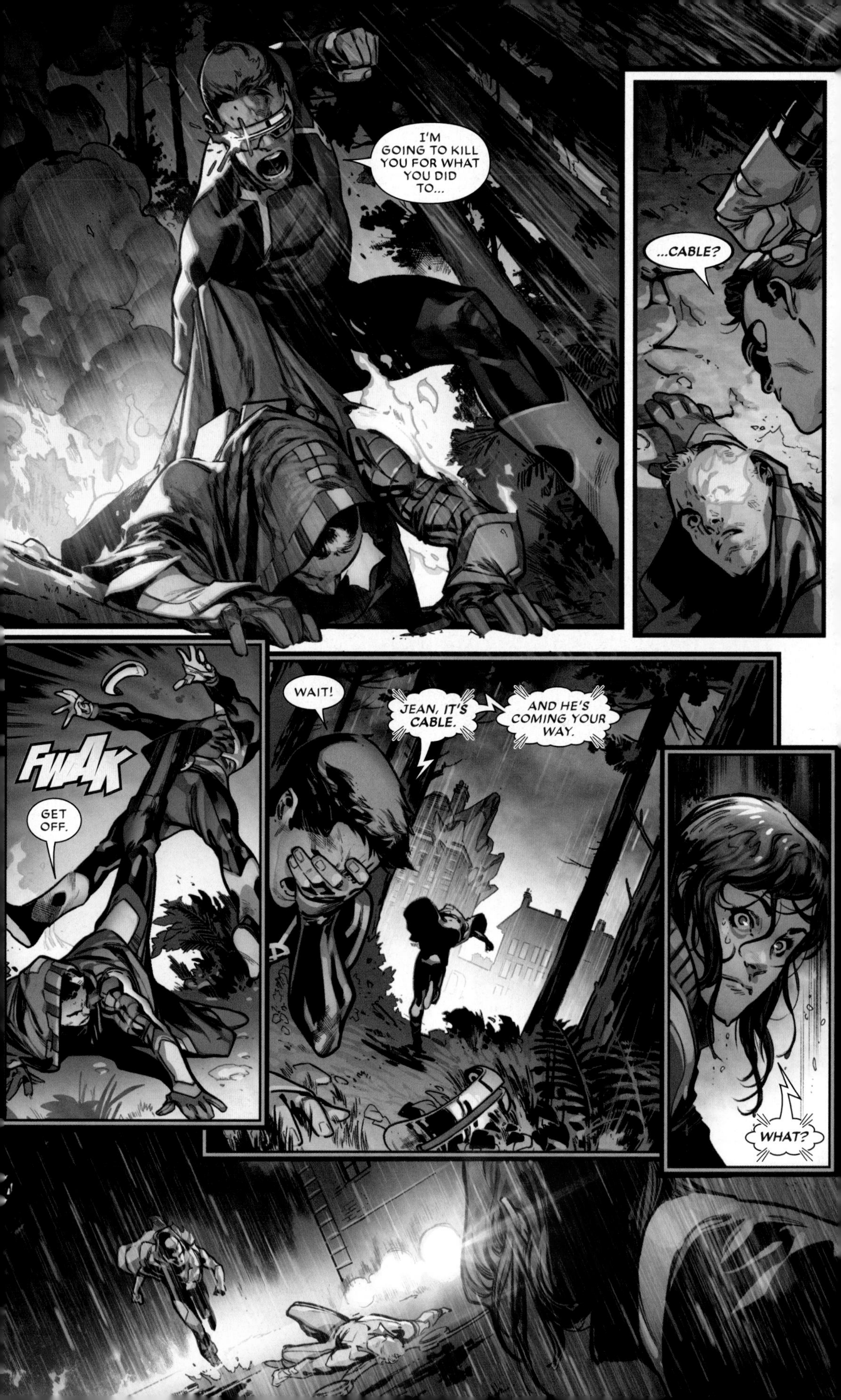
I'M GOING TO KILL YOU FOR WHAT YOU DID TO...
...CABLE?
FWAK
GET OFF.
WAIT!
JEAN, IT'S CABLE.
AND HE'S COMING YOUR WAY.
WHAT?

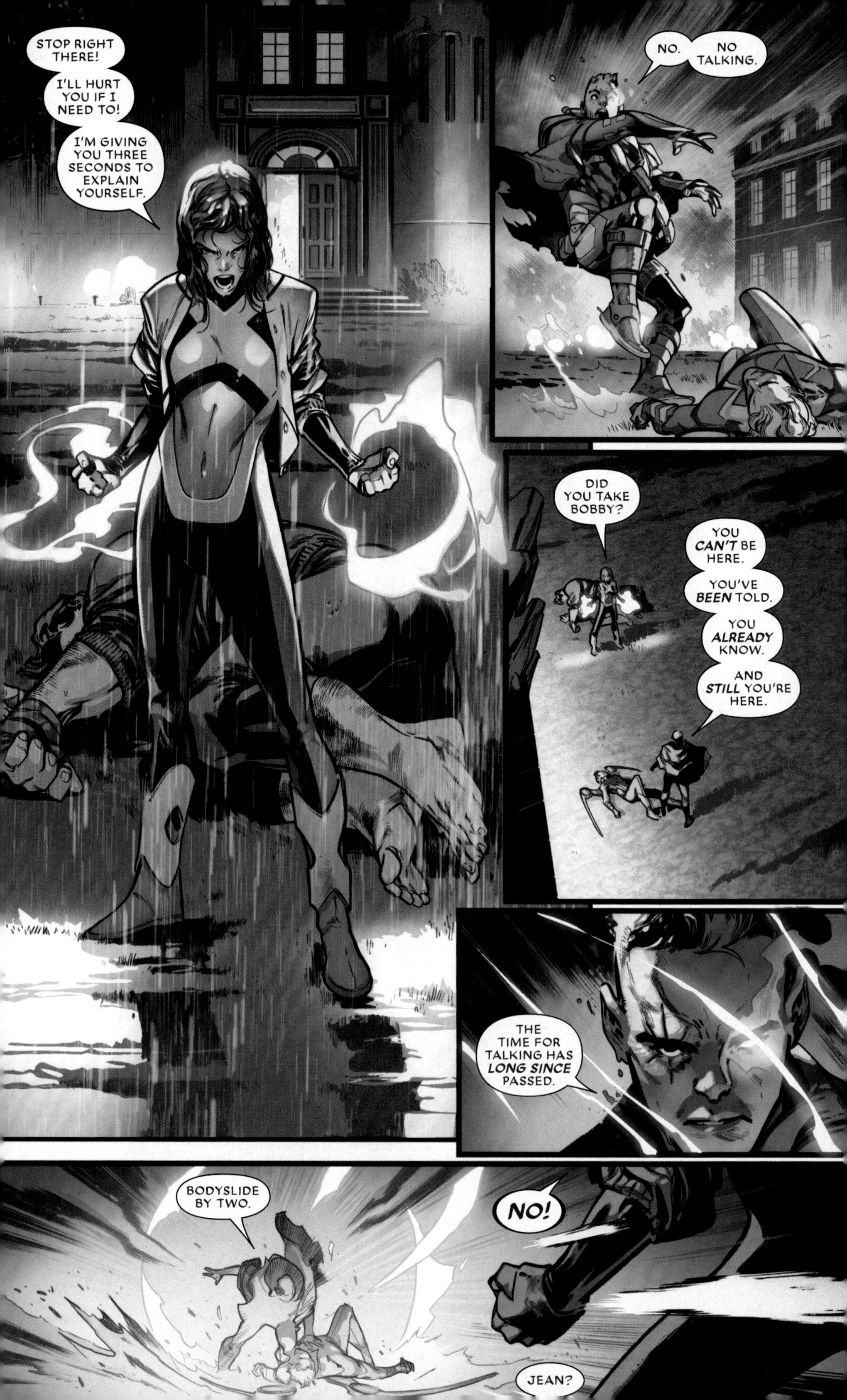
STOP RIGHT THERE!
I'LL HURT YOU IF I NEED TO!
I'M GIVING YOU THREE SECONDS TO EXPLAIN YOURSELF.
NO.
NO TALKING.
DID YOU TAKE BOBBY?
YOU CAN'T BE HERE.
YOU'VE BEEN TOLD.
YOU ALREADY KNOW.
AND STILL YOU'RE HERE.
THE TIME FOR TALKING HAS LONG SINCE PASSED.
BODYSLIDE BY TWO.
NO!
JEAN?

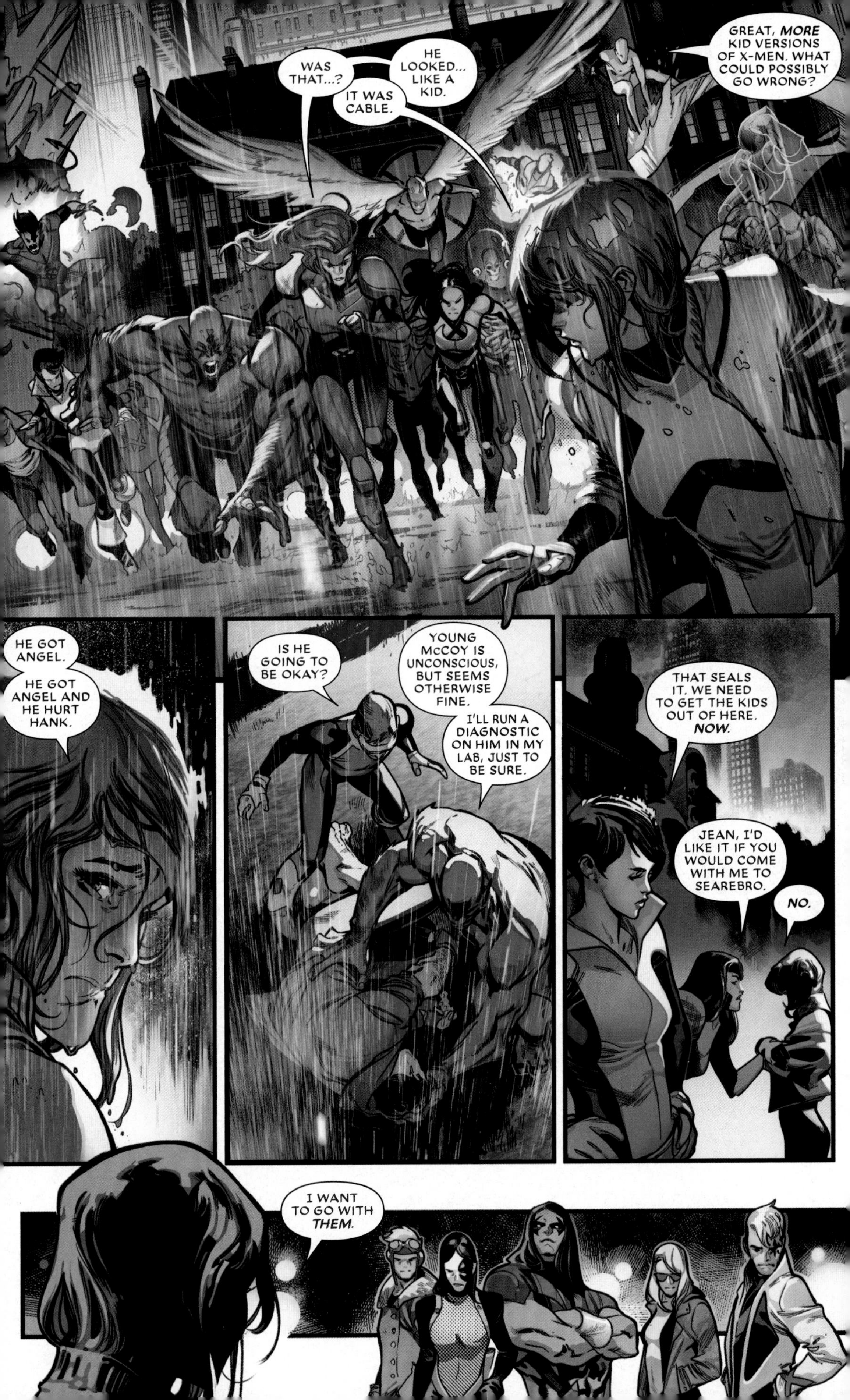
WAS THAT...?
HE LOOKED... LIKE A KID.
IT WAS CABLE.
GREAT, MORE KID VERSIONS OF X-MEN. WHAT COULD POSSIBLY GO WRONG?
HE GOT ANGEL.
HE GOT ANGEL AND HE HURT HANK.
IS HE GOING TO BE OKAY?
YOUNG McCOY IS UNCONSCIOUS, BUT SEEMS OTHERWISE FINE.
I'LL RUN A DIAGNOSTIC ON HIM IN MY LAB, JUST TO BE SURE.
THAT SEALS IT. WE NEED TO GET THE KIDS OUT OF HERE. NOW.
JEAN, I'D LIKE IT IF YOU WOULD COME WITH ME TO SEAREBRO.
NO.
I WANT TO GO WITH THEM.

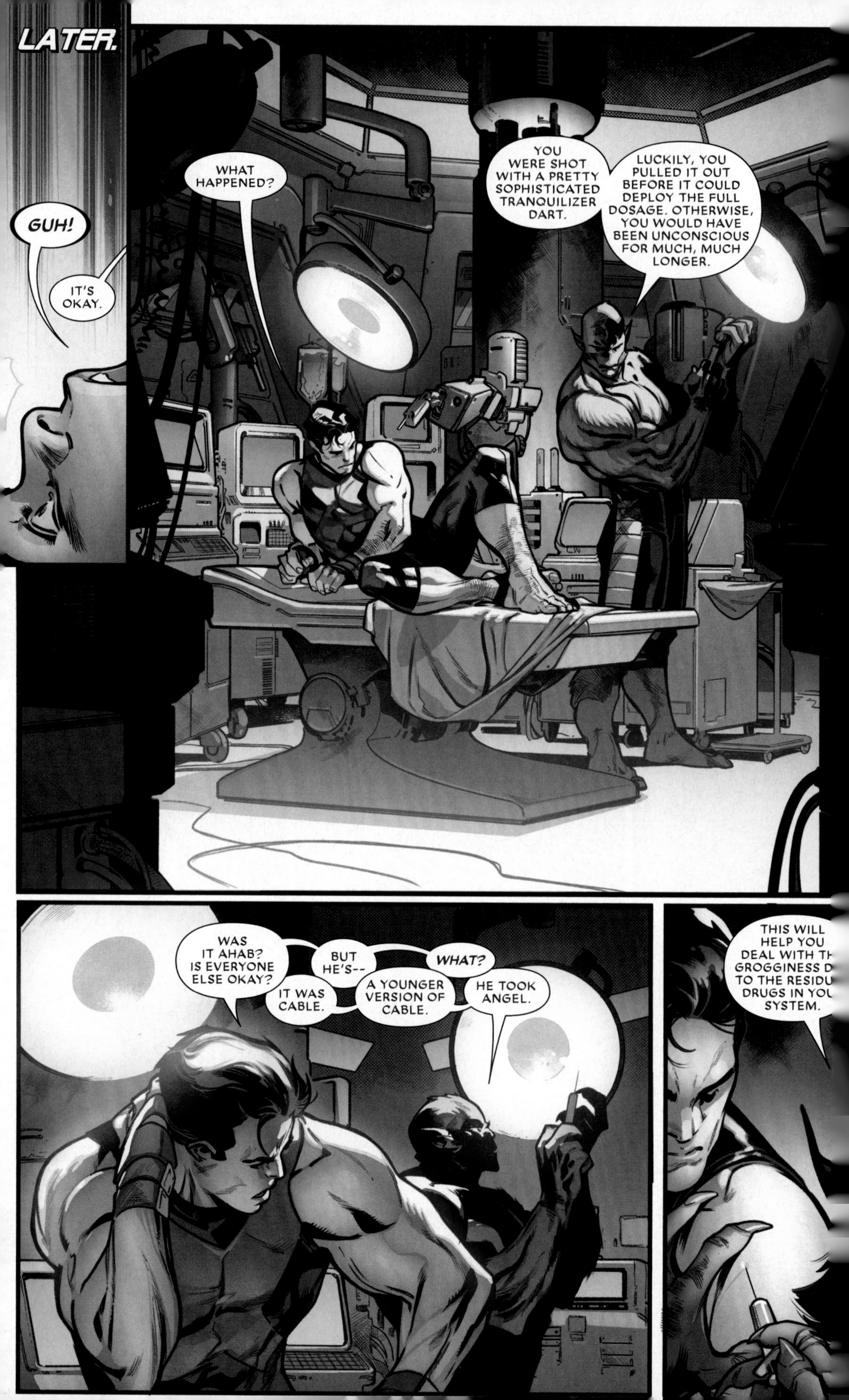

LATER.
GUH!
IT'S OKAY.
WHAT HAPPENED?
YOU WERE SHOT WITH A PRETTY SOPHISTICATED TRANQUILIZER DART.
LUCKILY, YOU PULLED IT OUT BEFORE IT COULD DEPLOY THE FULL DOSAGE. OTHERWISE, YOU WOULD HAVE BEEN UNCONSCIOUS FOR MUCH, MUCH LONGER.
WAS IT AHAB? IS EVERYONE ELSE OKAY?
IT WAS CABLE.
BUT HE'S--
A YOUNGER VERSION OF CABLE.
WHAT?
HE TOOK ANGEL.
THIS WILL HELP YOU DEAL WITH TH GROGGINESS D TO THE RESIDU DRUGS IN YOU SYSTEM.

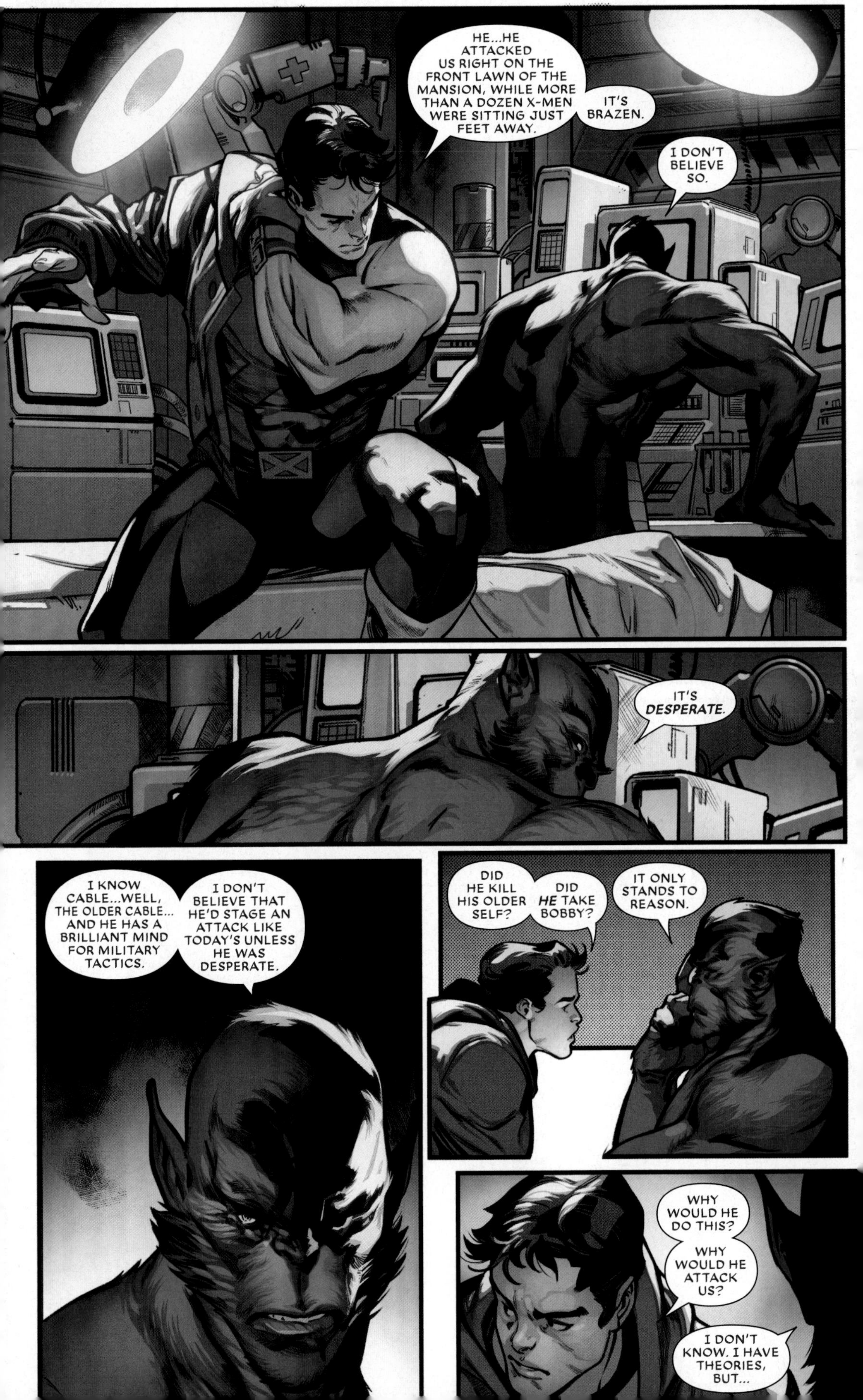
HE...HE ATTACKED US RIGHT ON THE FRONT LAWN OF THE MANSION, WHILE MORE THAN A DOZEN X-MEN WERE SITTING JUST FEET AWAY.
IT'S BRAZEN.
I DON'T BELIEVE SO.
IT'S *DESPERATE.*
I KNOW CABLE...WELL, THE OLDER CABLE... AND HE HAS A BRILLIANT MIND FOR MILITARY TACTICS.
I DON'T BELIEVE THAT HE'D STAGE AN ATTACK LIKE TODAY'S UNLESS HE WAS DESPERATE.
DID HE KILL HIS OLDER SELF?
DID *HE* TAKE BOBBY?
IT ONLY STANDS TO REASON.
WHY WOULD HE DO THIS?
WHY WOULD HE ATTACK US?
I DON'T KNOW. I HAVE THEORIES, BUT...

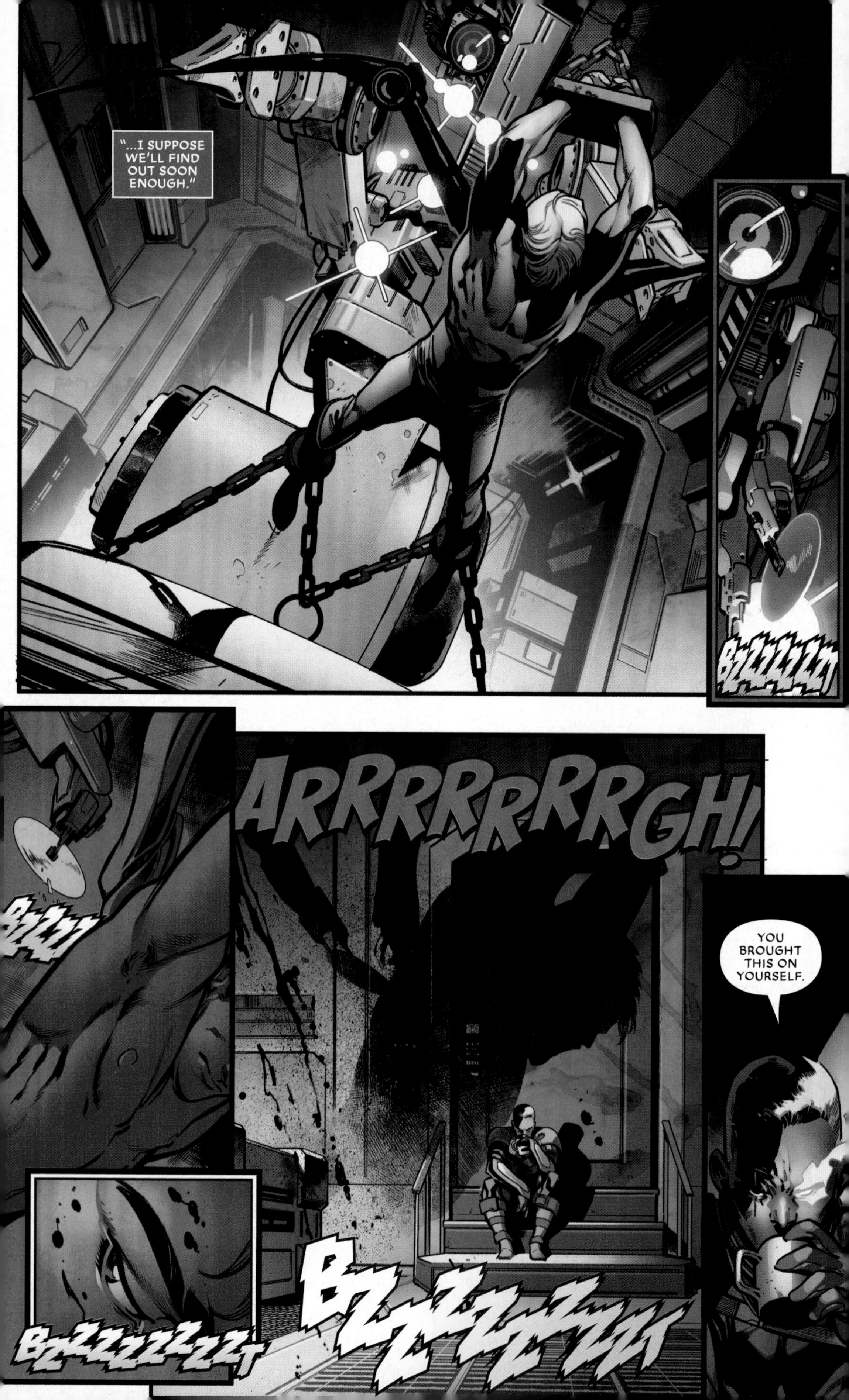
"...I SUPPOSE WE'LL FIND OUT SOON ENOUGH."
BZZZZZZZT
BZZZ
ARRRRRRRGH!
YOU BROUGHT THIS ON YOURSELF.
BZZZZZZZZZZT
BZZZZZZZT

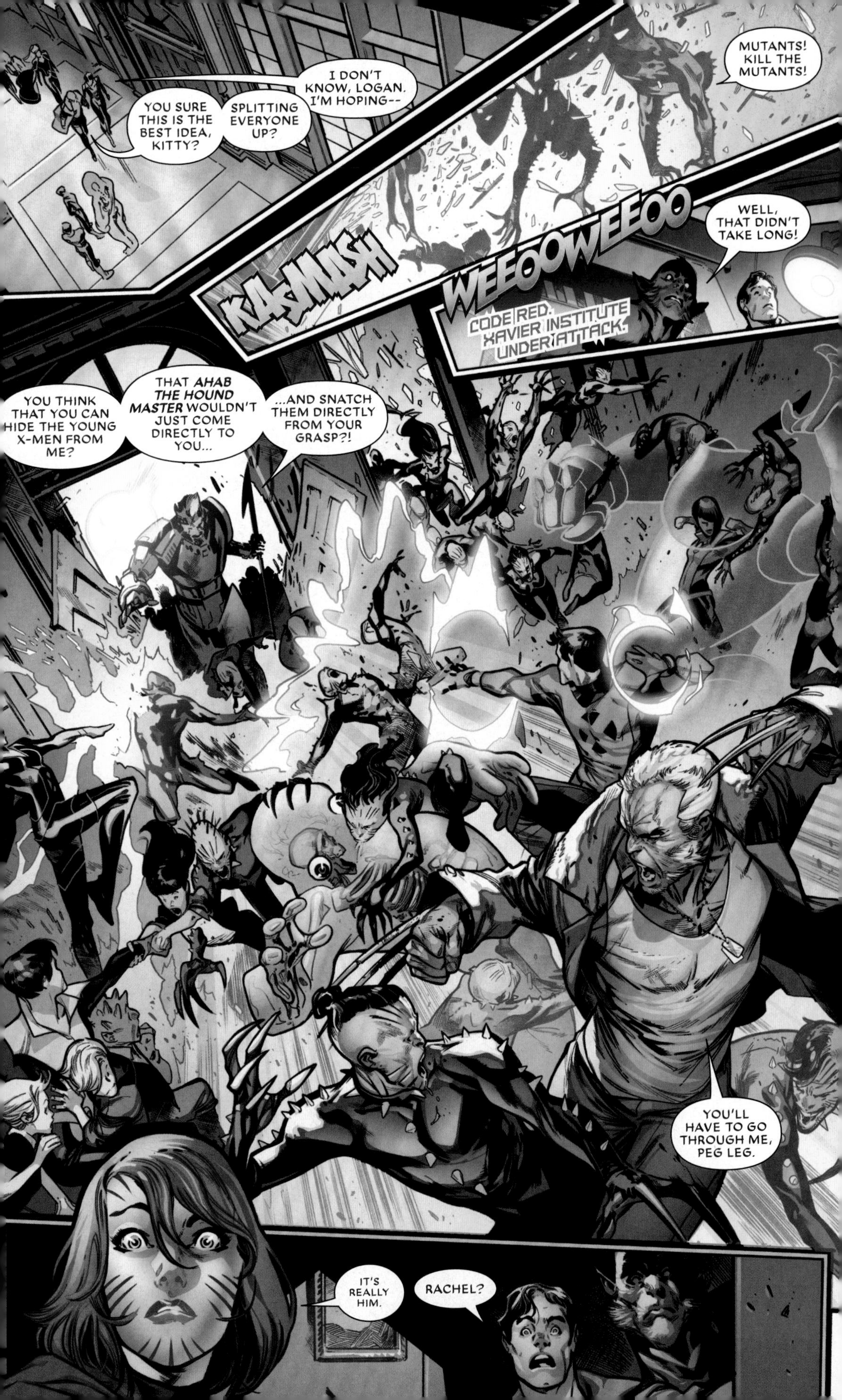
YOU SURE THIS IS THE BEST IDEA, KITTY?
SPLITTING EVERYONE UP?
I DON'T KNOW, LOGAN. I'M HOPING--
MUTANTS! KILL THE MUTANTS!
KASMASH
WEEOOWEEOO
CODE RED. XAVIER INSTITUTE UNDER ATTACK.
WELL, THAT DIDN'T TAKE LONG!
YOU THINK THAT YOU CAN HIDE THE YOUNG X-MEN FROM ME?
THAT AHAB THE HOUND MASTER WOULDN'T JUST COME DIRECTLY TO YOU...
...AND SNATCH THEM DIRECTLY FROM YOUR GRASP?!
YOU'LL HAVE TO GO THROUGH ME, PEG LEG.
IT'S REALLY HIM.
RACHEL?

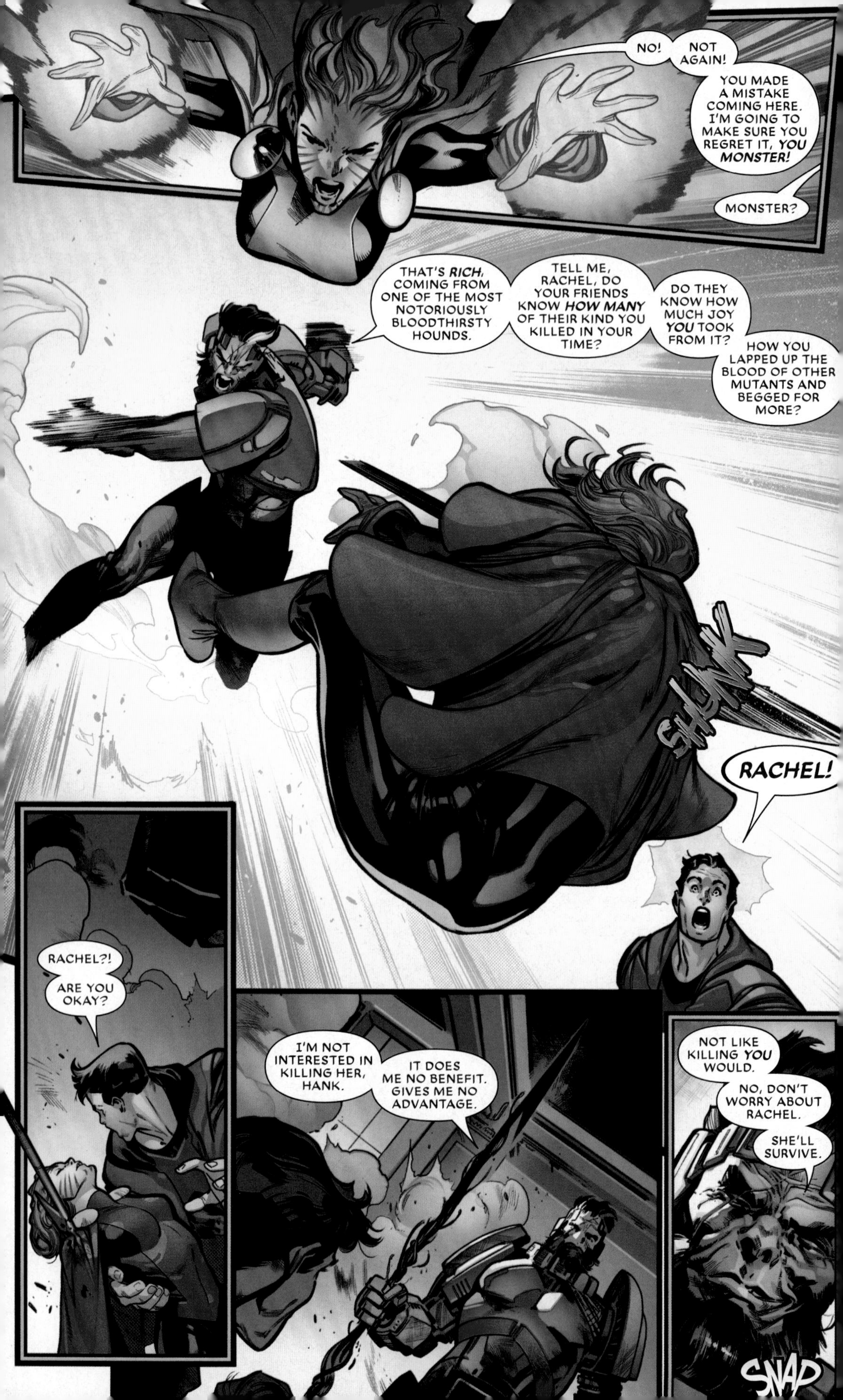
NO!
NOT AGAIN!
YOU MADE A MISTAKE COMING HERE. I'M GOING TO MAKE SURE YOU REGRET IT, YOU MONSTER!
MONSTER?
THAT'S RICH, COMING FROM ONE OF THE MOST NOTORIOUSLY BLOODTHIRSTY HOUNDS.
TELL ME, RACHEL, DO YOUR FRIENDS KNOW HOW MANY OF THEIR KIND YOU KILLED IN YOUR TIME?
DO THEY KNOW HOW MUCH JOY YOU TOOK FROM IT?
HOW YOU LAPPED UP THE BLOOD OF OTHER MUTANTS AND BEGGED FOR MORE?
SHUNK
RACHEL!
RACHEL?!
ARE YOU OKAY?
I'M NOT INTERESTED IN KILLING HER, HANK.
IT DOES ME NO BENEFIT. GIVES ME NO ADVANTAGE.
NOT LIKE KILLING YOU WOULD.
NO, DON'T WORRY ABOUT RACHEL.
SHE'LL SURVIVE.
SNAP

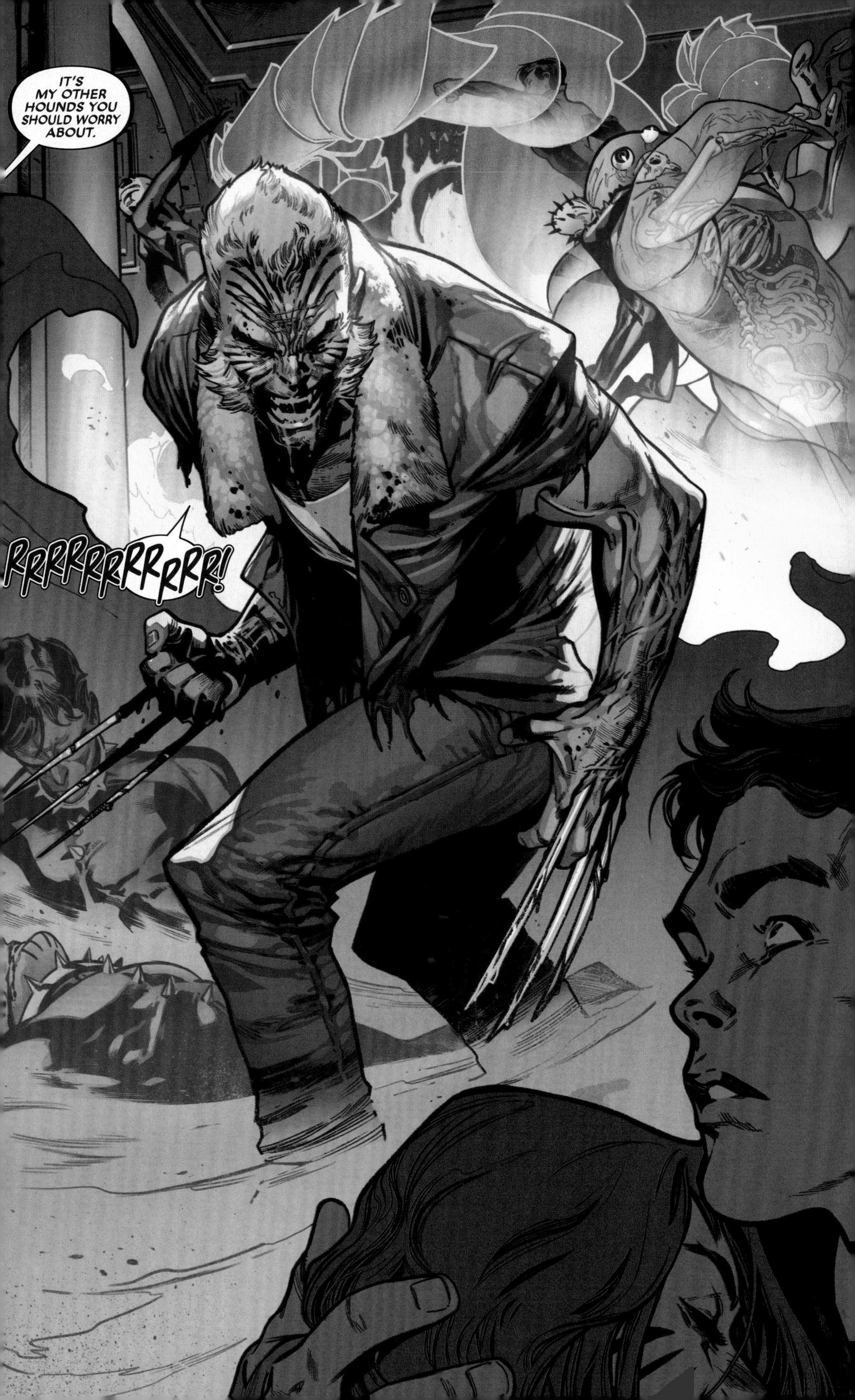
IT'S MY OTHER HOUNDS YOU SHOULD WORRY ABOUT.
RRRRRRRRRRR!

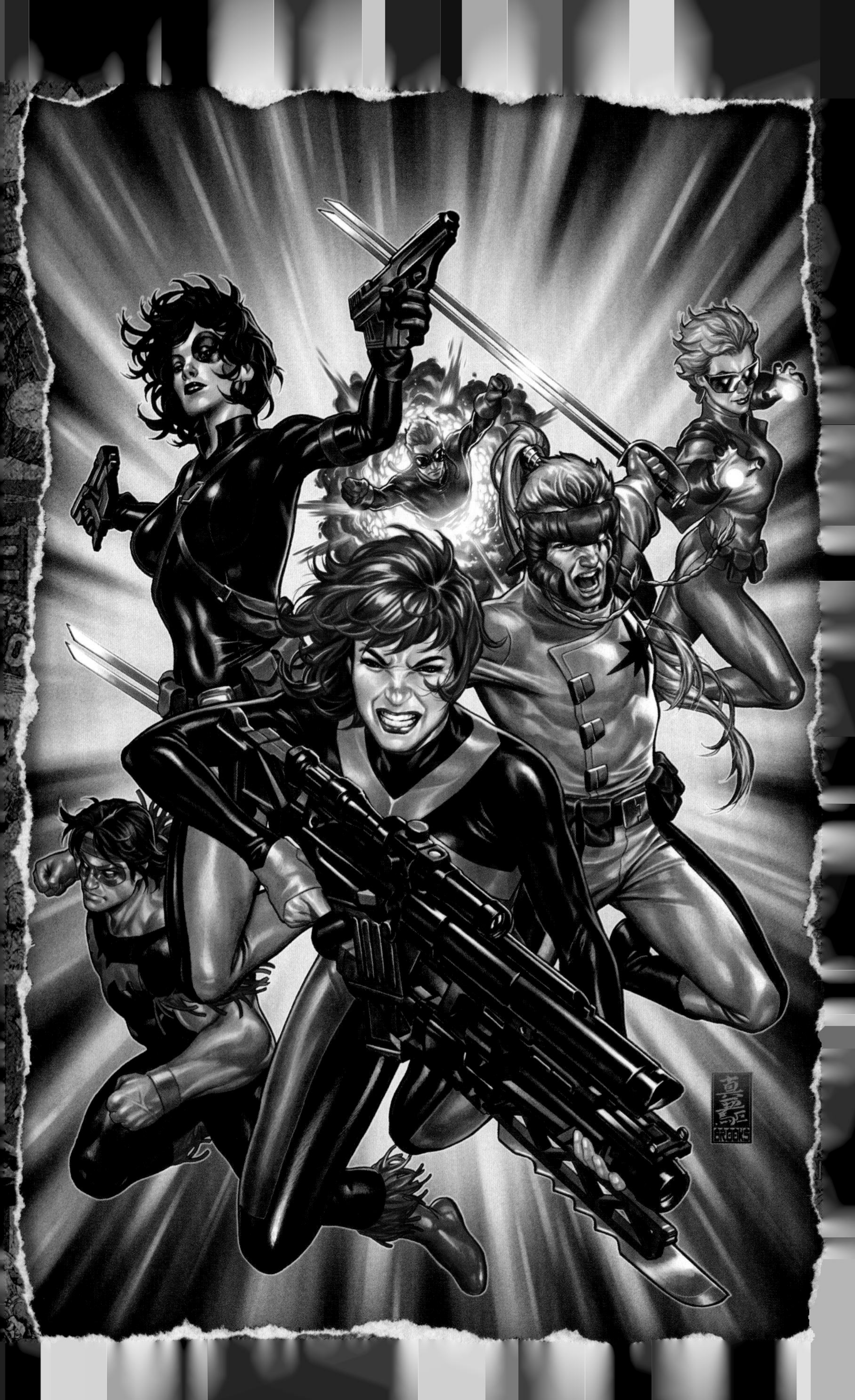
BROOKS

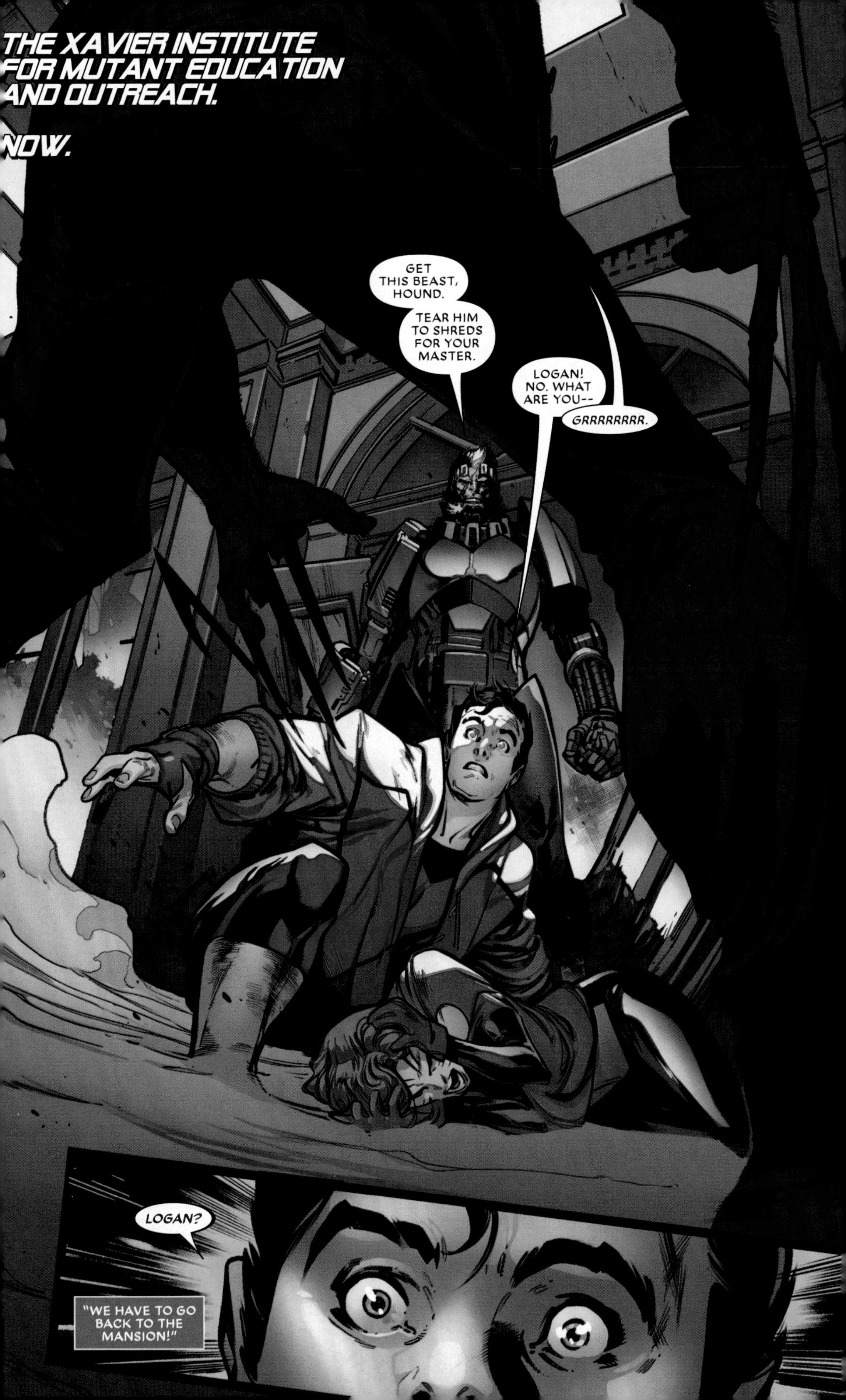
THE XAVIER INSTITUTE FOR MUTANT EDUCATION AND OUTREACH.
NOW.
GET THIS BEAST, HOUND.
TEAR HIM TO SHREDS FOR YOUR MASTER.
LOGAN! NO. WHAT ARE YOU--
GRRRRRRRR.
LOGAN?
"WE HAVE TO GO BACK TO THE MANSION!"

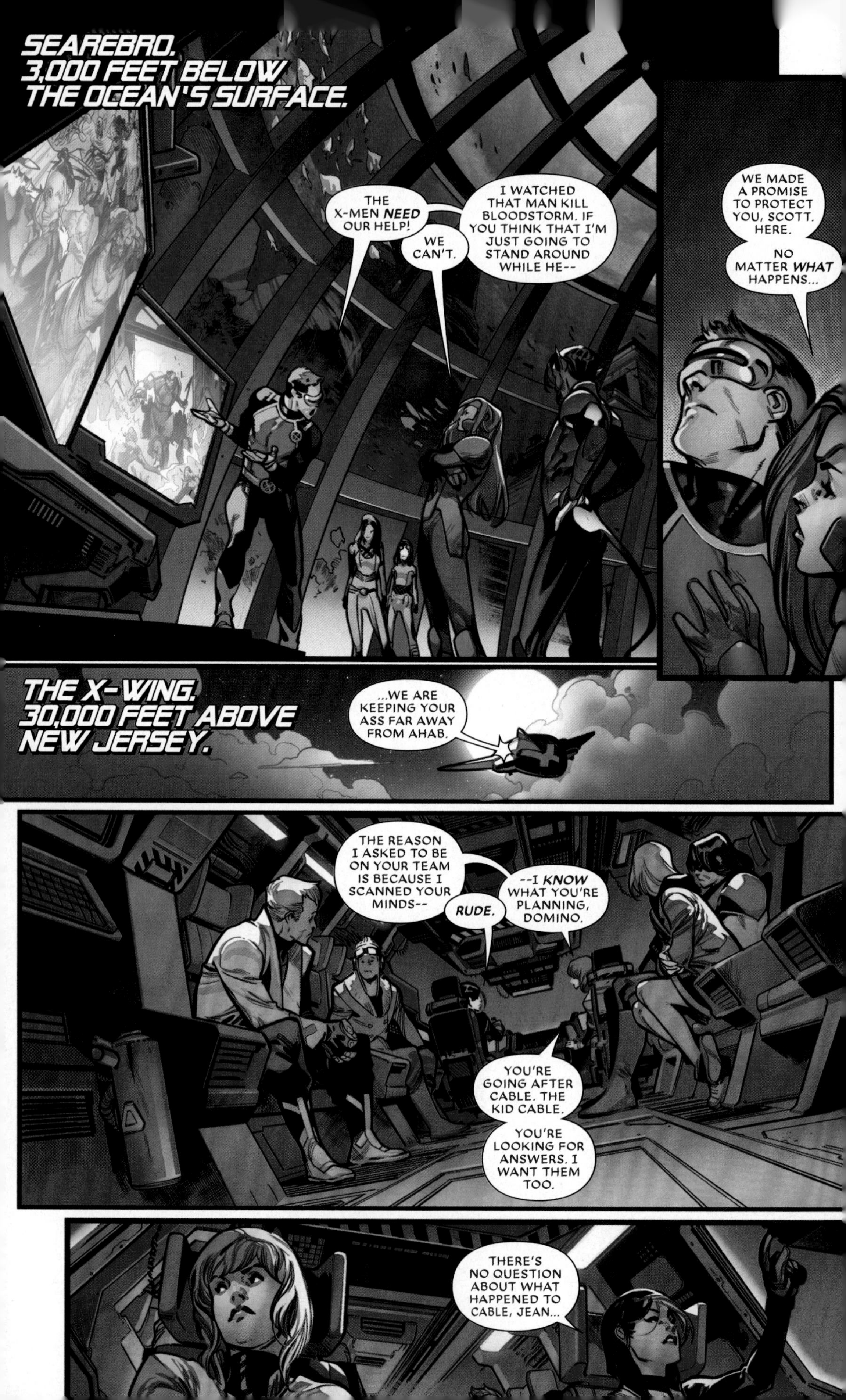
SEAREBRO.
3,000 FEET BELOW THE OCEAN'S SURFACE.
THE X-MEN NEED OUR HELP!
WE CAN'T.
I WATCHED THAT MAN KILL BLOODSTORM. IF YOU THINK THAT I'M JUST GOING TO STAND AROUND WHILE HE--
WE MADE A PROMISE TO PROTECT YOU, SCOTT. HERE.
NO MATTER WHAT HAPPENS...
THE X-WING.
30,000 FEET ABOVE NEW JERSEY.
...WE ARE KEEPING YOUR ASS FAR AWAY FROM AHAB.
THE REASON I ASKED TO BE ON YOUR TEAM IS BECAUSE I SCANNED YOUR MINDS--
RUDE.
--I KNOW WHAT YOU'RE PLANNING, DOMINO.
YOU'RE GOING AFTER CABLE. THE KID CABLE.
YOU'RE LOOKING FOR ANSWERS. I WANT THEM TOO.
THERE'S NO QUESTION ABOUT WHAT HAPPENED TO CABLE, JEAN...

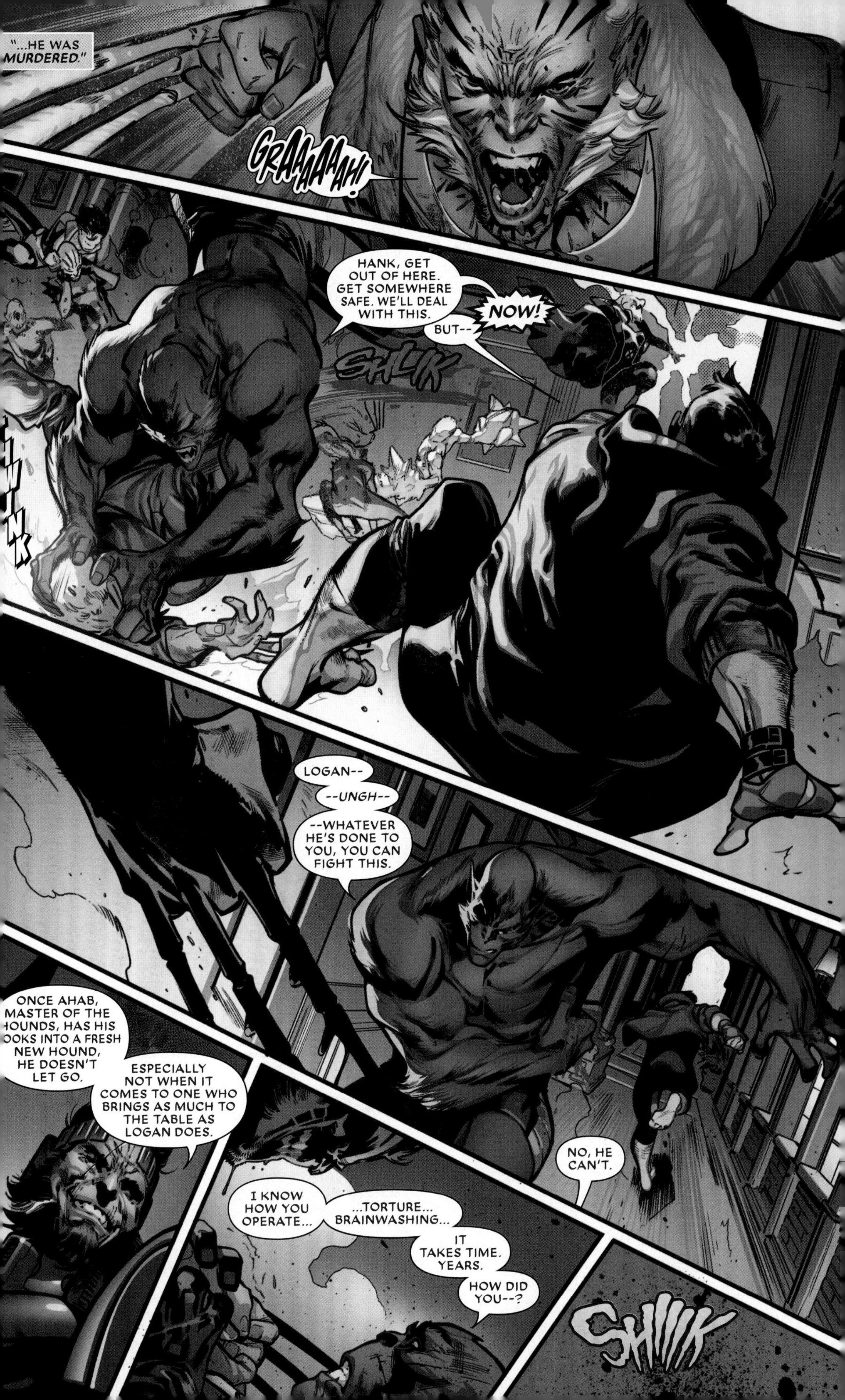
"...HE WAS MURDERED."
GRAAAAAAH!
HANK, GET OUT OF HERE. GET SOMEWHERE SAFE. WE'LL DEAL WITH THIS.
BUT--
NOW!
SHLIK
LOGAN--
--UNGH--
--WHATEVER HE'S DONE TO YOU, YOU CAN FIGHT THIS.
NO, HE CAN'T.
ONCE AHAB, MASTER OF THE OUNDS, HAS HIS OOKS INTO A FRESH NEW HOUND, HE DOESN'T LET GO.
ESPECIALLY NOT WHEN IT COMES TO ONE WHO BRINGS AS MUCH TO THE TABLE AS LOGAN DOES.
I KNOW HOW YOU OPERATE...
...TORTURE... BRAINWASHING...
IT TAKES TIME. YEARS.
HOW DID YOU--?
SHIIIK

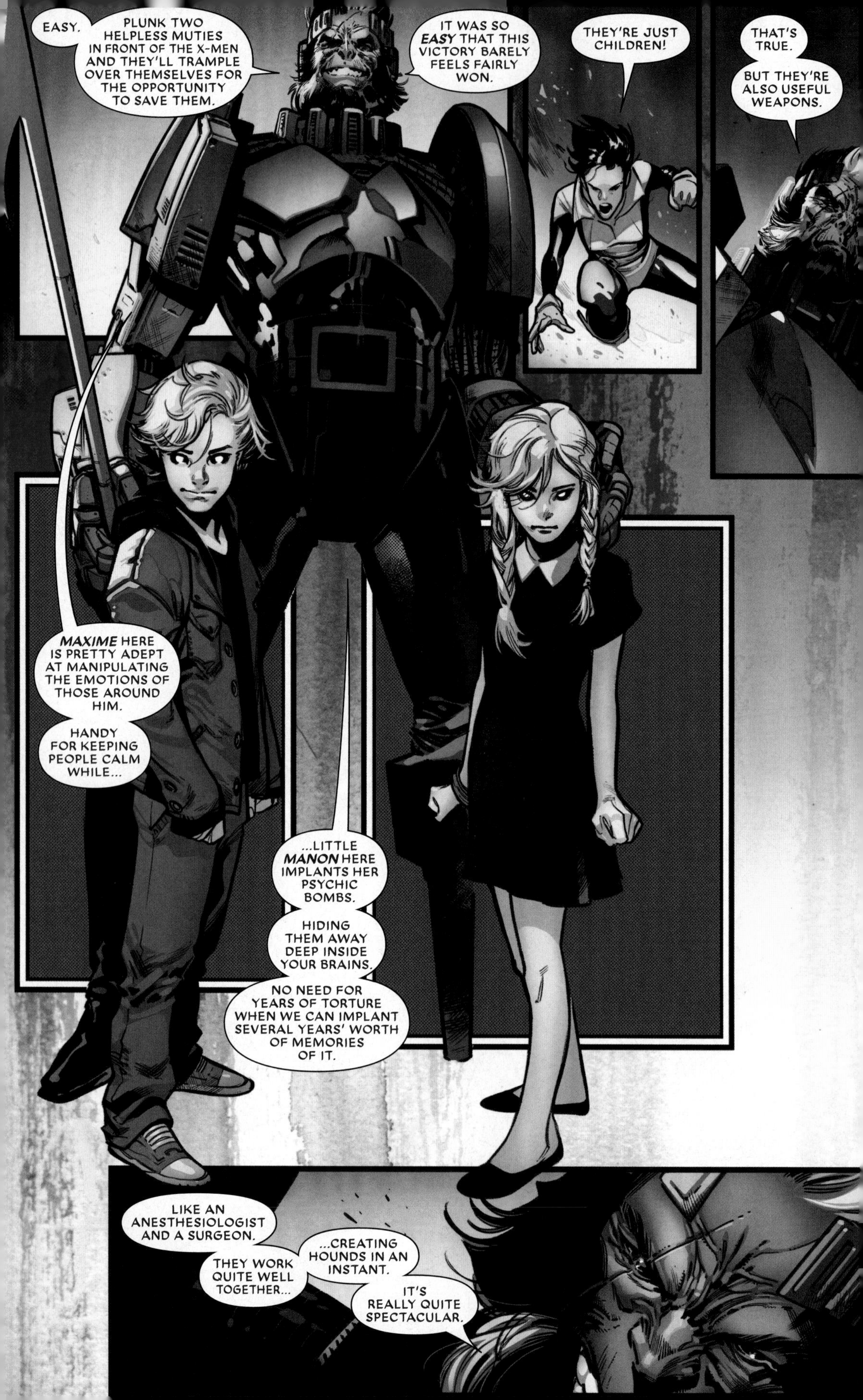
EASY.
PLUNK TWO HELPLESS MUTIES IN FRONT OF THE X-MEN AND THEY'LL TRAMPLE OVER THEMSELVES FOR THE OPPORTUNITY TO SAVE THEM.
IT WAS SO EASY THAT THIS VICTORY BARELY FEELS FAIRLY WON.
THEY'RE JUST CHILDREN!
THAT'S TRUE.
BUT THEY'RE ALSO USEFUL WEAPONS.
MAXIME HERE IS PRETTY ADEPT AT MANIPULATING THE EMOTIONS OF THOSE AROUND HIM.
HANDY FOR KEEPING PEOPLE CALM WHILE...
...LITTLE MANON HERE IMPLANTS HER PSYCHIC BOMBS.
HIDING THEM AWAY DEEP INSIDE YOUR BRAINS.
NO NEED FOR YEARS OF TORTURE WHEN WE CAN IMPLANT SEVERAL YEARS' WORTH OF MEMORIES OF IT.
LIKE AN ANESTHESIOLOGIST AND A SURGEON.
THEY WORK QUITE WELL TOGETHER...
...CREATING HOUNDS IN AN INSTANT.
IT'S REALLY QUITE SPECTACULAR.

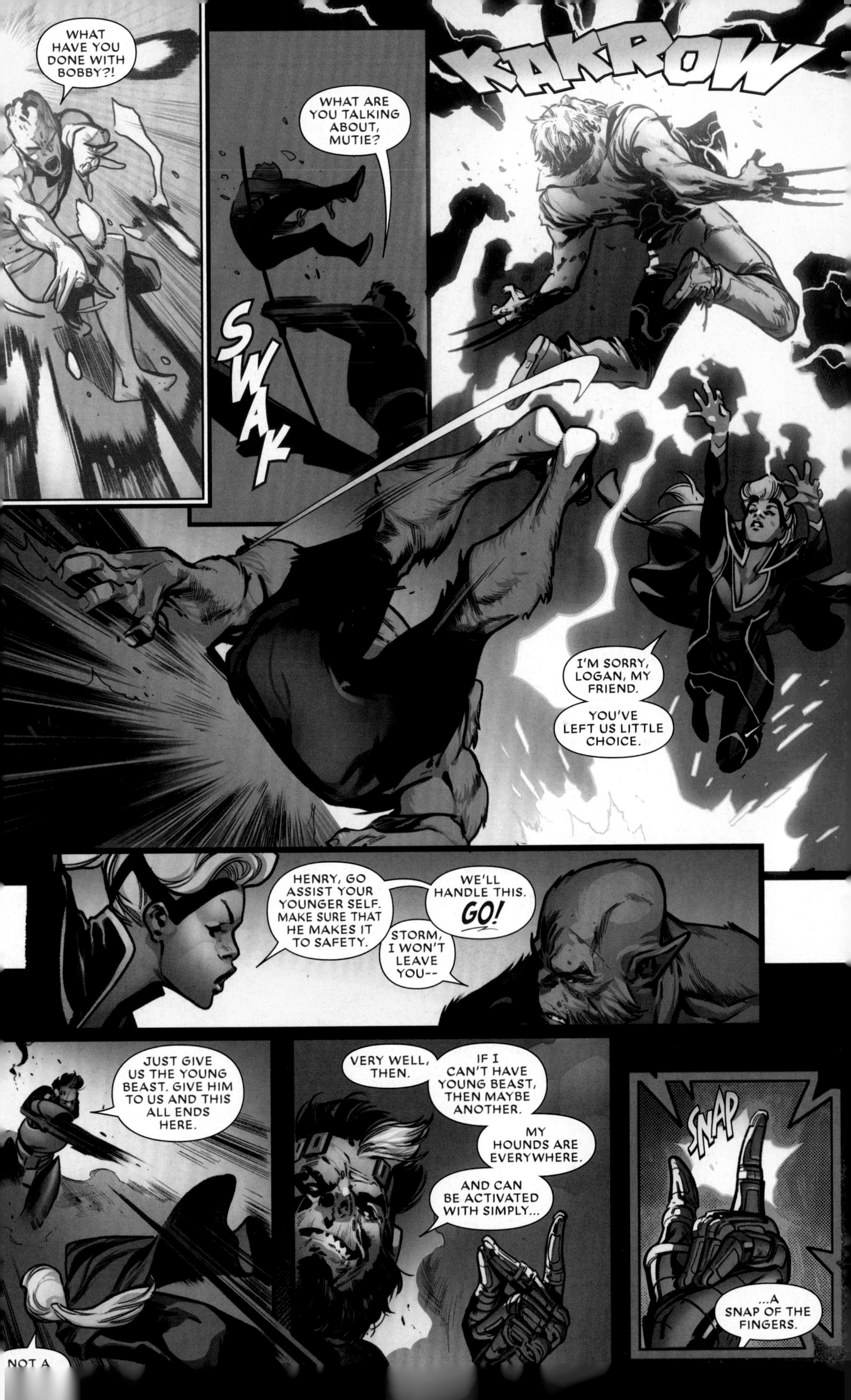

WHAT HAVE YOU DONE WITH BOBBY?!
WHAT ARE YOU TALKING ABOUT, MUTIE?
SWAK
KAKROW
I'M SORRY, LOGAN, MY FRIEND.
YOU'VE LEFT US LITTLE CHOICE.
HENRY, GO ASSIST YOUR YOUNGER SELF. MAKE SURE THAT HE MAKES IT TO SAFETY.
WE'LL HANDLE THIS. GO!
STORM, I WON'T LEAVE YOU--
JUST GIVE US THE YOUNG BEAST. GIVE HIM TO US AND THIS ALL ENDS HERE.
NOT A
VERY WELL, THEN.
IF I CAN'T HAVE YOUNG BEAST, THEN MAYBE ANOTHER.
MY HOUNDS ARE EVERYWHERE.
AND CAN BE ACTIVATED WITH SIMPLY...
SNAP
...A SNAP OF THE FINGERS.

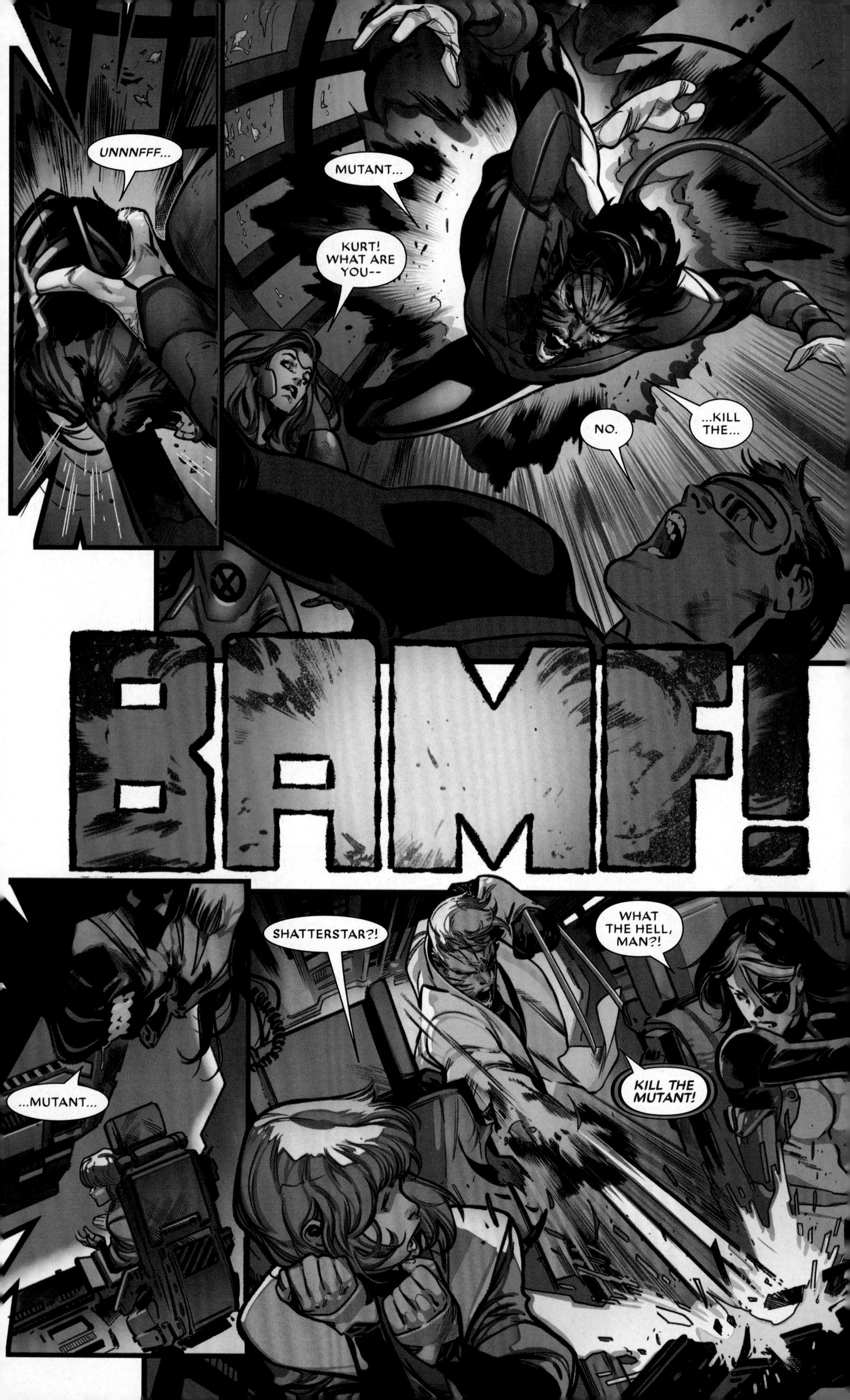
UNNNFFF...
MUTANT...
KURT! WHAT ARE YOU--
NO.
...KILL THE...
BAMF!
...MUTANT...
SHATTERSTAR?!
WHAT THE HELL, MAN?!
KILL THE MUTANT!

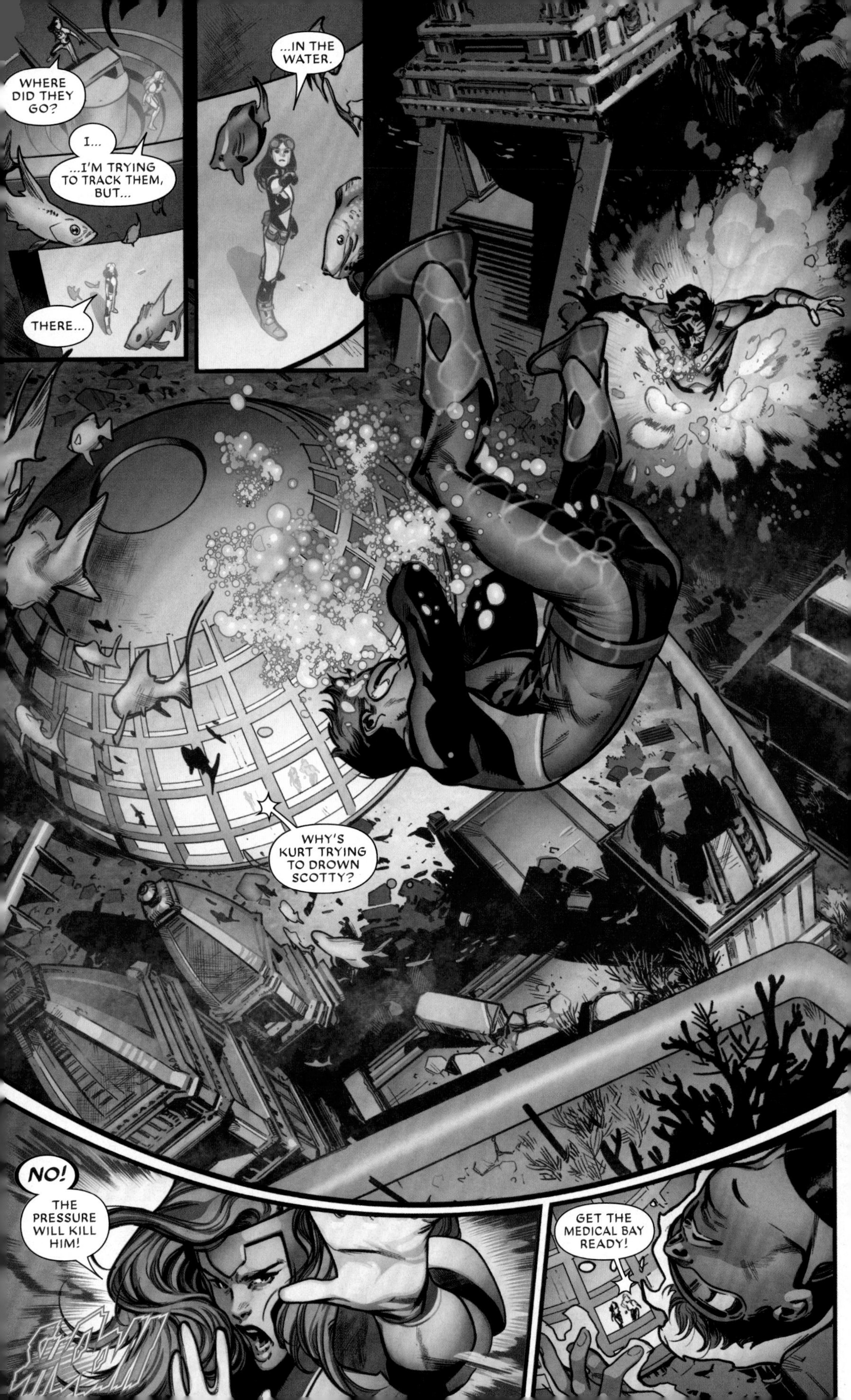

WHERE DID THEY GO?
I...
...I'M TRYING TO TRACK THEM, BUT...
THERE...
...IN THE WATER.
WHY'S KURT TRYING TO DROWN SCOTTY?
NO!
THE PRESSURE WILL KILL HIM!
GET THE MEDICAL BAY READY!

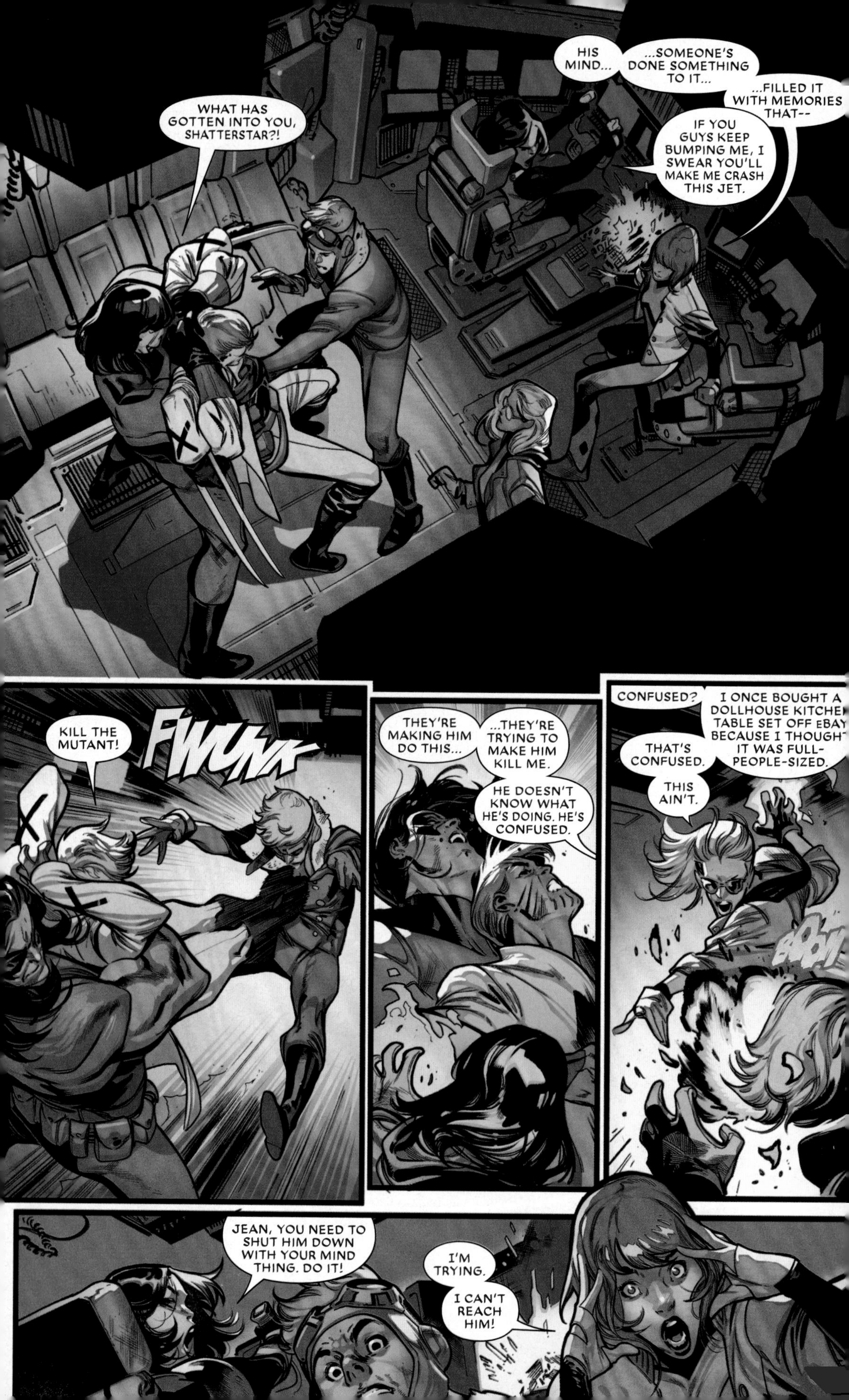
WHAT HAS GOTTEN INTO YOU, SHATTERSTAR?!
HIS MIND...
...SOMEONE'S DONE SOMETHING TO IT...
...FILLED IT WITH MEMORIES THAT--
IF YOU GUYS KEEP BUMPING ME, I SWEAR YOU'LL MAKE ME CRASH THIS JET.
KILL THE MUTANT!
FWUNK
THEY'RE MAKING HIM DO THIS...
...THEY'RE TRYING TO MAKE HIM KILL ME.
HE DOESN'T KNOW WHAT HE'S DOING. HE'S CONFUSED.
CONFUSED?
I ONCE BOUGHT A DOLLHOUSE KITCHEN TABLE SET OFF EBAY BECAUSE I THOUGHT IT WAS FULL-PEOPLE-SIZED.
THAT'S CONFUSED.
THIS AIN'T.
BOOM
JEAN, YOU NEED TO SHUT HIM DOWN WITH YOUR MIND THING. DO IT!
I'M TRYING.
I CAN'T REACH HIM!

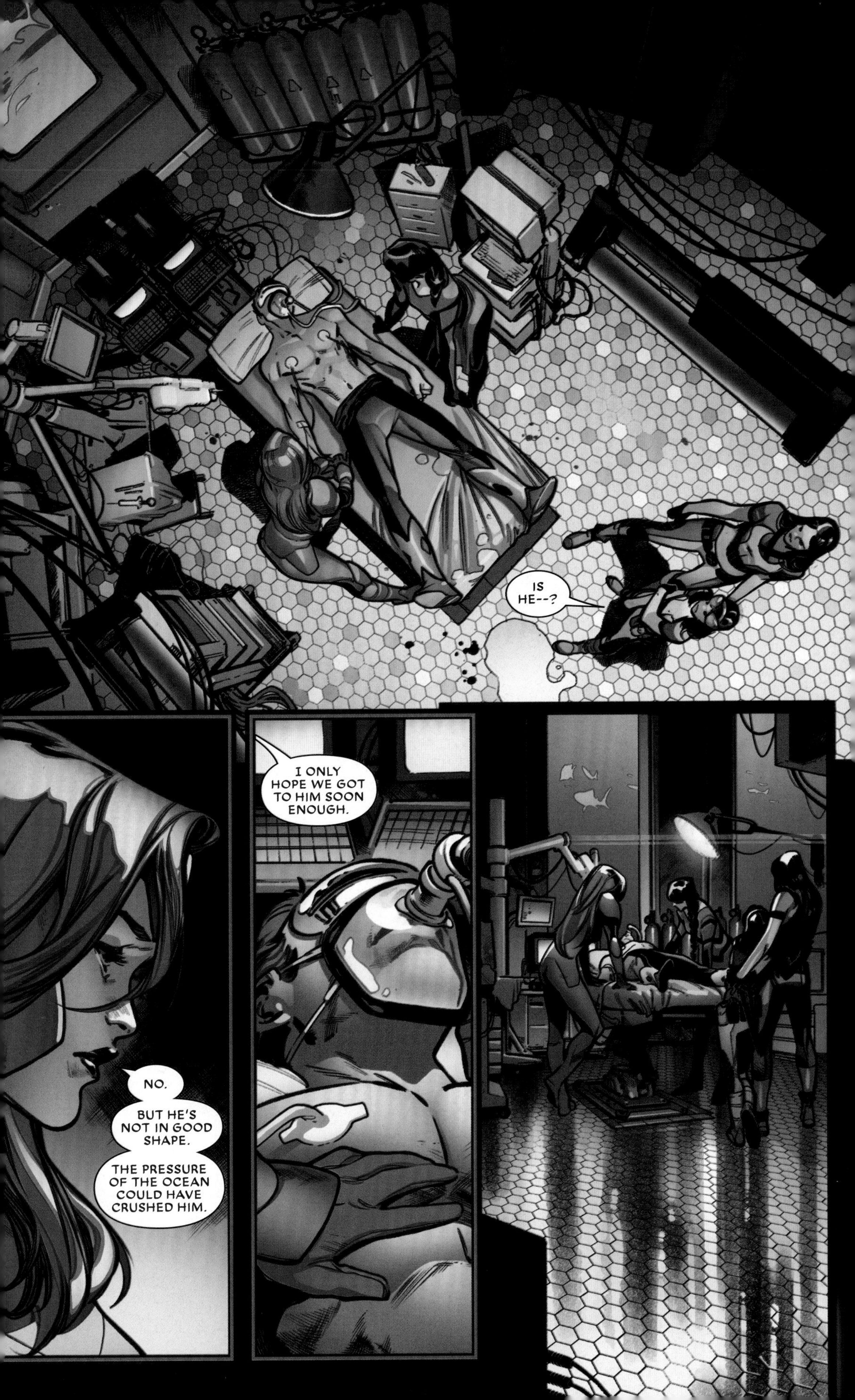
IS HE--?
NO.
BUT HE'S NOT IN GOOD SHAPE.
THE PRESSURE OF THE OCEAN COULD HAVE CRUSHED HIM.
I ONLY HOPE WE GOT TO HIM SOON ENOUGH.

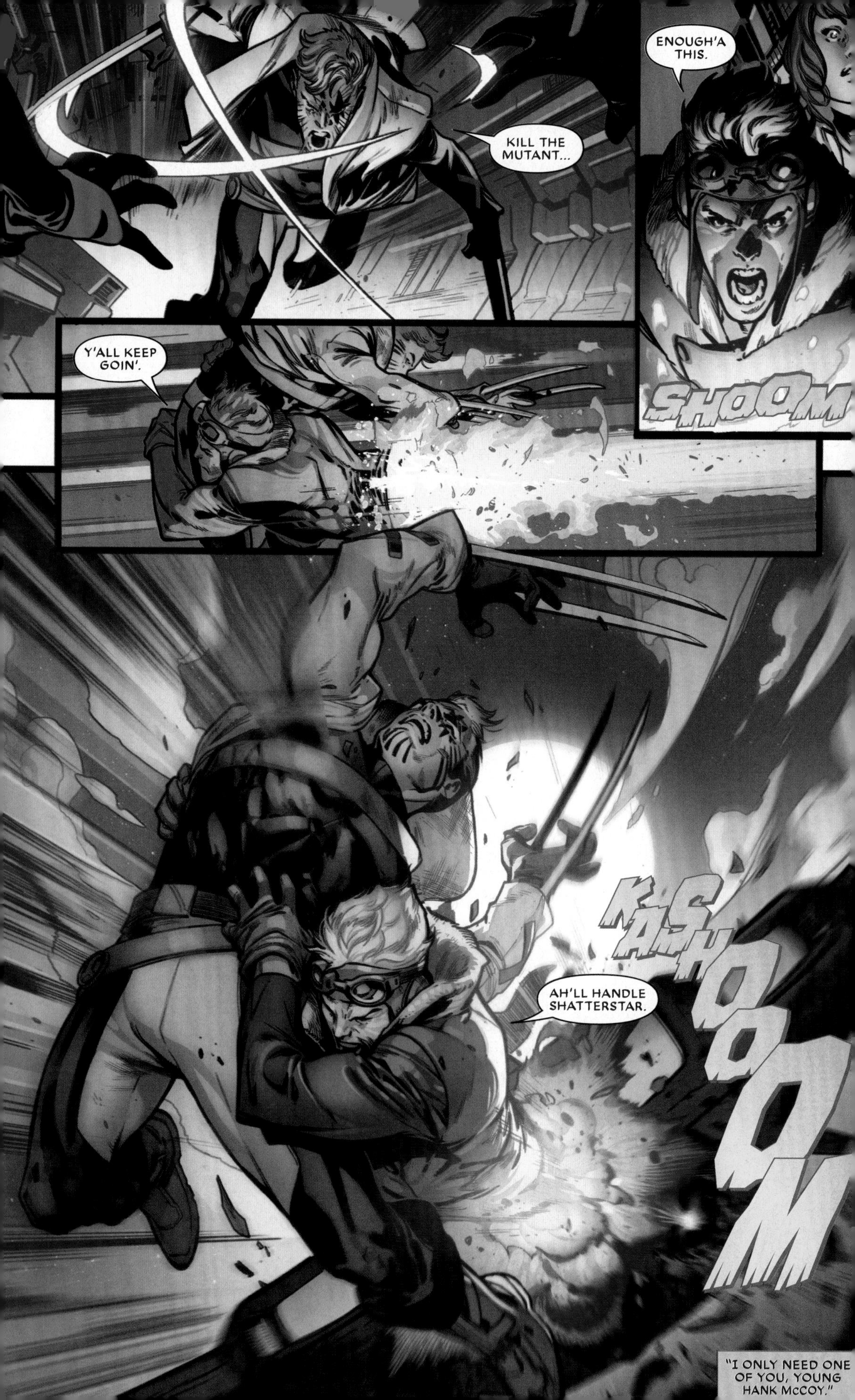
KILL THE MUTANT...
ENOUGH'A THIS.
SHOOM
Y'ALL KEEP GOIN'.
AH'LL HANDLE SHATTERSTAR.
KASHAMHOOOOM
"I ONLY NEED ONE OF YOU, YOUNG HANK McCOY."

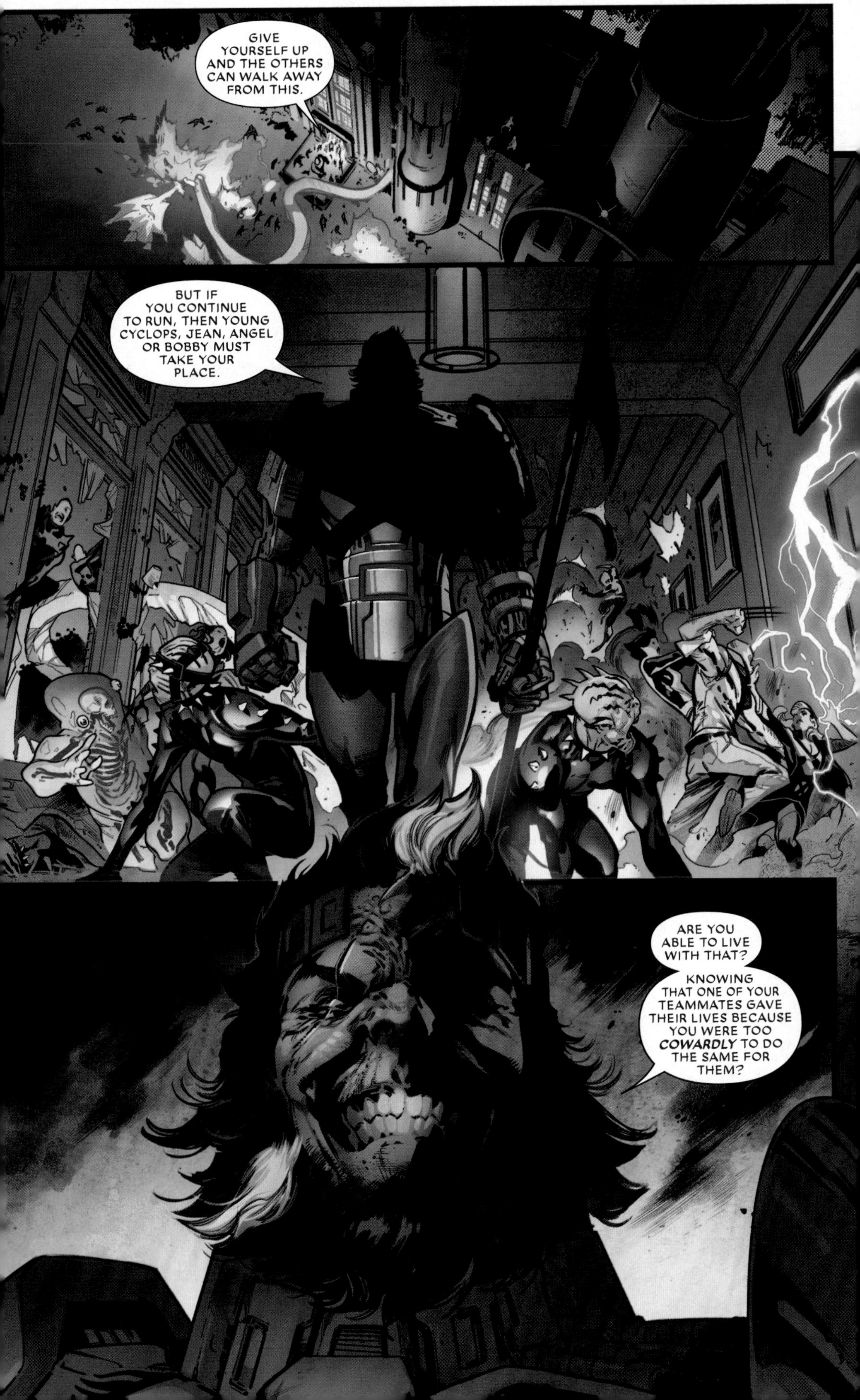
GIVE YOURSELF UP AND THE OTHERS CAN WALK AWAY FROM THIS.
BUT IF YOU CONTINUE TO RUN, THEN YOUNG CYCLOPS, JEAN, ANGEL OR BOBBY MUST TAKE YOUR PLACE.
ARE YOU ABLE TO LIVE WITH THAT?
KNOWING THAT ONE OF YOUR TEAMMATES GAVE THEIR LIVES BECAUSE YOU WERE TOO COWARDLY TO DO THE SAME FOR THEM?

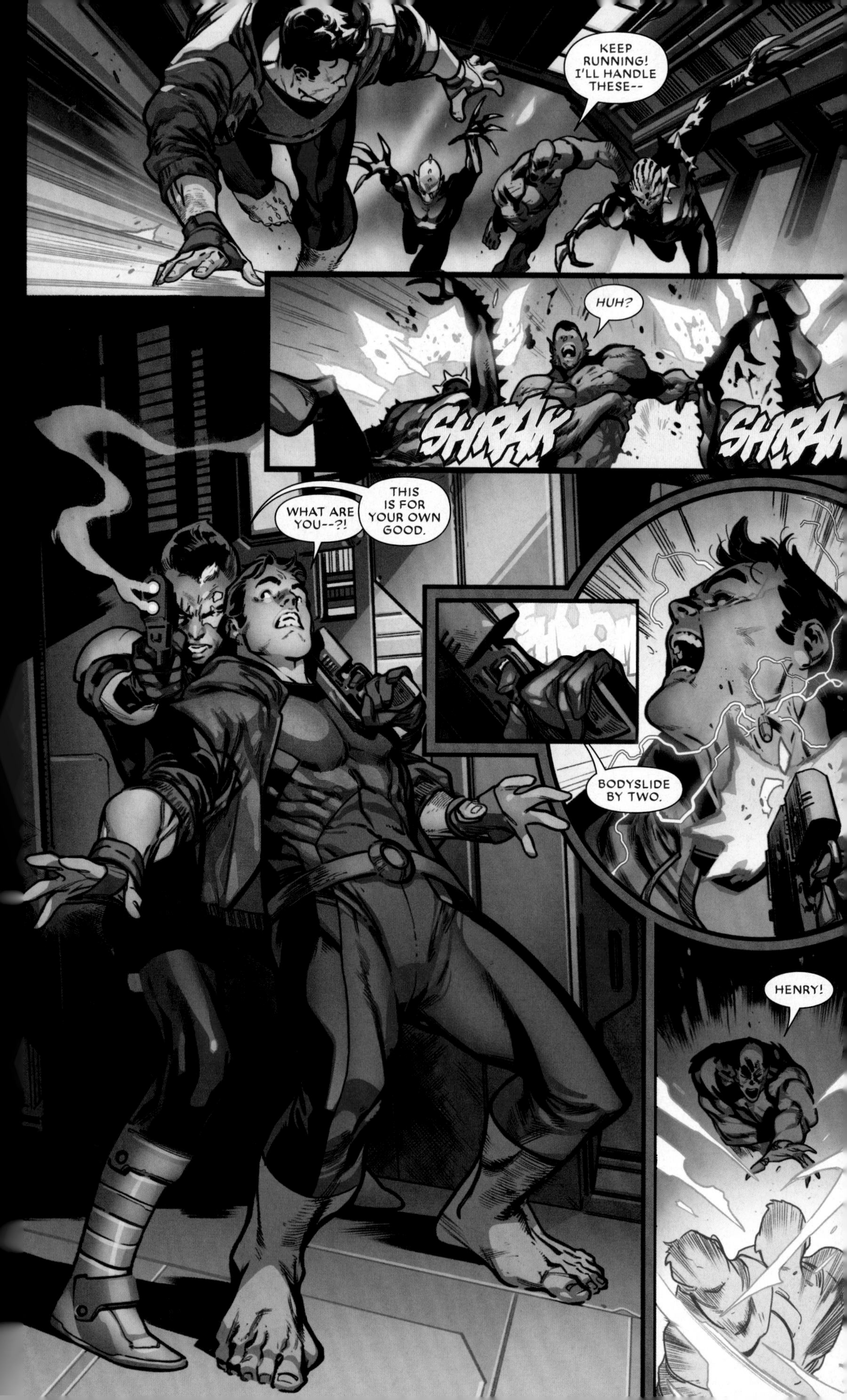
KEEP RUNNING! I'LL HANDLE THESE--
HUH?
SHRAK
WHAT ARE YOU--?!
THIS IS FOR YOUR OWN GOOD.
BODYSLIDE BY TWO.
HENRY!

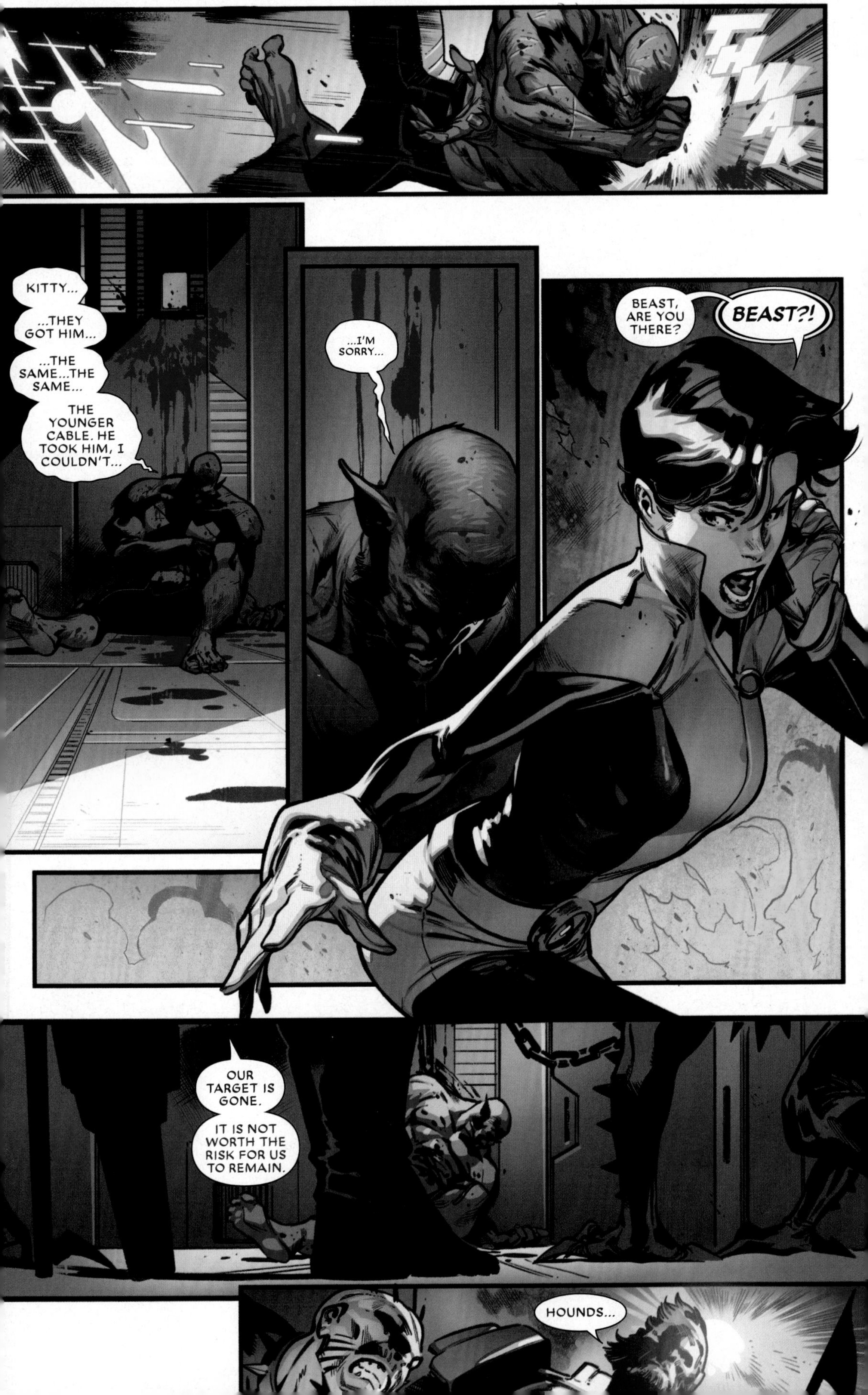
THWAK
KITTY...
...THEY GOT HIM...
...THE SAME...THE SAME...
THE YOUNGER CABLE. HE TOOK HIM, I COULDN'T...
...I'M SORRY...
BEAST, ARE YOU THERE?
BEAST?!
OUR TARGET IS GONE.
IT IS NOT WORTH THE RISK FOR US TO REMAIN.
HOUNDS...

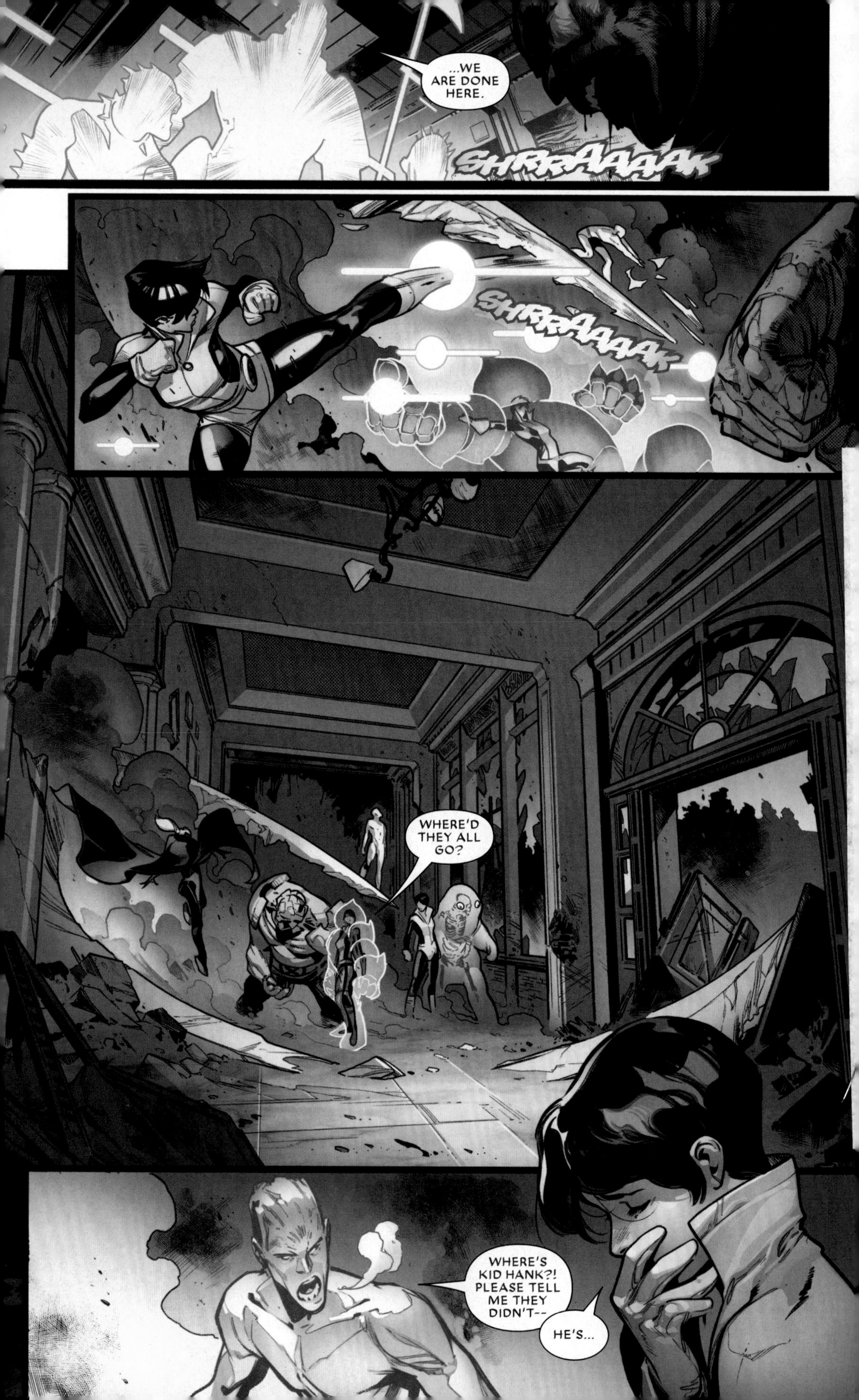

...WE ARE DONE HERE.
SHRRAAAAK
SHRRAAAAK
WHERE'D THEY ALL GO?
WHERE'S KID HANK?! PLEASE TELL ME THEY DIDN'T--
HE'S...

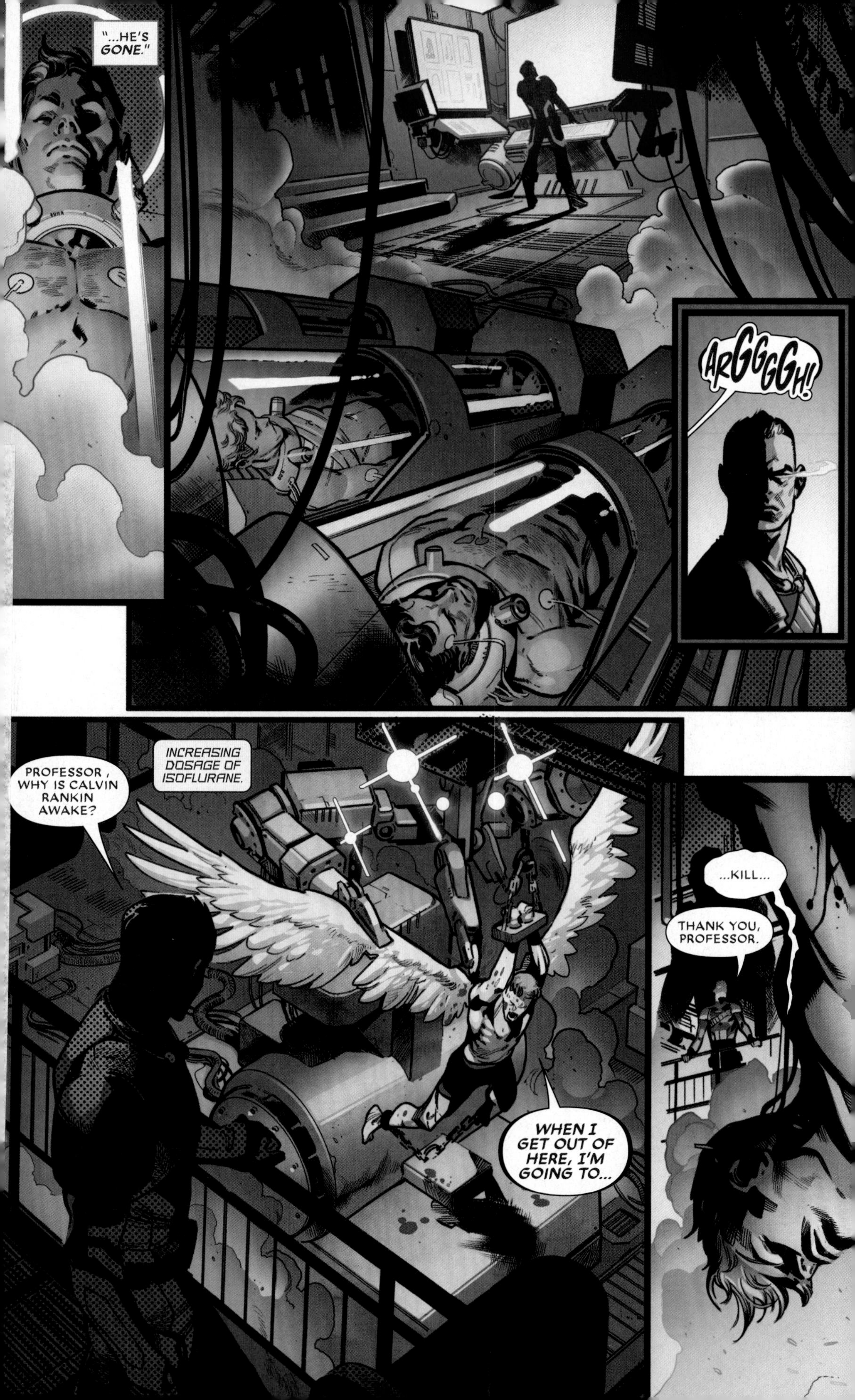
"...HE'S GONE."
ARGGGGH!
PROFESSOR, WHY IS CALVIN RANKIN AWAKE?
INCREASING DOSAGE OF ISOFLURANE.
WHEN I GET OUT OF HERE, I'M GOING TO...
...KILL...
THANK YOU, PROFESSOR.

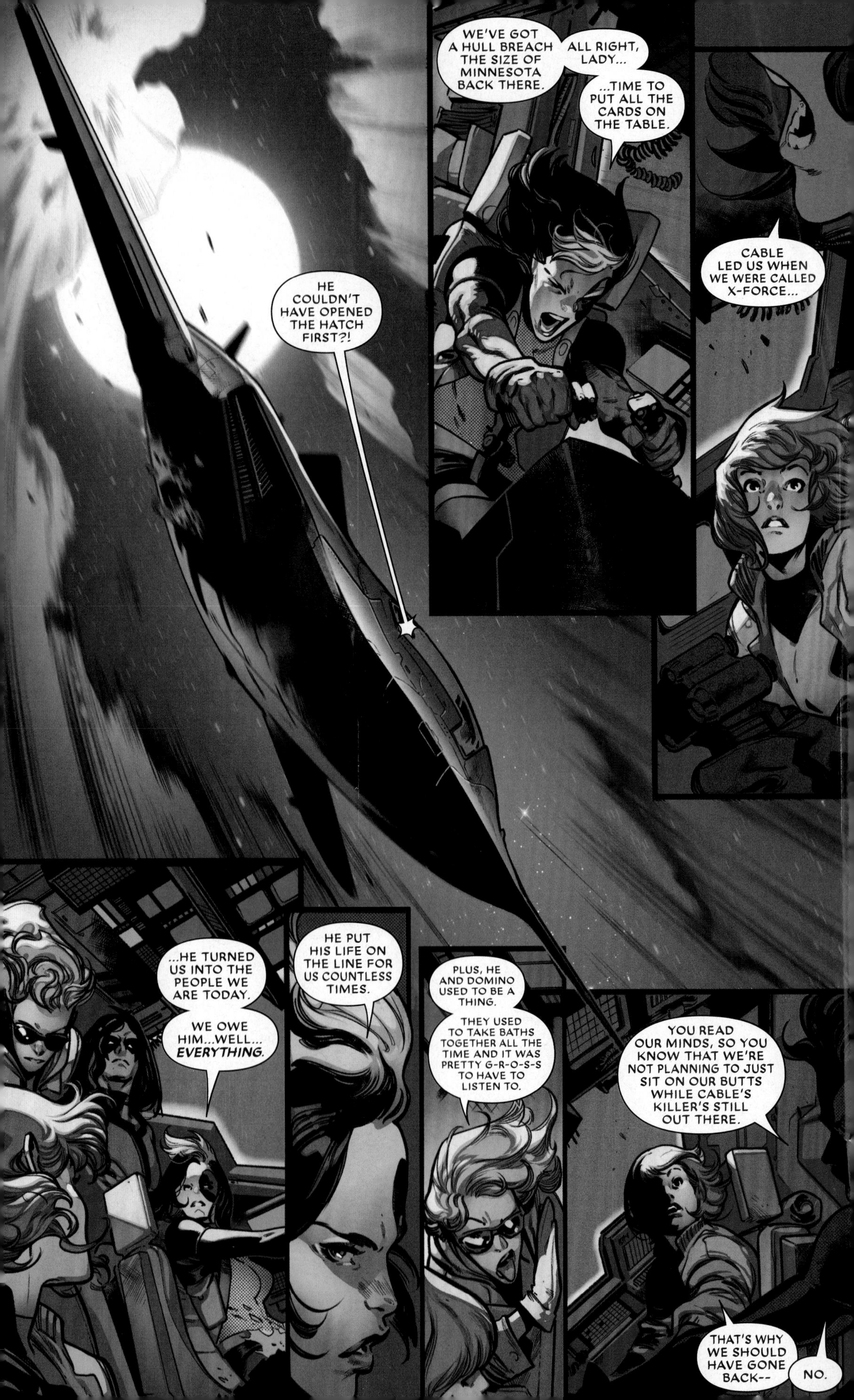
HE COULDN'T HAVE OPENED THE HATCH FIRST?!
WE'VE GOT A HULL BREACH THE SIZE OF MINNESOTA BACK THERE.
ALL RIGHT, LADY...
...TIME TO PUT ALL THE CARDS ON THE TABLE.
CABLE LED US WHEN WE WERE CALLED X-FORCE...
...HE TURNED US INTO THE PEOPLE WE ARE TODAY.
WE OWE HIM...WELL... *EVERYTHING*.
HE PUT HIS LIFE ON THE LINE FOR US COUNTLESS TIMES.
PLUS, HE AND DOMINO USED TO BE A THING.
THEY USED TO TAKE BATHS TOGETHER ALL THE TIME AND IT WAS PRETTY G-R-O-S-S TO HAVE TO LISTEN TO.
YOU READ OUR MINDS, SO YOU KNOW THAT WE'RE NOT PLANNING TO JUST SIT ON OUR BUTTS WHILE CABLE'S KILLER'S STILL OUT THERE.
THAT'S WHY WE SHOULD HAVE GONE BACK--
NO.

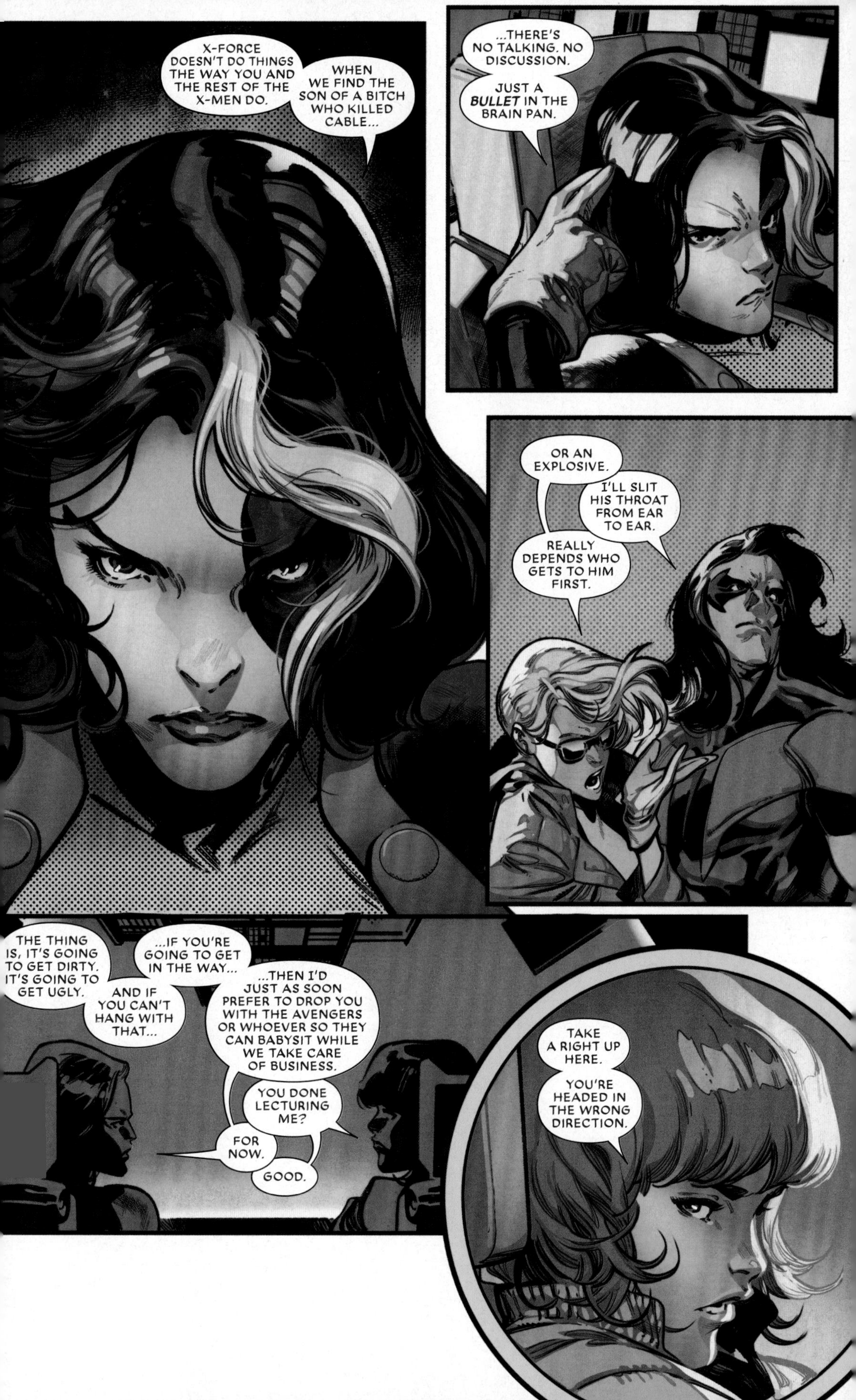
X-FORCE DOESN'T DO THINGS THE WAY YOU AND THE REST OF THE X-MEN DO.
WHEN WE FIND THE SON OF A BITCH WHO KILLED CABLE...
...THERE'S NO TALKING. NO DISCUSSION.
JUST A *BULLET* IN THE BRAIN PAN.
OR AN EXPLOSIVE.
I'LL SLIT HIS THROAT FROM EAR TO EAR.
REALLY DEPENDS WHO GETS TO HIM FIRST.
THE THING IS, IT'S GOING TO GET DIRTY. IT'S GOING TO GET UGLY.
AND IF YOU CAN'T HANG WITH THAT...
...IF YOU'RE GOING TO GET IN THE WAY...
...THEN I'D JUST AS SOON PREFER TO DROP YOU WITH THE AVENGERS OR WHOEVER SO THEY CAN BABYSIT WHILE WE TAKE CARE OF BUSINESS.
YOU DONE LECTURING ME?
FOR NOW.
GOOD.
TAKE A RIGHT UP HERE.
YOU'RE HEADED IN THE WRONG DIRECTION.

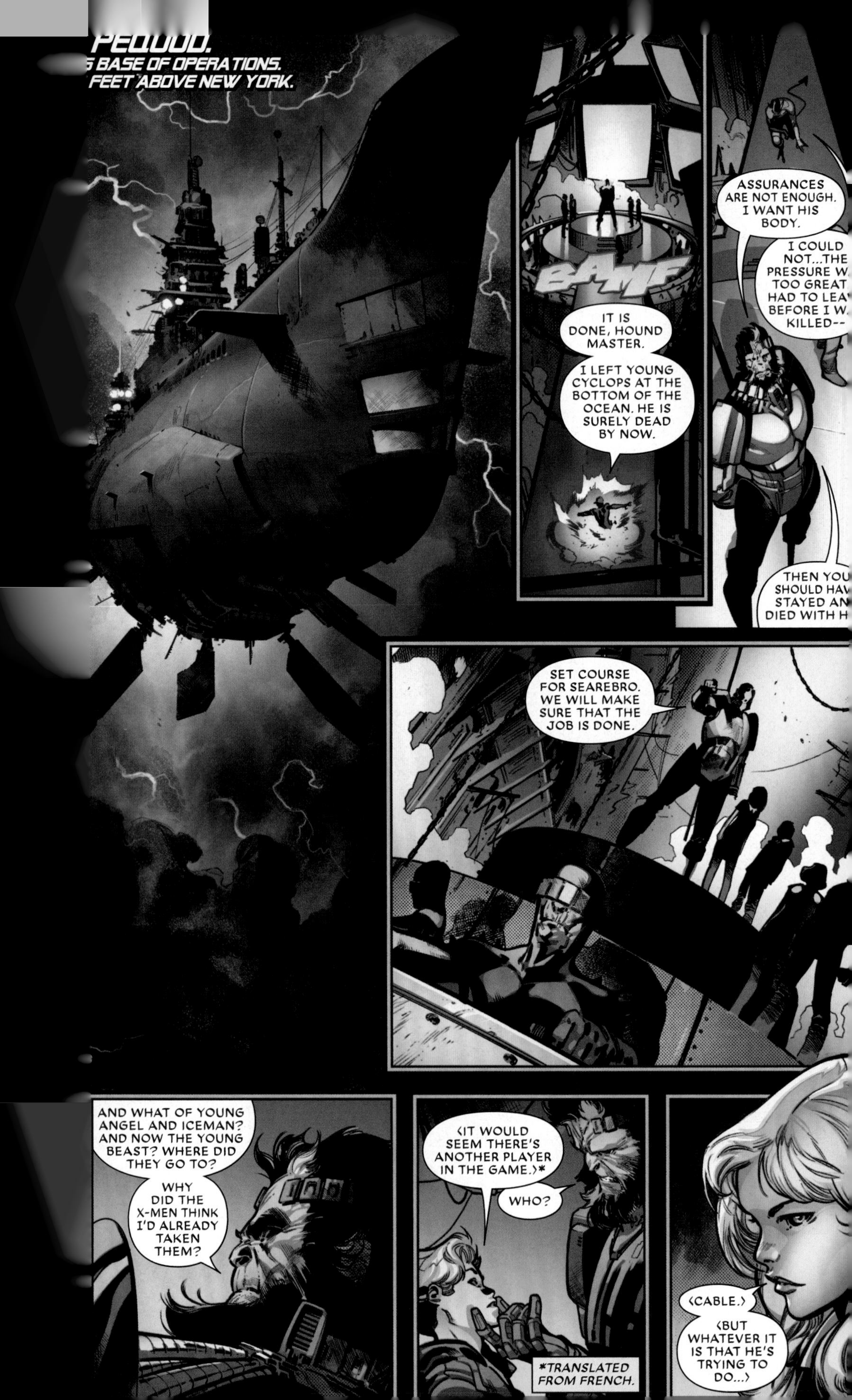
PEQUOD.
S BASE OF OPERATIONS.
FEET ABOVE NEW YORK.
BAMF
IT IS DONE, HOUND MASTER.
I LEFT YOUNG CYCLOPS AT THE BOTTOM OF THE OCEAN. HE IS SURELY DEAD BY NOW.
ASSURANCES ARE NOT ENOUGH. I WANT HIS BODY.
I COULD NOT...THE PRESSURE W TOO GREAT HAD TO LEA BEFORE I W KILLED--
THEN YOU SHOULD HAV STAYED AN DIED WITH H
SET COURSE FOR SEAREBRO. WE WILL MAKE SURE THAT THE JOB IS DONE.
AND WHAT OF YOUNG ANGEL AND ICEMAN? AND NOW THE YOUNG BEAST? WHERE DID THEY GO TO?
WHY DID THE X-MEN THINK I'D ALREADY TAKEN THEM?
‹IT WOULD SEEM THERE'S ANOTHER PLAYER IN THE GAME.›*
WHO?
*TRANSLATED FROM FRENCH.
‹CABLE.›
‹BUT WHATEVER IT IS THAT HE'S TRYING TO DO...›

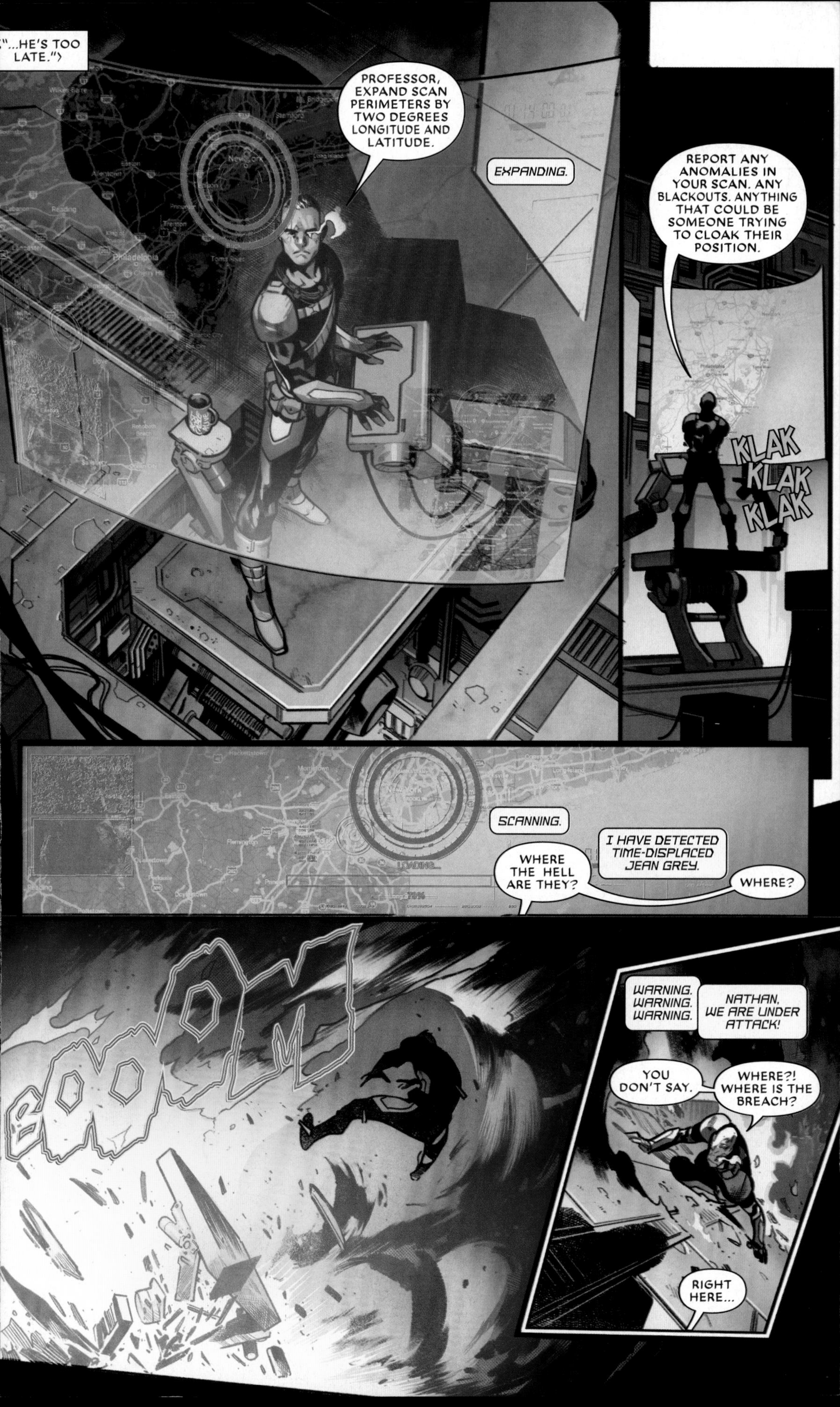

‹"...HE'S TOO LATE."›
PROFESSOR, EXPAND SCAN PERIMETERS BY TWO DEGREES LONGITUDE AND LATITUDE.
EXPANDING.
REPORT ANY ANOMALIES IN YOUR SCAN. ANY BLACKOUTS. ANYTHING THAT COULD BE SOMEONE TRYING TO CLOAK THEIR POSITION.
KLAK KLAK KLAK
SCANNING.
WHERE THE HELL ARE THEY?
I HAVE DETECTED TIME-DISPLACED JEAN GREY.
WHERE?
BOOOOM
WARNING. WARNING. WARNING.
NATHAN, WE ARE UNDER ATTACK!
YOU DON'T SAY.
WHERE?! WHERE IS THE BREACH?
RIGHT HERE...

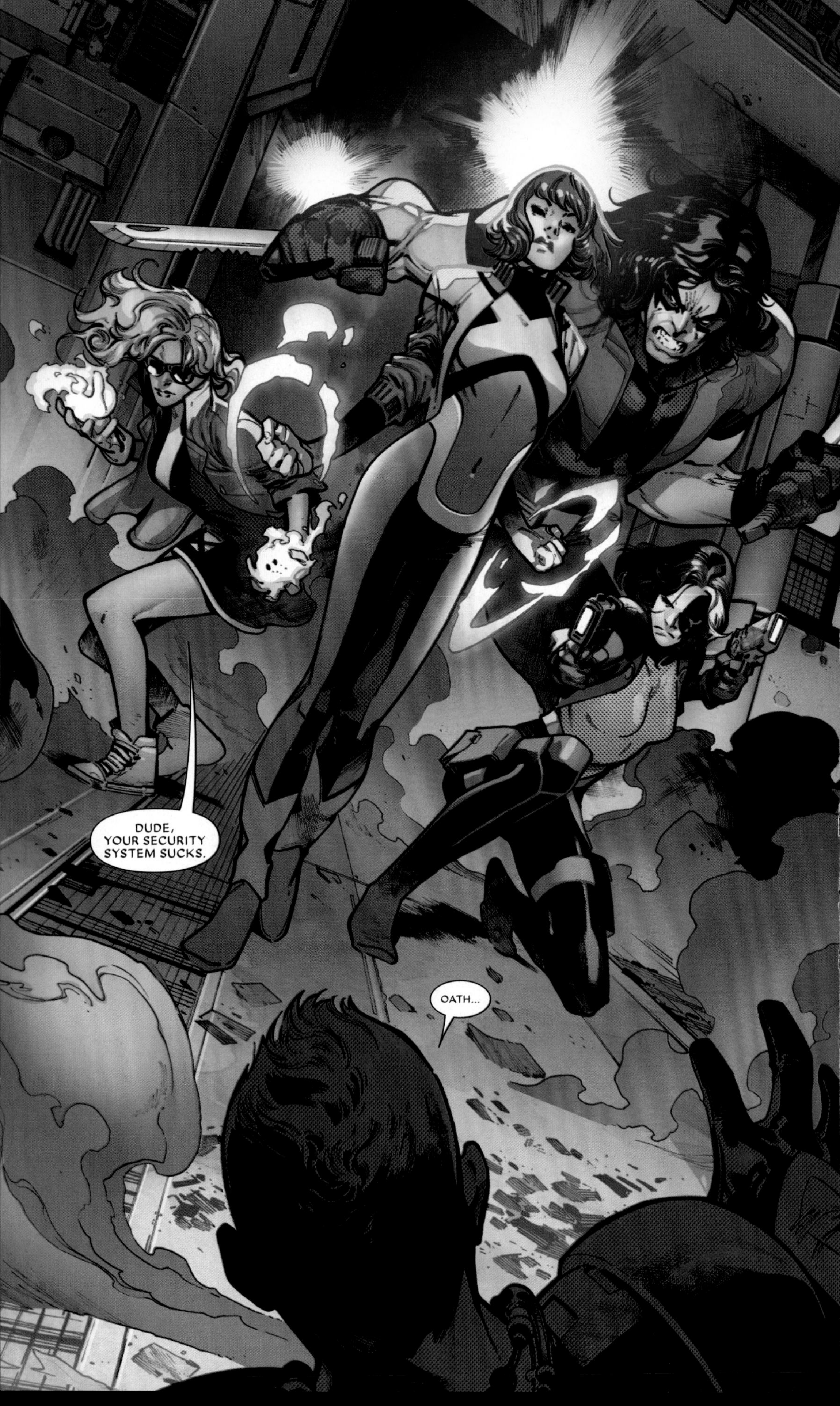
DUDE, YOUR SECURITY SYSTEM SUCKS.
OATH...

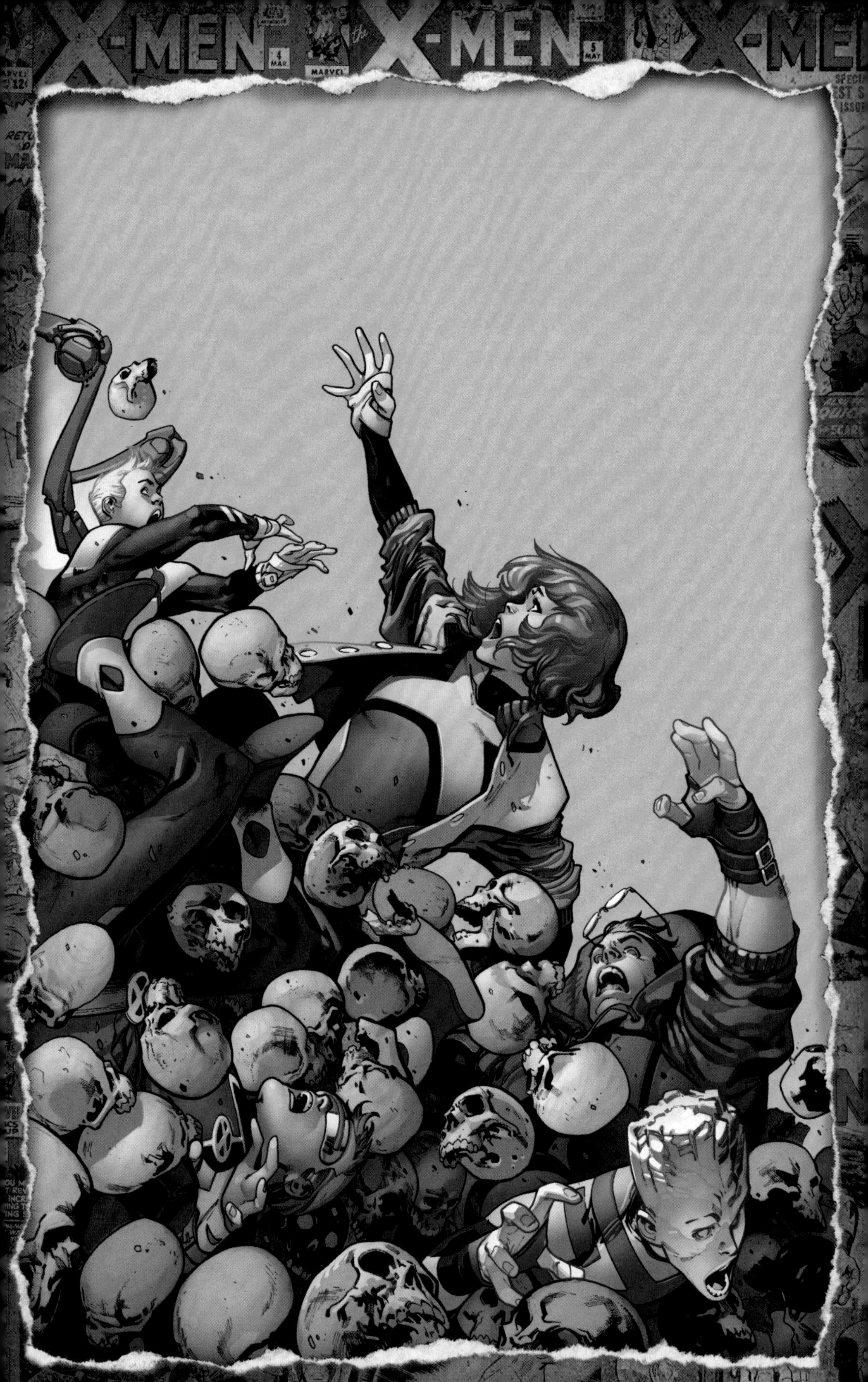
X-MEN
X-MEN

#1 VARIANT *Pepe Larraz* & *Marte Gracia*

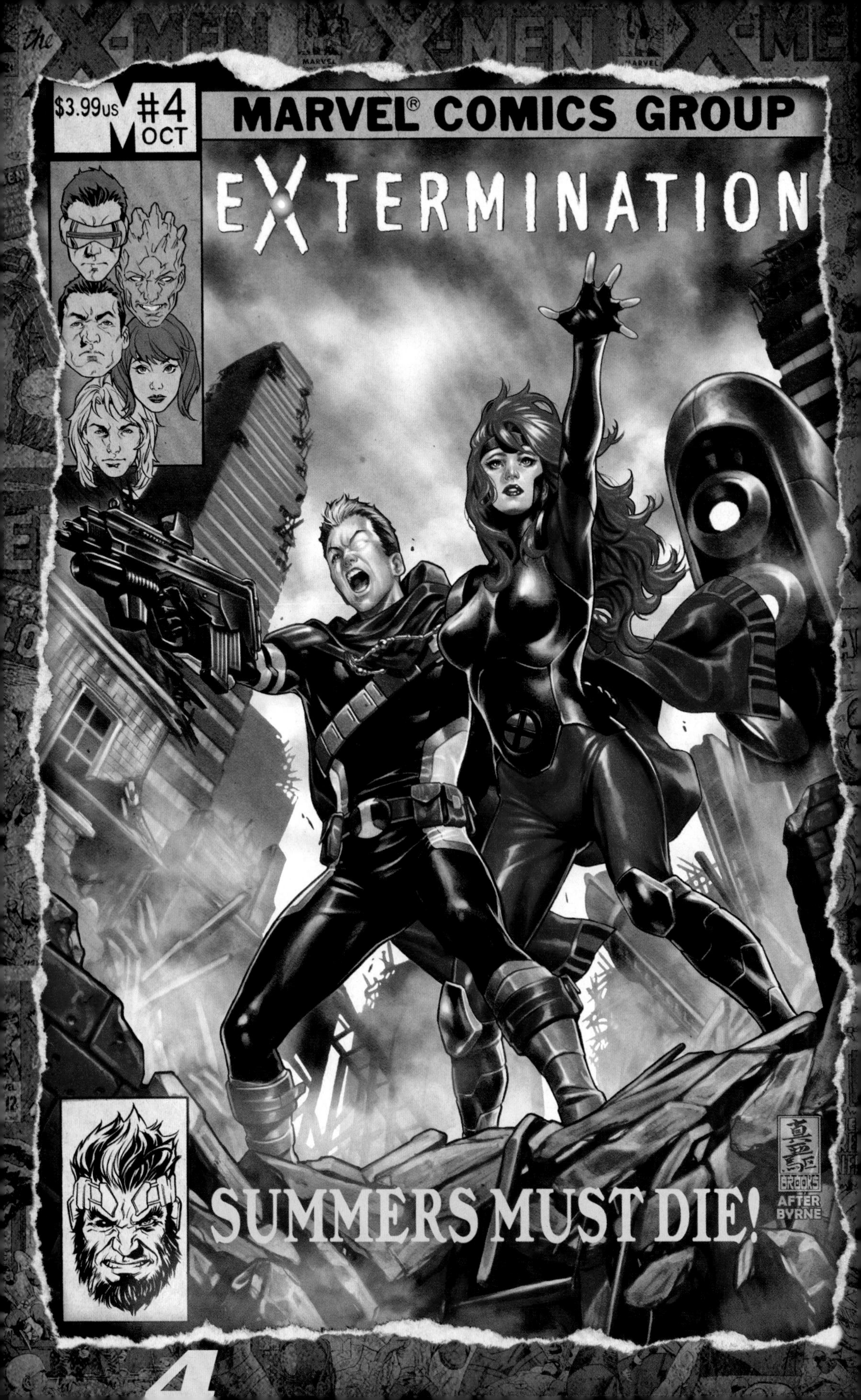

X-MEN
$3.99US
#4
OCT
MARVEL® COMICS GROUP
EXTERMINATION
SUMMERS MUST DIE!
BROOKS
AFTER BYRNE
4

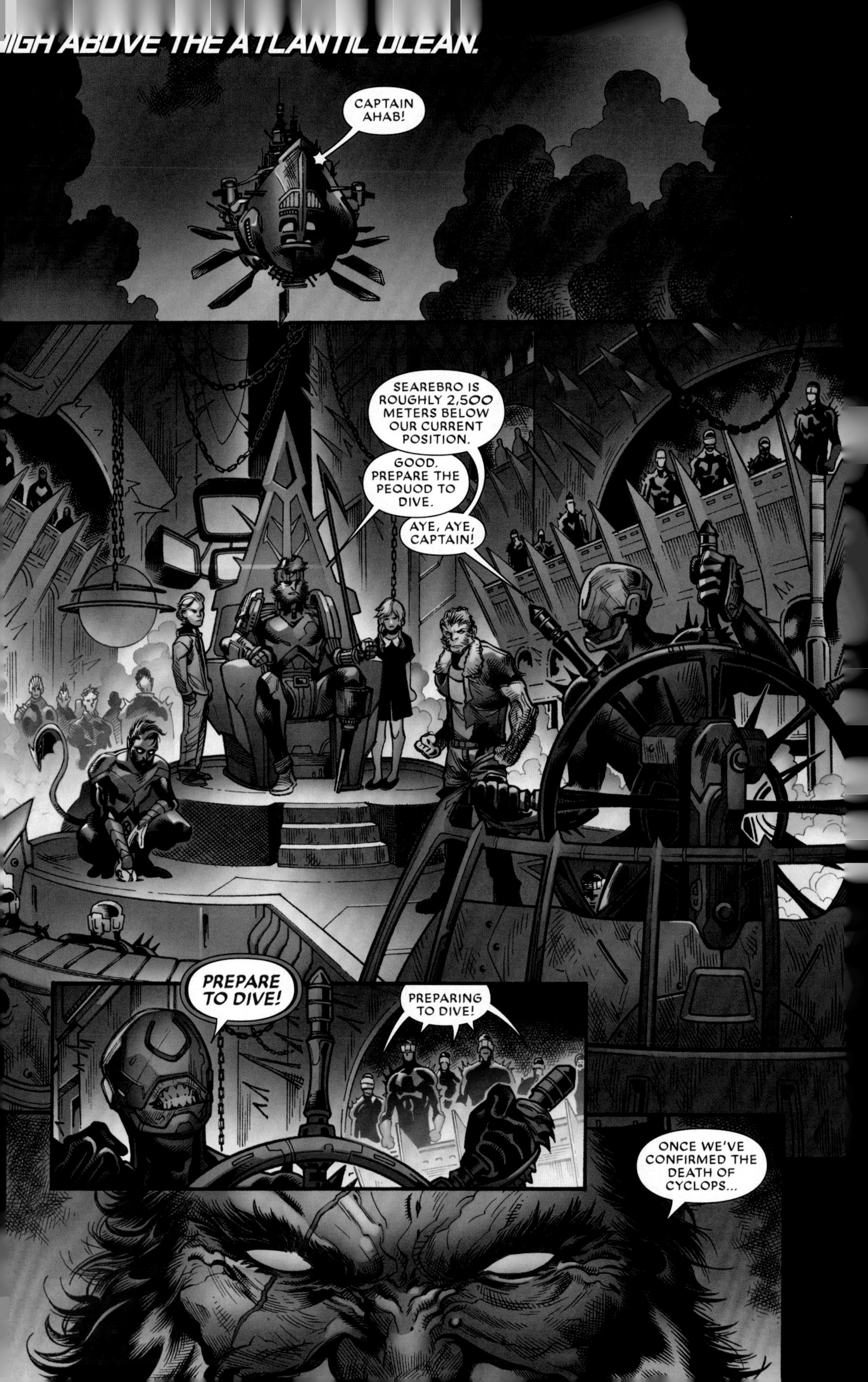
HIGH ABOVE THE ATLANTIC OCEAN.
CAPTAIN AHAB!
SEAREBRO IS ROUGHLY 2,500 METERS BELOW OUR CURRENT POSITION.
GOOD. PREPARE THE PEQUOD TO DIVE.
AYE, AYE, CAPTAIN!
PREPARE TO DIVE!
PREPARING TO DIVE!
ONCE WE'VE CONFIRMED THE DEATH OF CYCLOPS...

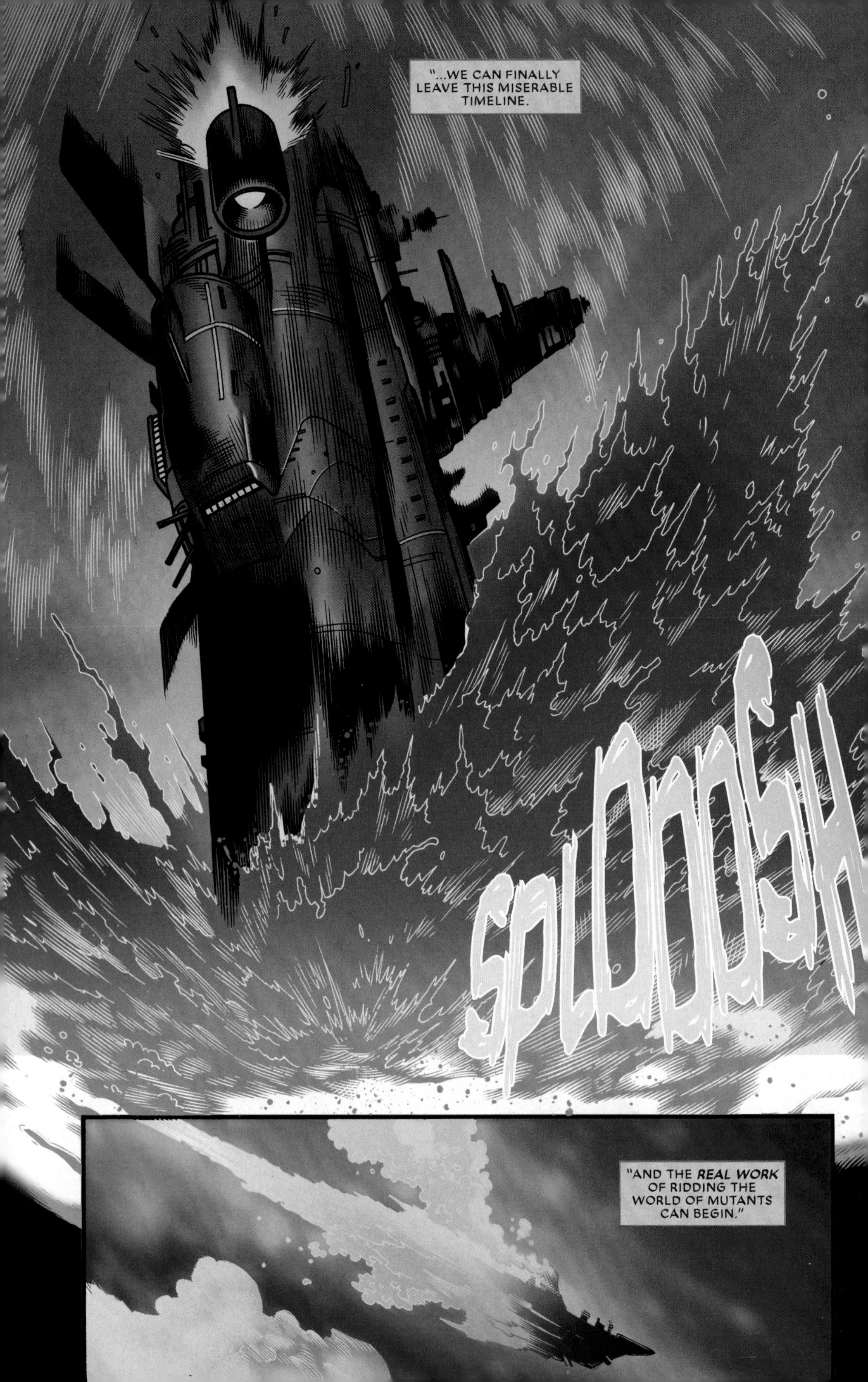
"...WE CAN FINALLY LEAVE THIS MISERABLE TIMELINE.
SPLOOOSH
"AND THE *REAL WORK* OF RIDDING THE WORLD OF MUTANTS CAN BEGIN."

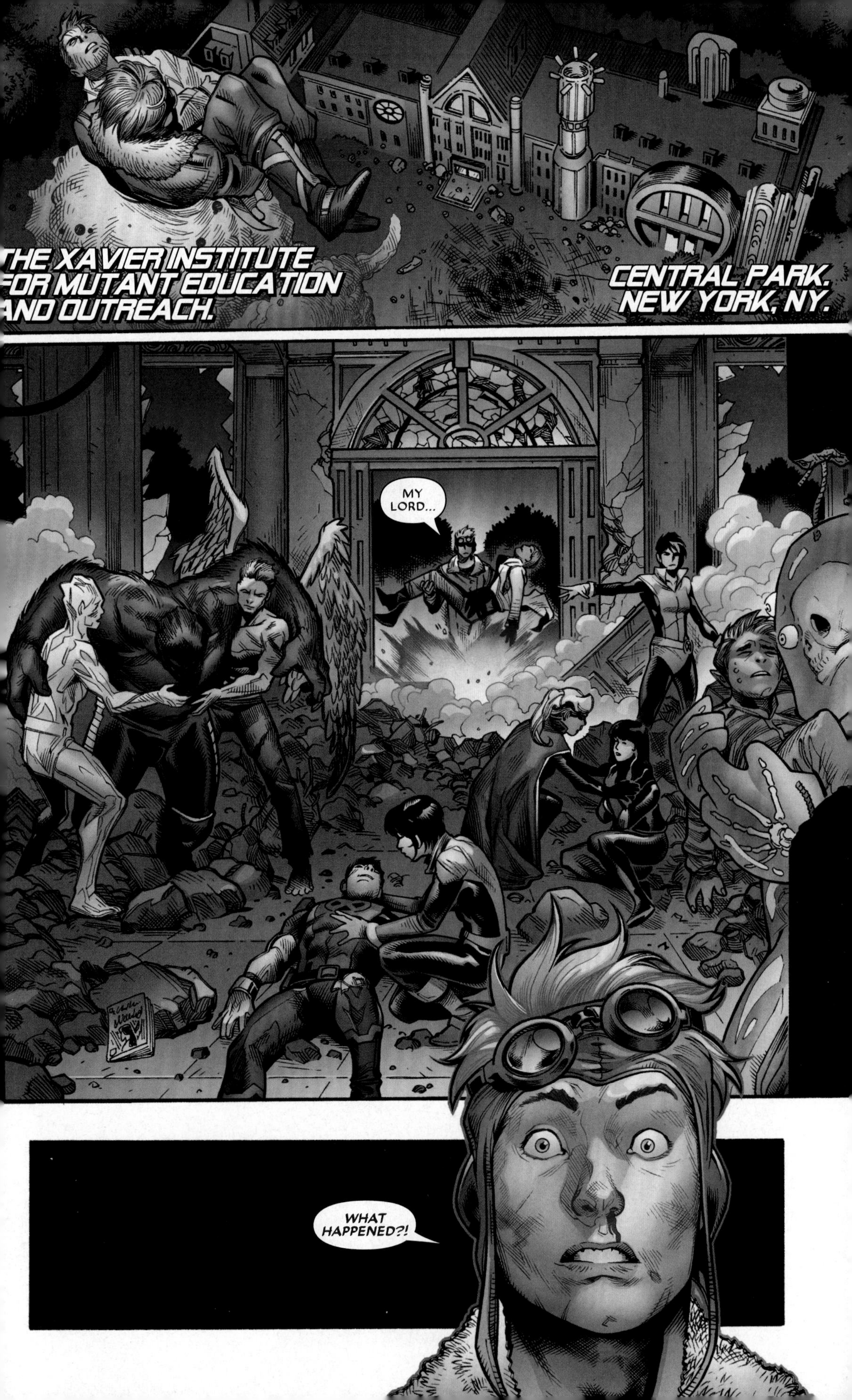
THE XAVIER INSTITUTE FOR MUTANT EDUCATION AND OUTREACH.
CENTRAL PARK. NEW YORK, NY.
MY LORD...
WHAT HAPPENED?!

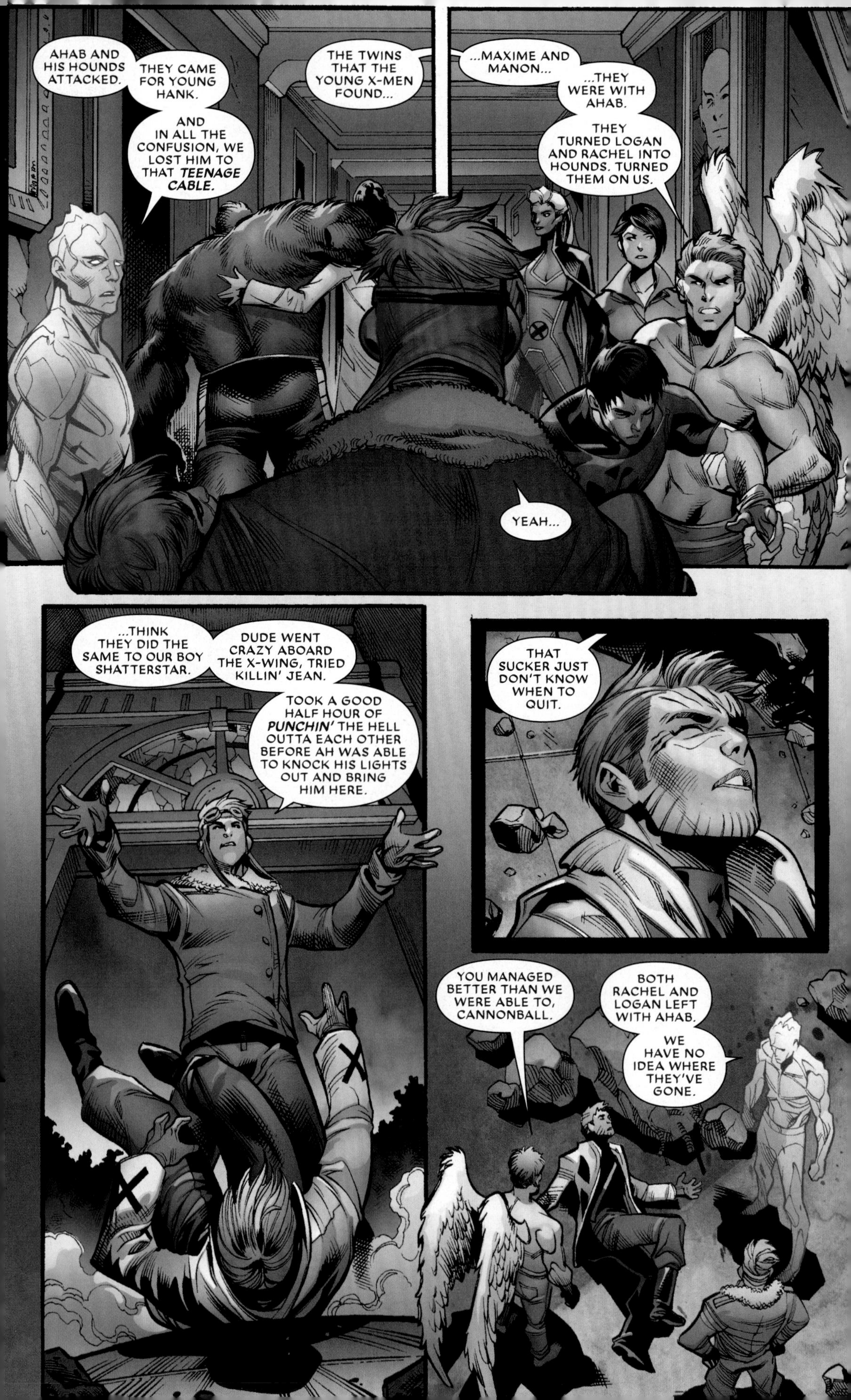
AHAB AND HIS HOUNDS ATTACKED.
THEY CAME FOR YOUNG HANK.
AND IN ALL THE CONFUSION, WE LOST HIM TO THAT *TEENAGE CABLE.*
THE TWINS THAT THE YOUNG X-MEN FOUND...
...MAXIME AND MANON...
...THEY WERE WITH AHAB.
THEY TURNED LOGAN AND RACHEL INTO HOUNDS. TURNED THEM ON US.
YEAH...
...THINK THEY DID THE SAME TO OUR BOY SHATTERSTAR.
DUDE WENT CRAZY ABOARD THE X-WING, TRIED KILLIN' JEAN.
TOOK A GOOD HALF HOUR OF *PUNCHIN'* THE HELL OUTTA EACH OTHER BEFORE AH WAS ABLE TO KNOCK HIS LIGHTS OUT AND BRING HIM HERE.
THAT SUCKER JUST DON'T KNOW WHEN TO QUIT.
YOU MANAGED BETTER THAN WE WERE ABLE TO, CANNONBALL.
BOTH RACHEL AND LOGAN LEFT WITH AHAB.
WE HAVE NO IDEA WHERE THEY'VE GONE.

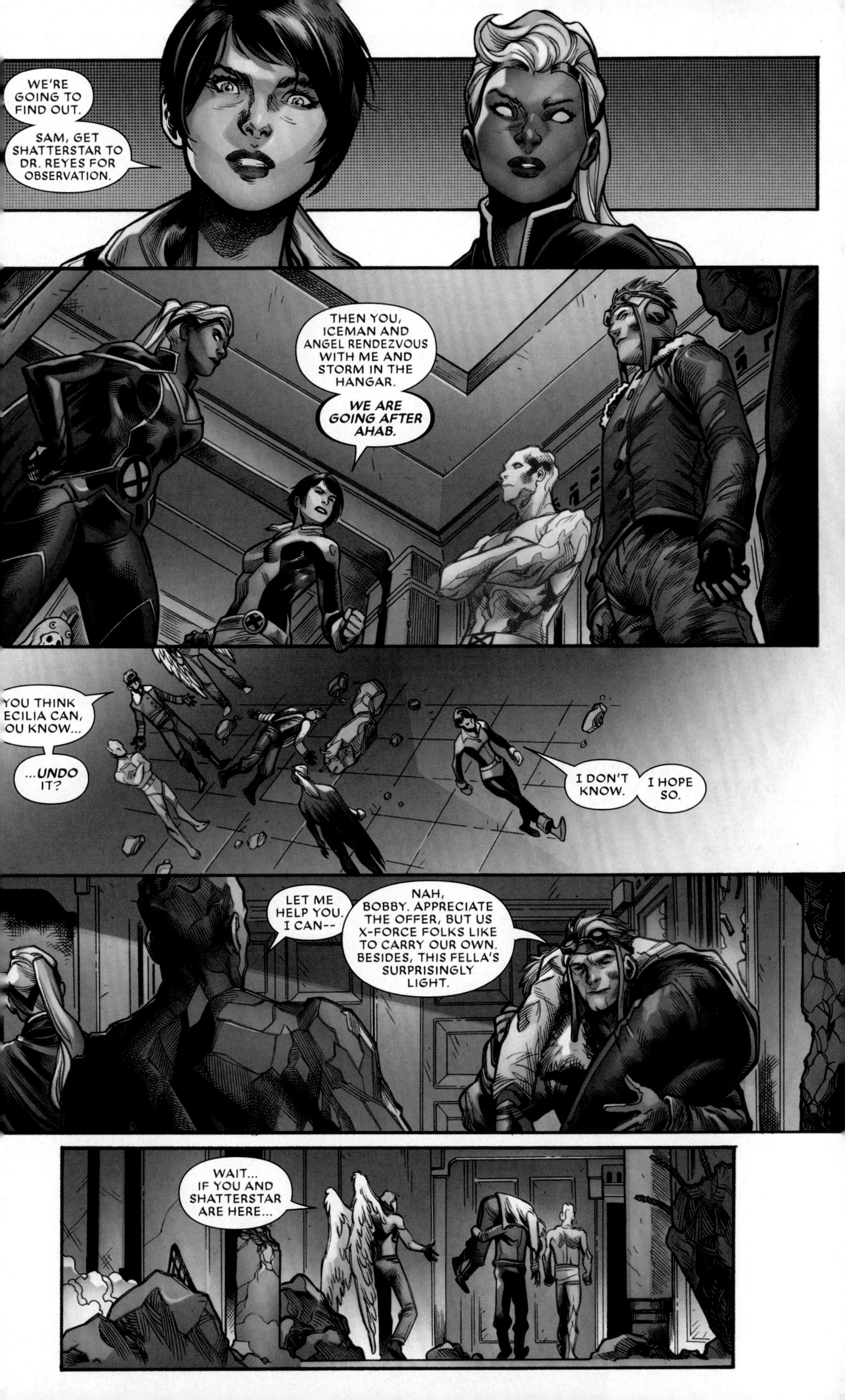
WE'RE GOING TO FIND OUT.
SAM, GET SHATTERSTAR TO DR. REYES FOR OBSERVATION.
THEN YOU, ICEMAN AND ANGEL RENDEZVOUS WITH ME AND STORM IN THE HANGAR.
WE ARE GOING AFTER AHAB.
YOU THINK ECILIA CAN, OU KNOW...
...UNDO IT?
I DON'T KNOW.
I HOPE SO.
LET ME HELP YOU. I CAN--
NAH, BOBBY. APPRECIATE THE OFFER, BUT US X-FORCE FOLKS LIKE TO CARRY OUR OWN. BESIDES, THIS FELLA'S SURPRISINGLY LIGHT.
WAIT... IF YOU AND SHATTERSTAR ARE HERE...

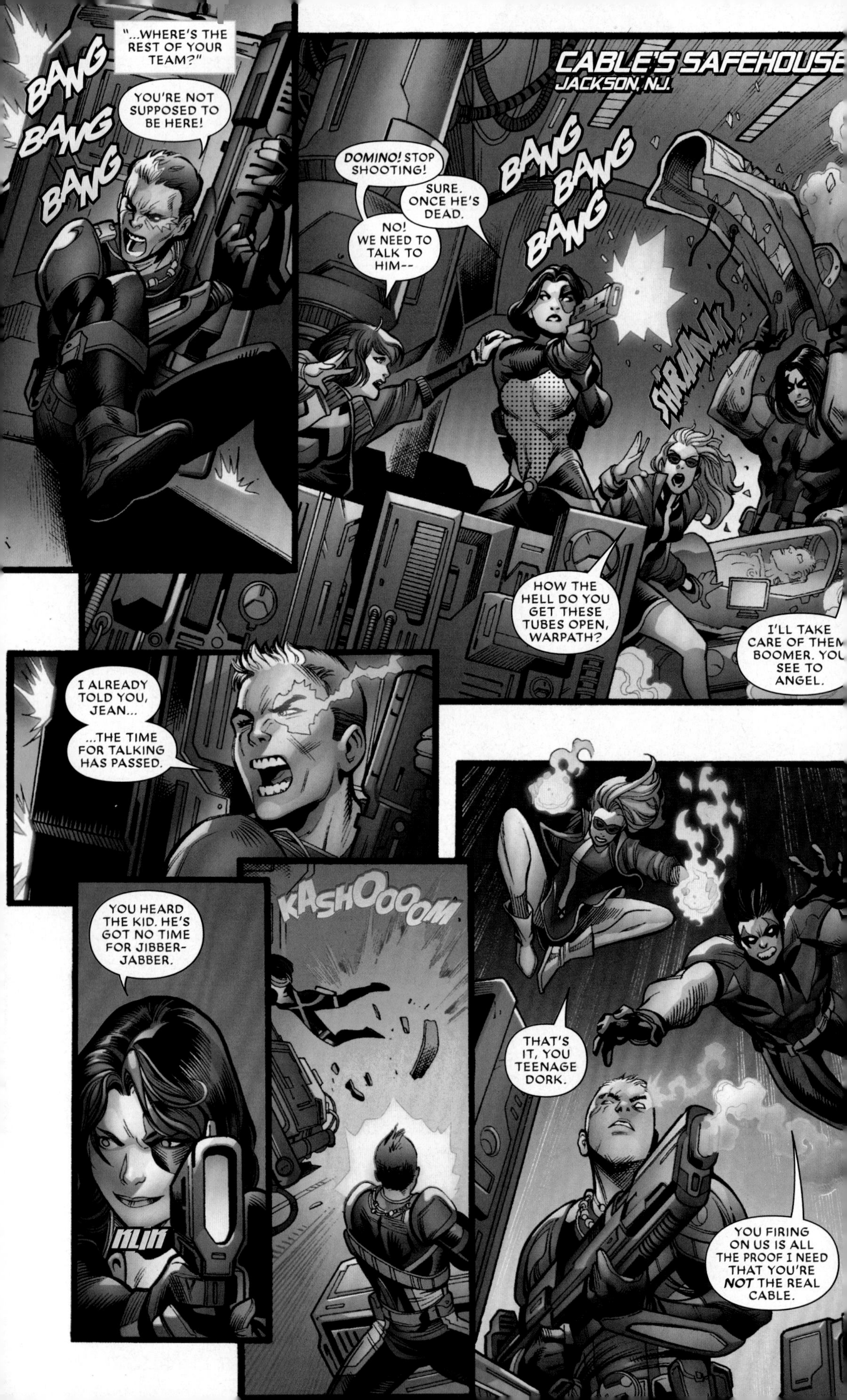
"...WHERE'S THE REST OF YOUR TEAM?"
BANG BANG BANG
YOU'RE NOT SUPPOSED TO BE HERE!
CABLE'S SAFEHOUSE
JACKSON, N.J.
DOMINO! STOP SHOOTING!
SURE. ONCE HE'S DEAD.
NO! WE NEED TO TALK TO HIM--
BANG BANG BANG
SHRAAAAK
HOW THE HELL DO YOU GET THESE TUBES OPEN, WARPATH?
I'LL TAKE CARE OF THEM BOOMER. YOU SEE TO ANGEL.
I ALREADY TOLD YOU, JEAN...
...THE TIME FOR TALKING HAS PASSED.
YOU HEARD THE KID. HE'S GOT NO TIME FOR JIBBER-JABBER.
KLIK
KASHOOOOM
THAT'S IT, YOU TEENAGE DORK.
YOU FIRING ON US IS ALL THE PROOF I NEED THAT YOU'RE NOT THE REAL CABLE.

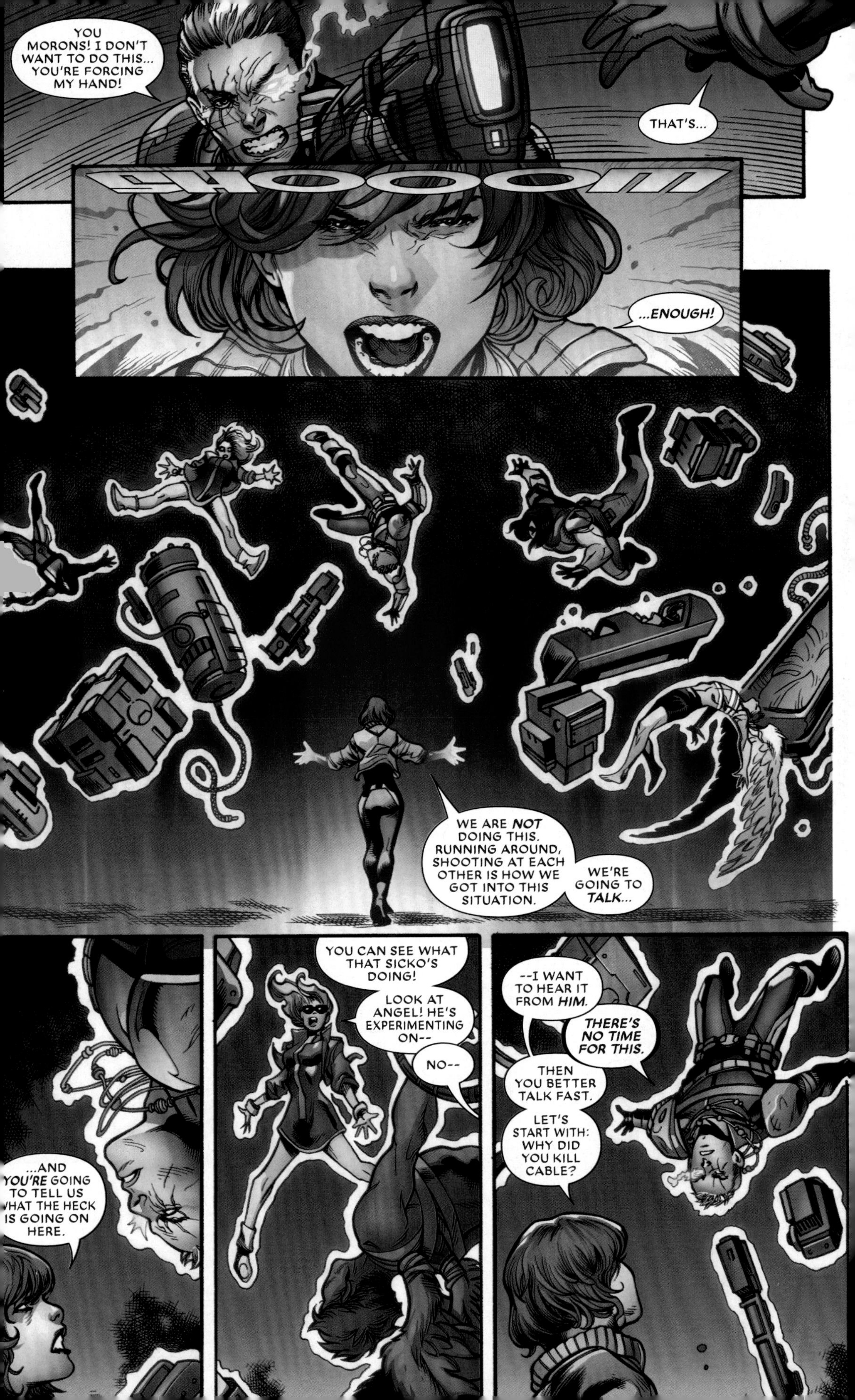
YOU MORONS! I DON'T WANT TO DO THIS... YOU'RE FORCING MY HAND!
THAT'S...
...ENOUGH!
WE ARE NOT DOING THIS. RUNNING AROUND, SHOOTING AT EACH OTHER IS HOW WE GOT INTO THIS SITUATION.
WE'RE GOING TO TALK...
...AND YOU'RE GOING TO TELL US WHAT THE HECK IS GOING ON HERE.
YOU CAN SEE WHAT THAT SICKO'S DOING!
LOOK AT ANGEL! HE'S EXPERIMENTING ON--
NO--
--I WANT TO HEAR IT FROM HIM.
THERE'S NO TIME FOR THIS.
THEN YOU BETTER TALK FAST.
LET'S START WITH: WHY DID YOU KILL CABLE?

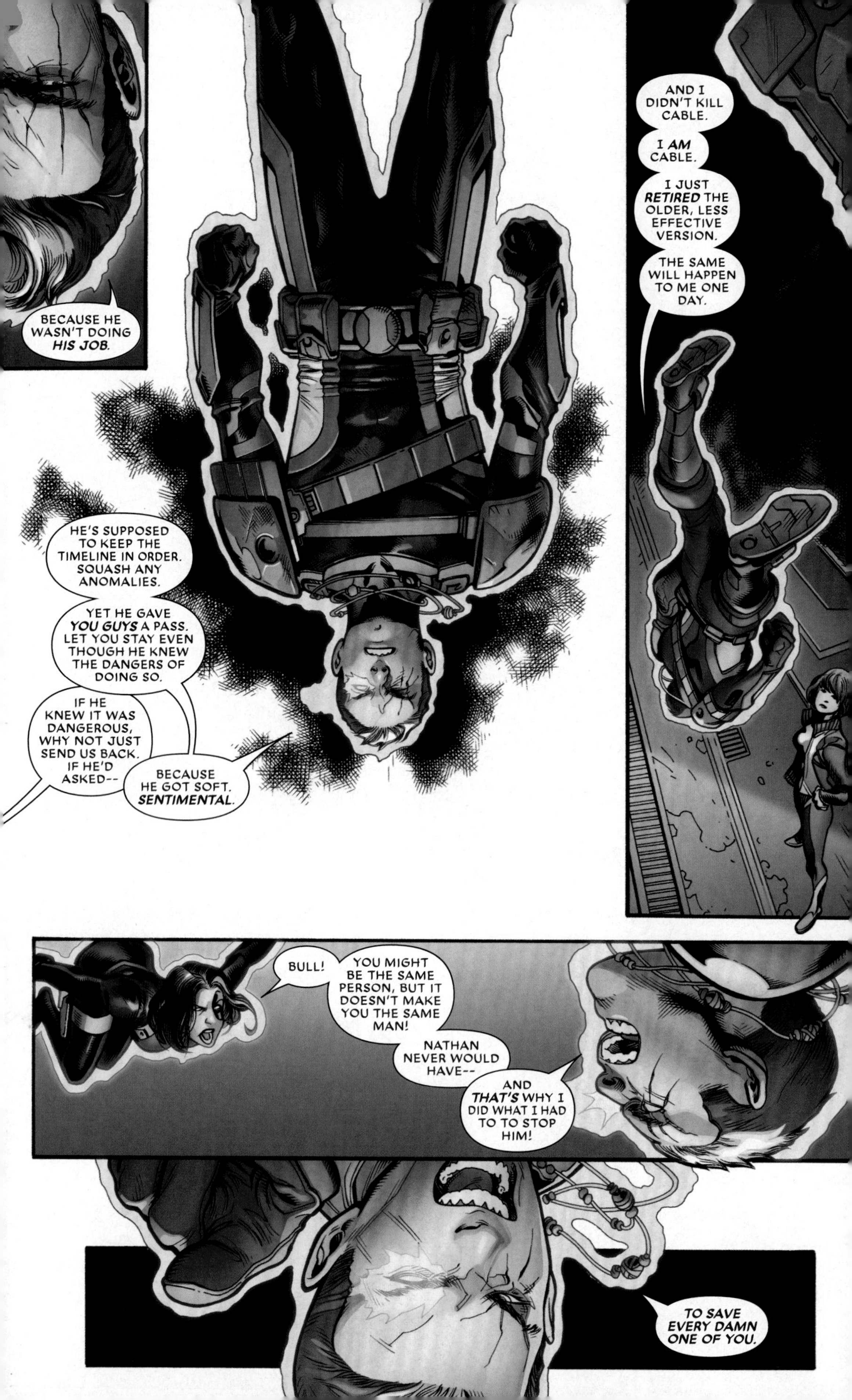

BECAUSE HE WASN'T DOING HIS JOB.
HE'S SUPPOSED TO KEEP THE TIMELINE IN ORDER. SQUASH ANY ANOMALIES.
YET HE GAVE YOU GUYS A PASS. LET YOU STAY EVEN THOUGH HE KNEW THE DANGERS OF DOING SO.
IF HE KNEW IT WAS DANGEROUS, WHY NOT JUST SEND US BACK. IF HE'D ASKED--
BECAUSE HE GOT SOFT. SENTIMENTAL.
AND I DIDN'T KILL CABLE.
I AM CABLE.
I JUST RETIRED THE OLDER, LESS EFFECTIVE VERSION.
THE SAME WILL HAPPEN TO ME ONE DAY.
BULL!
YOU MIGHT BE THE SAME PERSON, BUT IT DOESN'T MAKE YOU THE SAME MAN!
NATHAN NEVER WOULD HAVE--
AND THAT'S WHY I DID WHAT I HAD TO TO STOP HIM!
TO SAVE EVERY DAMN ONE OF YOU.

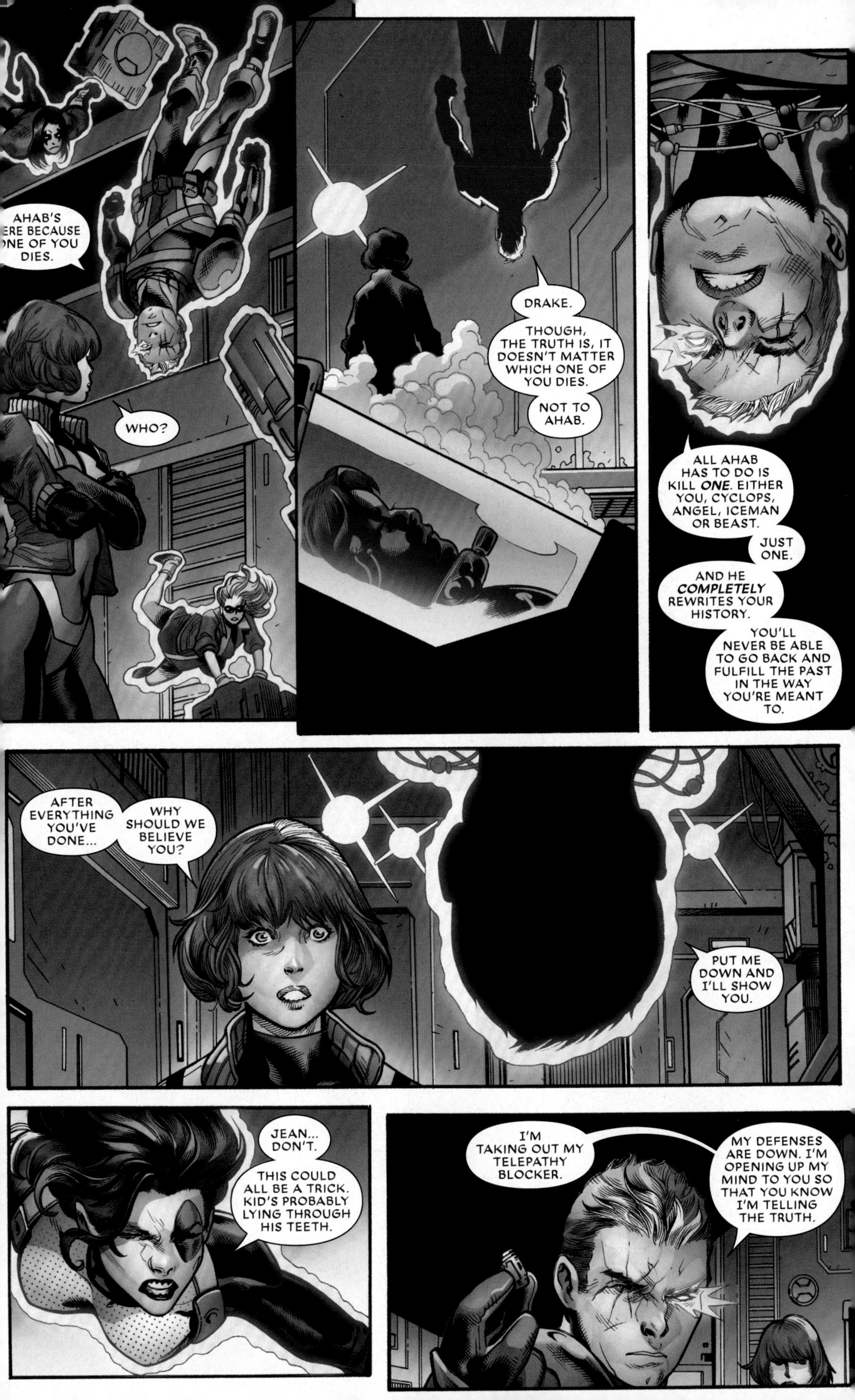
AHAB'S
ERE BECAUSE
NE OF YOU
DIES.
WHO?
DRAKE.
THOUGH, THE TRUTH IS, IT DOESN'T MATTER WHICH ONE OF YOU DIES.
NOT TO AHAB.
ALL AHAB HAS TO DO IS KILL ONE. EITHER YOU, CYCLOPS, ANGEL, ICEMAN OR BEAST.
JUST ONE.
AND HE COMPLETELY REWRITES YOUR HISTORY.
YOU'LL NEVER BE ABLE TO GO BACK AND FULFILL THE PAST IN THE WAY YOU'RE MEANT TO.
AFTER EVERYTHING YOU'VE DONE...
WHY SHOULD WE BELIEVE YOU?
PUT ME DOWN AND I'LL SHOW YOU.
JEAN... DON'T.
THIS COULD ALL BE A TRICK. KID'S PROBABLY LYING THROUGH HIS TEETH.
I'M TAKING OUT MY TELEPATHY BLOCKER.
MY DEFENSES ARE DOWN. I'M OPENING UP MY MIND TO YOU SO THAT YOU KNOW I'M TELLING THE TRUTH.

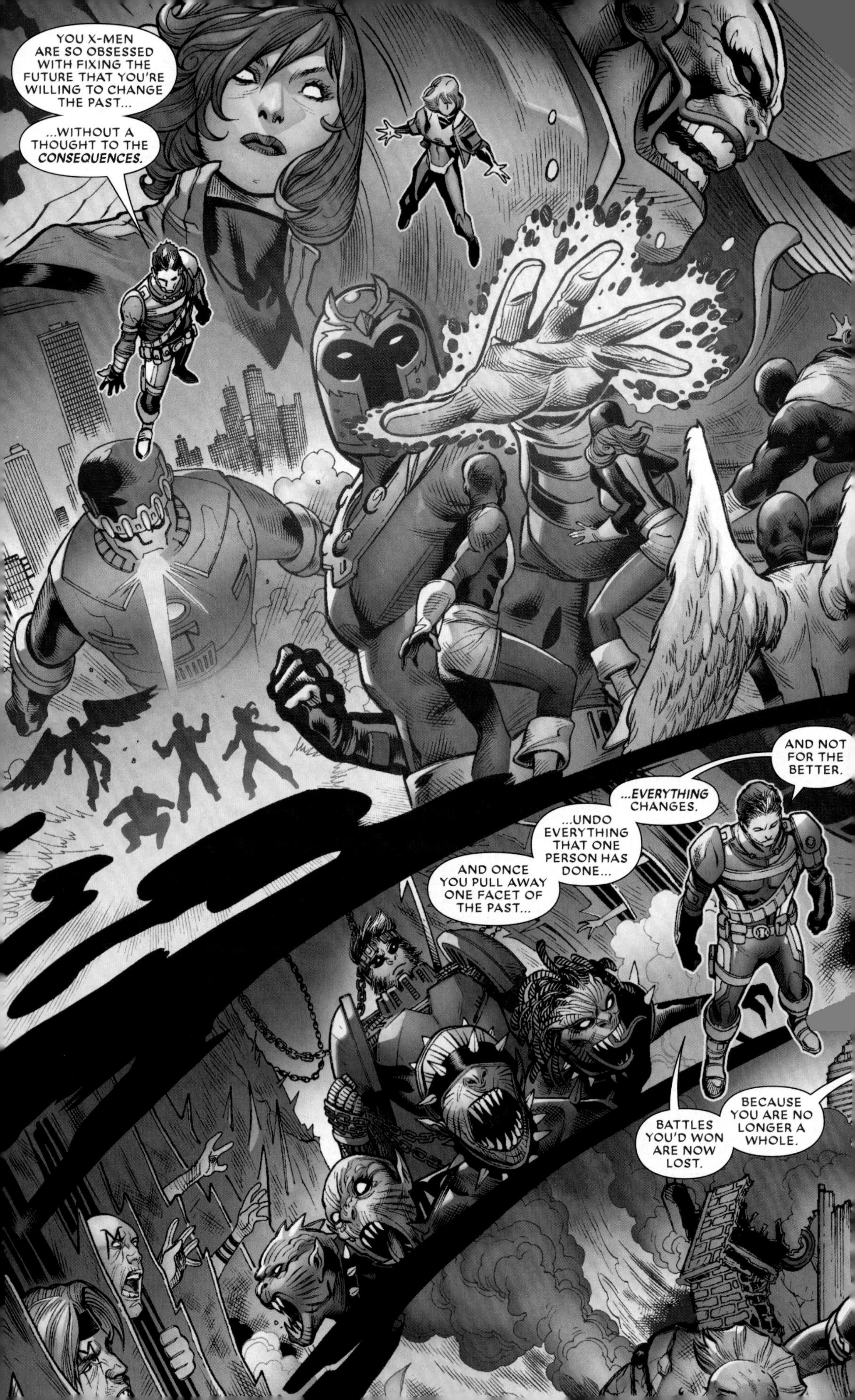
YOU X-MEN ARE SO OBSESSED WITH FIXING THE FUTURE THAT YOU'RE WILLING TO CHANGE THE PAST...
...WITHOUT A THOUGHT TO THE *CONSEQUENCES.*
AND ONCE YOU PULL AWAY ONE FACET OF THE PAST...
...UNDO EVERYTHING THAT ONE PERSON HAS DONE...
*...EVERYTHING* CHANGES.
AND NOT FOR THE BETTER.
BATTLES YOU'D WON ARE NOW LOST.
BECAUSE YOU ARE NO LONGER A WHOLE.

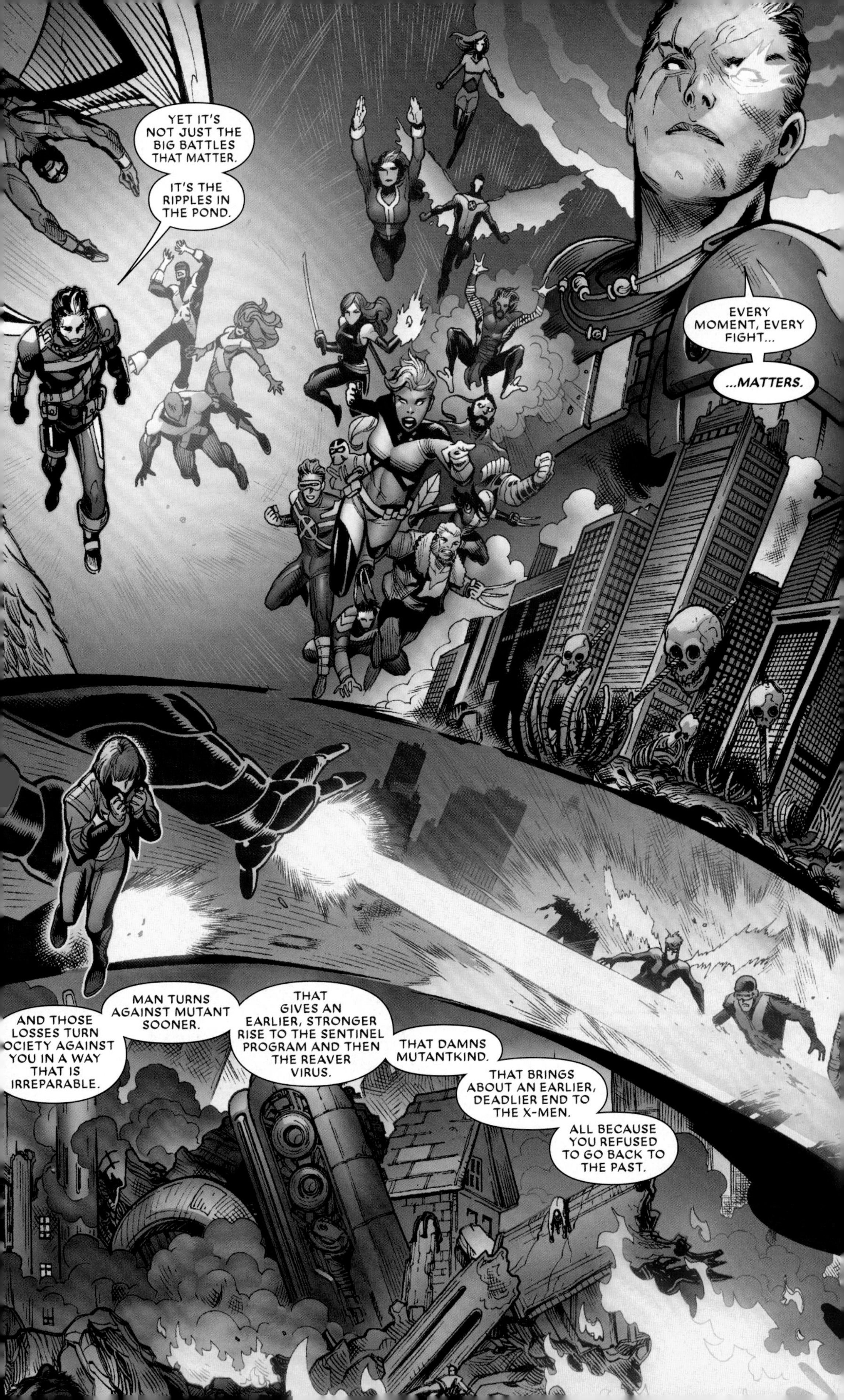
YET IT'S NOT JUST THE BIG BATTLES THAT MATTER.
IT'S THE RIPPLES IN THE POND.
EVERY MOMENT, EVERY FIGHT...
...MATTERS.
AND THOSE LOSSES TURN OCIETY AGAINST YOU IN A WAY THAT IS IRREPARABLE.
MAN TURNS AGAINST MUTANT SOONER.
THAT GIVES AN EARLIER, STRONGER RISE TO THE SENTINEL PROGRAM AND THEN THE REAVER VIRUS.
THAT DAMNS MUTANTKIND.
THAT BRINGS ABOUT AN EARLIER, DEADLIER END TO THE X-MEN.
ALL BECAUSE YOU REFUSED TO GO BACK TO THE PAST.

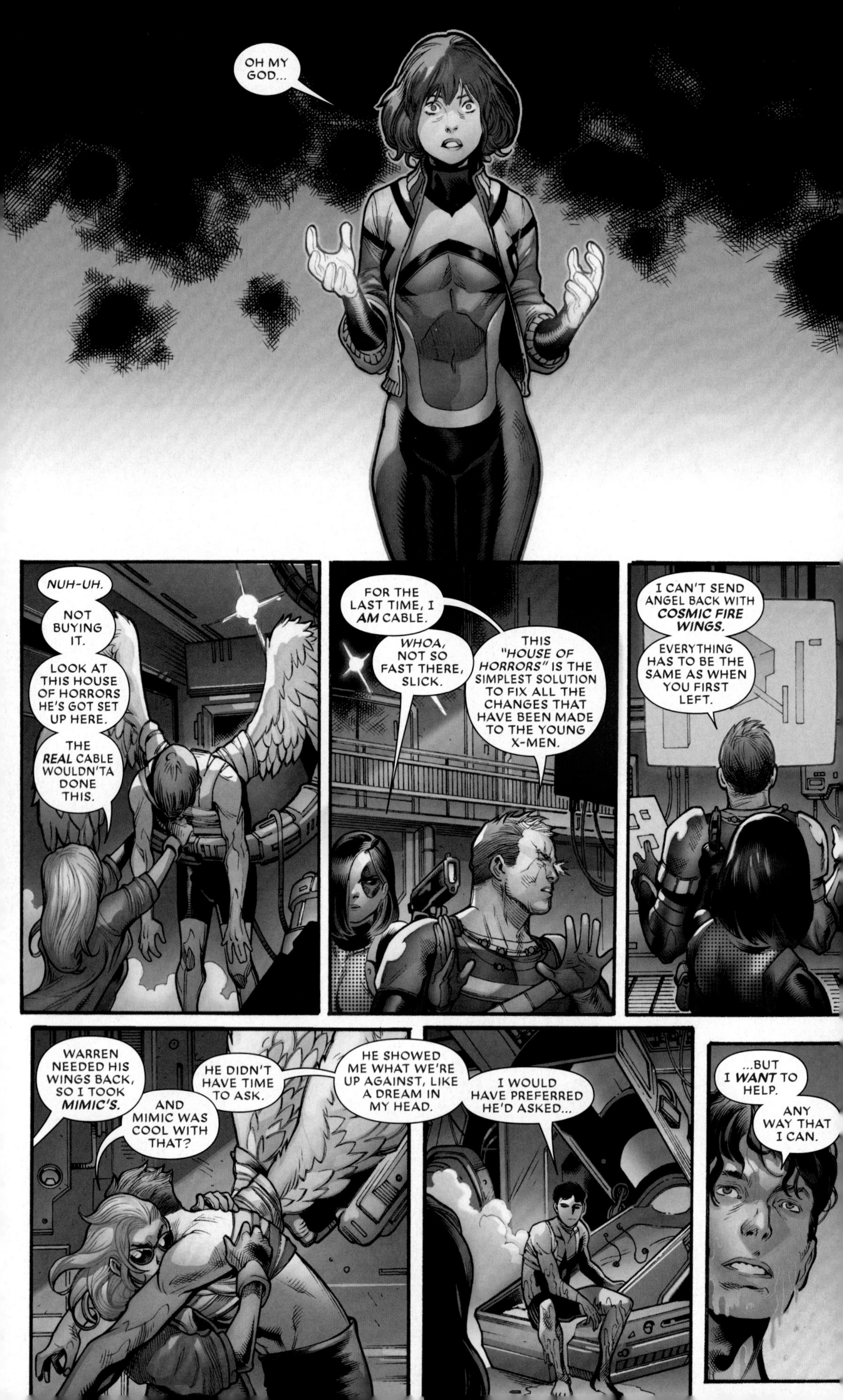

OH MY GOD...
NUH-UH.
NOT BUYING IT.
LOOK AT THIS HOUSE OF HORRORS HE'S GOT SET UP HERE.
THE *REAL* CABLE WOULDN'TA DONE THIS.
FOR THE LAST TIME, I *AM* CABLE.
*WHOA,* NOT SO FAST THERE, SLICK.
THIS *"HOUSE OF HORRORS"* IS THE SIMPLEST SOLUTION TO FIX ALL THE CHANGES THAT HAVE BEEN MADE TO THE YOUNG X-MEN.
I CAN'T SEND ANGEL BACK WITH ***COSMIC FIRE WINGS.***
EVERYTHING HAS TO BE THE SAME AS WHEN YOU FIRST LEFT.
WARREN NEEDED HIS WINGS BACK, SO I TOOK ***MIMIC'S.***
AND MIMIC WAS COOL WITH THAT?
HE DIDN'T HAVE TIME TO ASK.
HE SHOWED ME WHAT WE'RE UP AGAINST, LIKE A DREAM IN MY HEAD.
I WOULD HAVE PREFERRED HE'D ASKED...
...BUT I *WANT* TO HELP.
ANY WAY THAT I CAN.

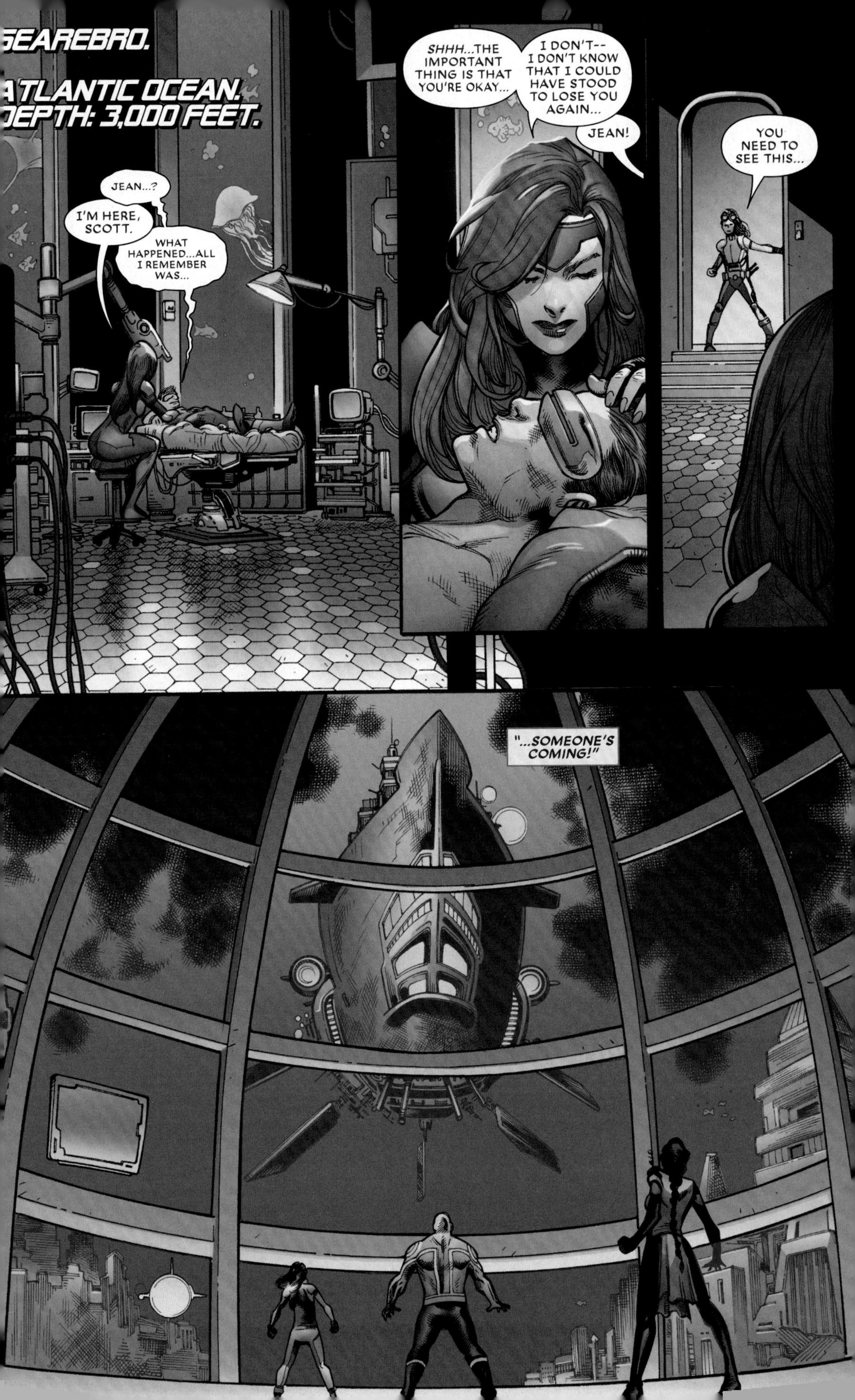

CEAREBRO.
ATLANTIC OCEAN.
DEPTH: 3,000 FEET.
JEAN...?
I'M HERE, SCOTT.
WHAT HAPPENED...ALL I REMEMBER WAS...
SHHH...THE IMPORTANT THING IS THAT YOU'RE OKAY...
I DON'T-- I DON'T KNOW THAT I COULD HAVE STOOD TO LOSE YOU AGAIN...
JEAN!
YOU NEED TO SEE THIS...
"...SOMEONE'S COMING!"

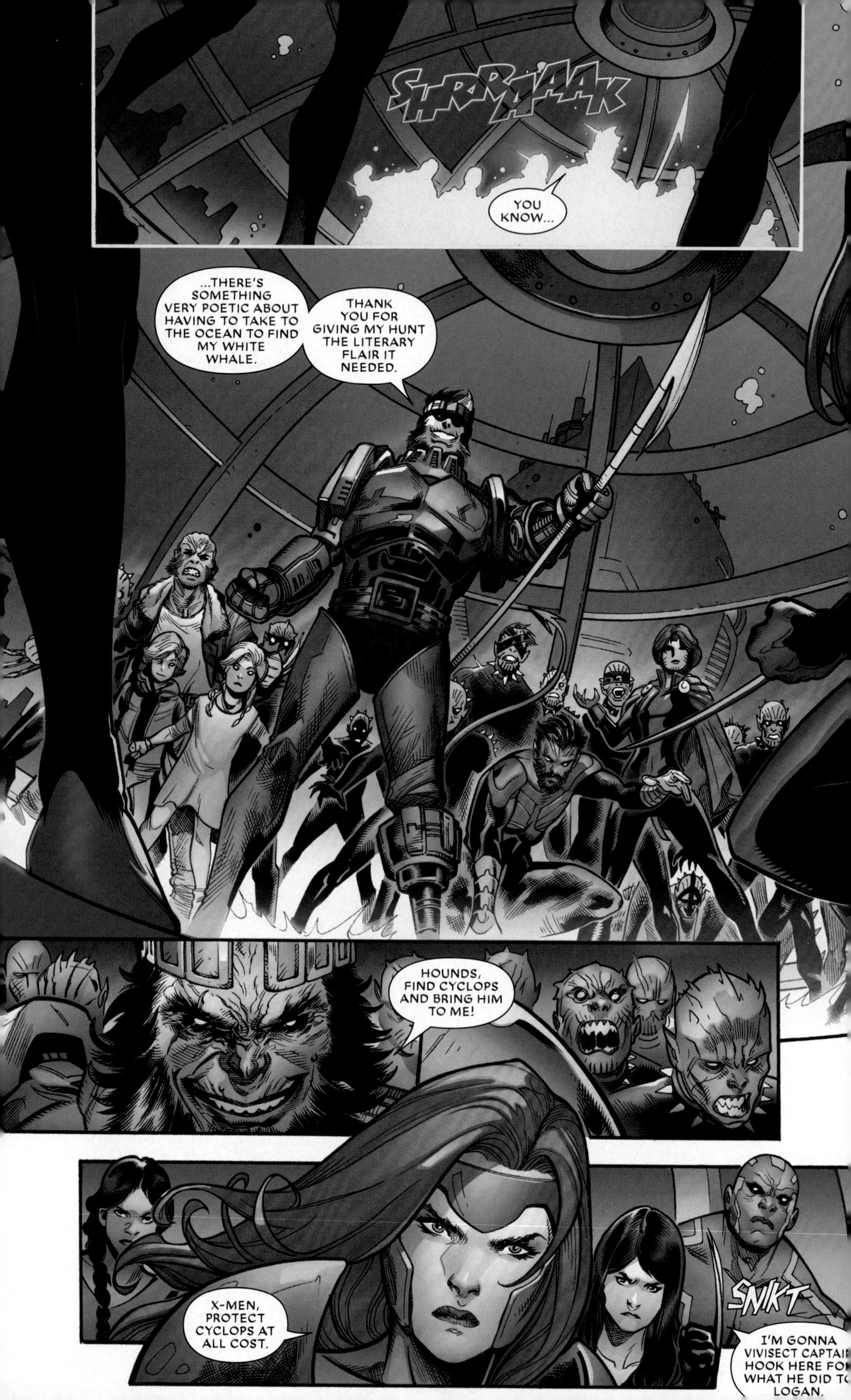
SHRRAAAK
YOU KNOW...
...THERE'S SOMETHING VERY POETIC ABOUT HAVING TO TAKE TO THE OCEAN TO FIND MY WHITE WHALE.
THANK YOU FOR GIVING MY HUNT THE LITERARY FLAIR IT NEEDED.
HOUNDS, FIND CYCLOPS AND BRING HIM TO ME!
X-MEN, PROTECT CYCLOPS AT ALL COST.
SNIKT
I'M GONNA VIVISECT CAPTAI HOOK HERE FO WHAT HE DID T LOGAN.

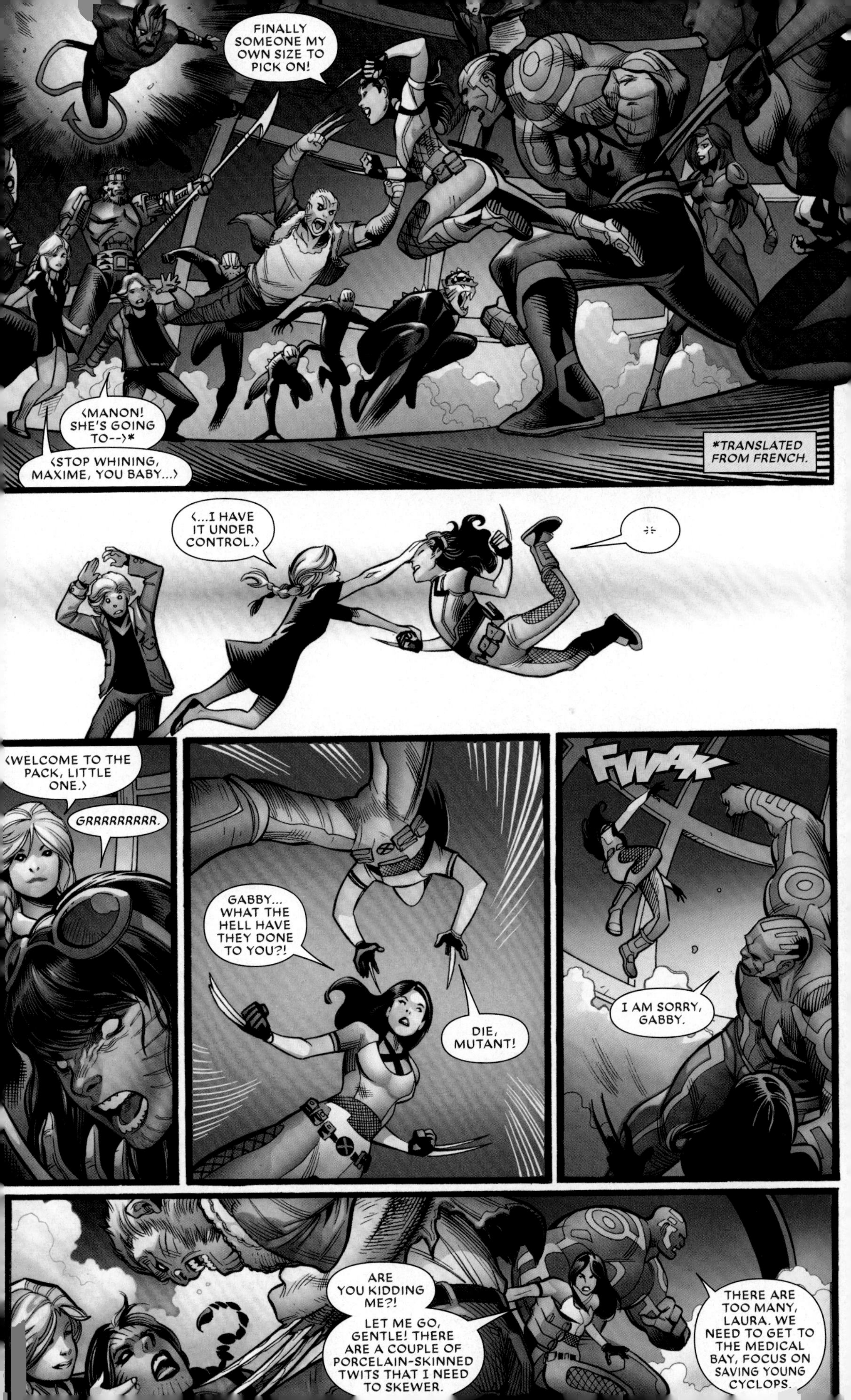
FINALLY SOMEONE MY OWN SIZE TO PICK ON!
‹MANON! SHE'S GOING TO--›*
‹STOP WHINING, MAXIME, YOU BABY...›
*TRANSLATED FROM FRENCH.
‹...I HAVE IT UNDER CONTROL.›
‹WELCOME TO THE PACK, LITTLE ONE.›
GRRRRRRRRR.
GABBY... WHAT THE HELL HAVE THEY DONE TO YOU?!
DIE, MUTANT!
FWAK
I AM SORRY, GABBY.
ARE YOU KIDDING ME?!
LET ME GO, GENTLE! THERE ARE A COUPLE OF PORCELAIN-SKINNED TWITS THAT I NEED TO SKEWER.
THERE ARE TOO MANY, LAURA. WE NEED TO GET TO THE MEDICAL BAY, FOCUS ON SAVING YOUNG CYCLOPS.

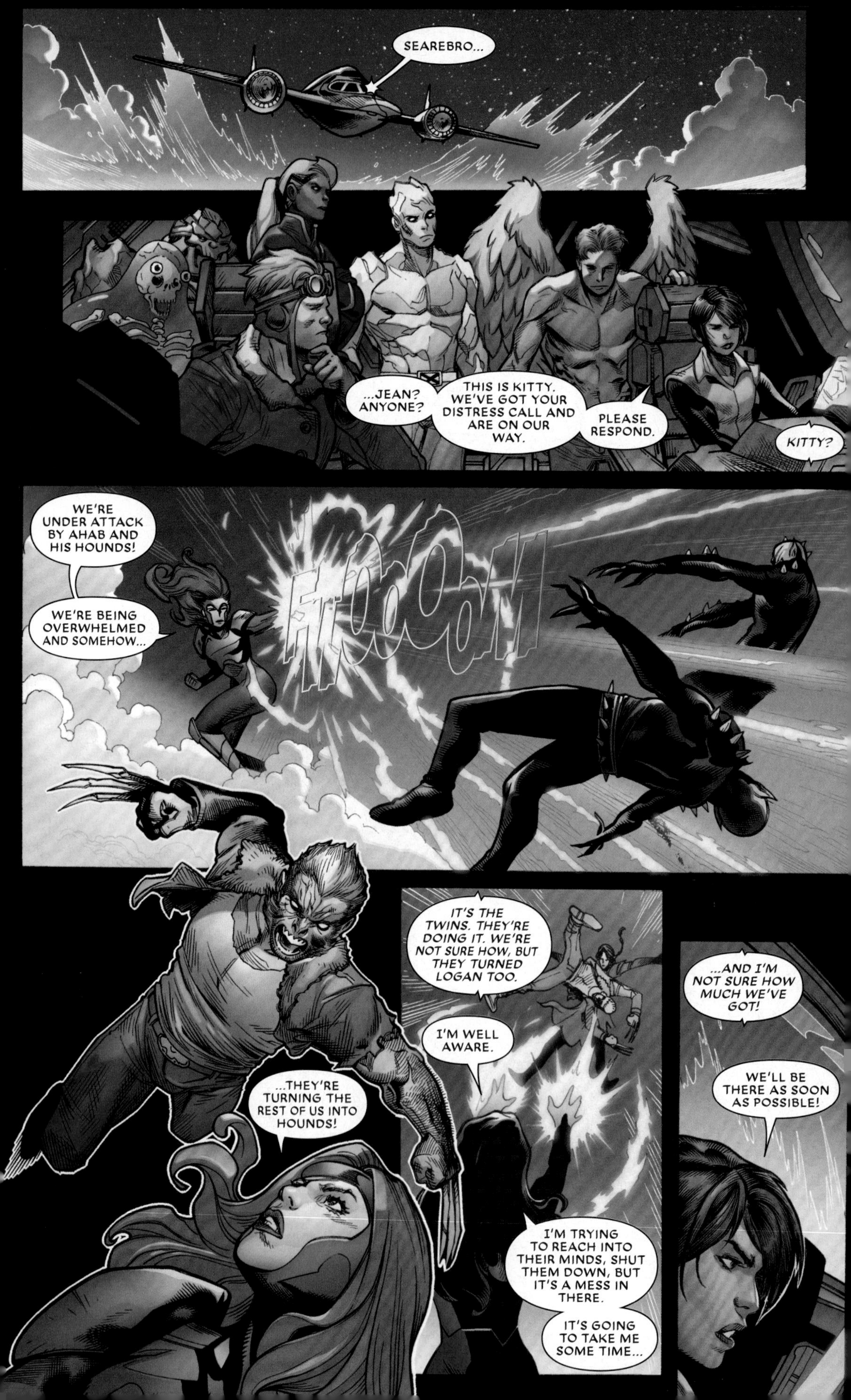
SEAREBRO...
...JEAN? ANYONE?
THIS IS KITTY. WE'VE GOT YOUR DISTRESS CALL AND ARE ON OUR WAY.
PLEASE RESPOND.
KITTY?
WE'RE UNDER ATTACK BY AHAB AND HIS HOUNDS!
WE'RE BEING OVERWHELMED AND SOMEHOW...
FTOOOOM
...THEY'RE TURNING THE REST OF US INTO HOUNDS!
IT'S THE TWINS. THEY'RE DOING IT. WE'RE NOT SURE HOW, BUT THEY TURNED LOGAN TOO.
I'M WELL AWARE.
I'M TRYING TO REACH INTO THEIR MINDS, SHUT THEM DOWN, BUT IT'S A MESS IN THERE.
IT'S GOING TO TAKE ME SOME TIME...
...AND I'M NOT SURE HOW MUCH WE'VE GOT!
WE'LL BE THERE AS SOON AS POSSIBLE!

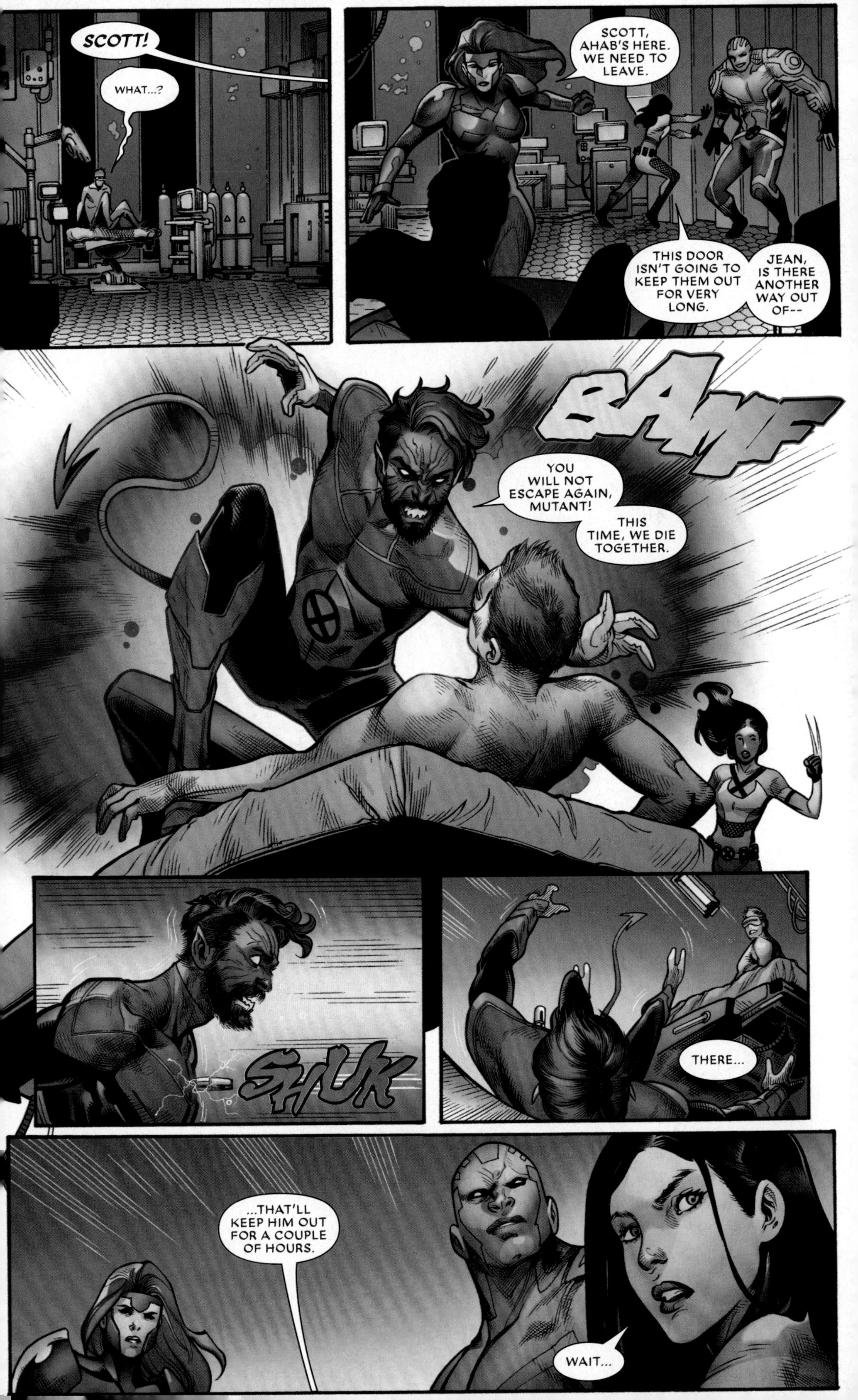
SCOTT!
WHAT...?
SCOTT, AHAB'S HERE. WE NEED TO LEAVE.
THIS DOOR ISN'T GOING TO KEEP THEM OUT FOR VERY LONG.
JEAN, IS THERE ANOTHER WAY OUT OF--
BAMF
YOU WILL NOT ESCAPE AGAIN, MUTANT!
THIS TIME, WE DIE TOGETHER.
SHUK
THERE...
...THAT'LL KEEP HIM OUT FOR A COUPLE OF HOURS.
WAIT...

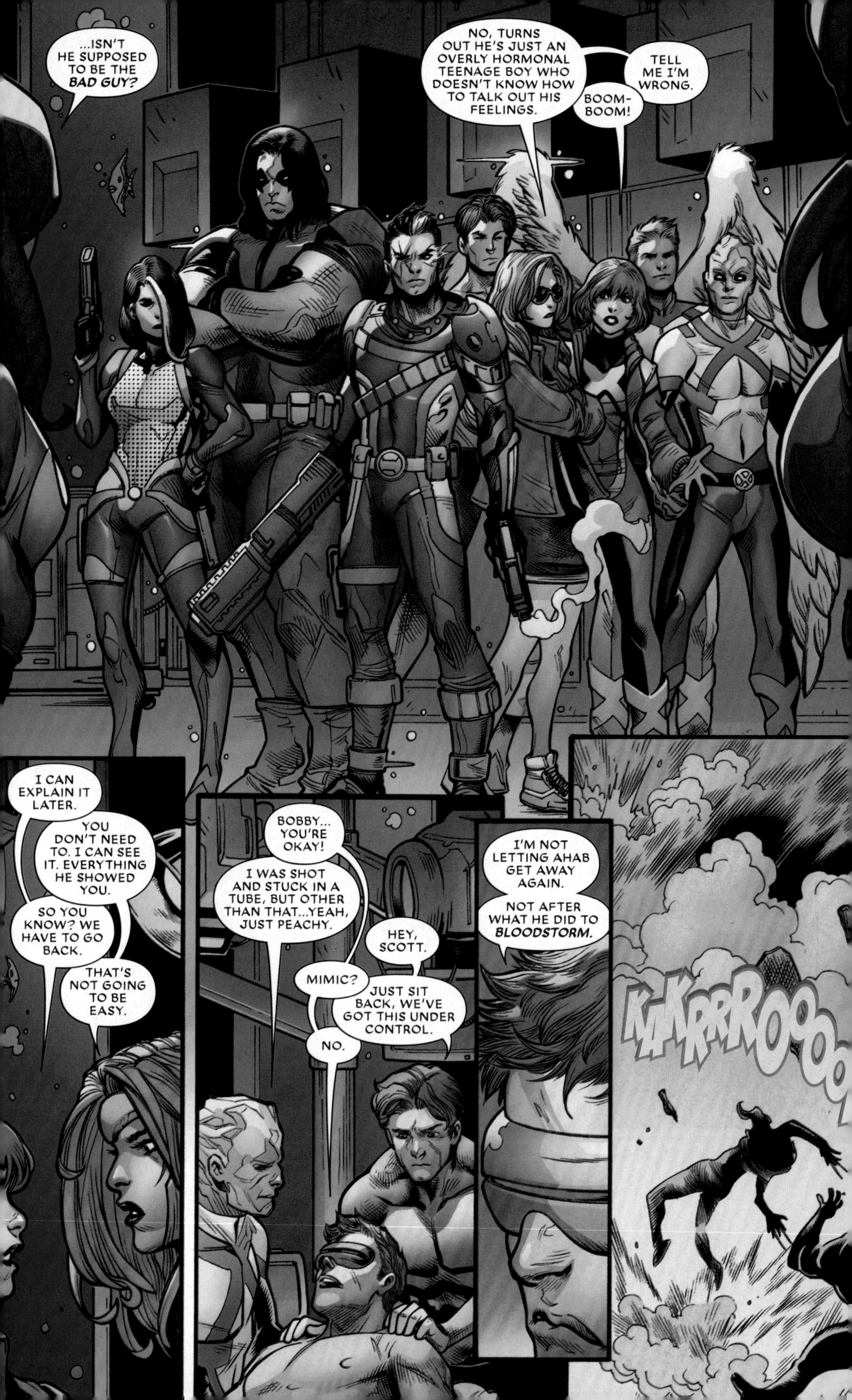
...ISN'T HE SUPPOSED TO BE THE *BAD GUY?*
NO, TURNS OUT HE'S JUST AN OVERLY HORMONAL TEENAGE BOY WHO DOESN'T KNOW HOW TO TALK OUT HIS FEELINGS.
TELL ME I'M WRONG.
BOOM-BOOM!
I CAN EXPLAIN IT LATER.
YOU DON'T NEED TO. I CAN SEE IT. EVERYTHING HE SHOWED YOU.
SO YOU KNOW? WE HAVE TO GO BACK.
THAT'S NOT GOING TO BE EASY.
BOBBY... YOU'RE OKAY!
I WAS SHOT AND STUCK IN A TUBE, BUT OTHER THAN THAT...YEAH, JUST PEACHY.
HEY, SCOTT.
MIMIC?
JUST SIT BACK, WE'VE GOT THIS UNDER CONTROL.
NO.
I'M NOT LETTING AHAB GET AWAY AGAIN.
NOT AFTER WHAT HE DID TO *BLOODSTORM.*
KKKRRROOOO

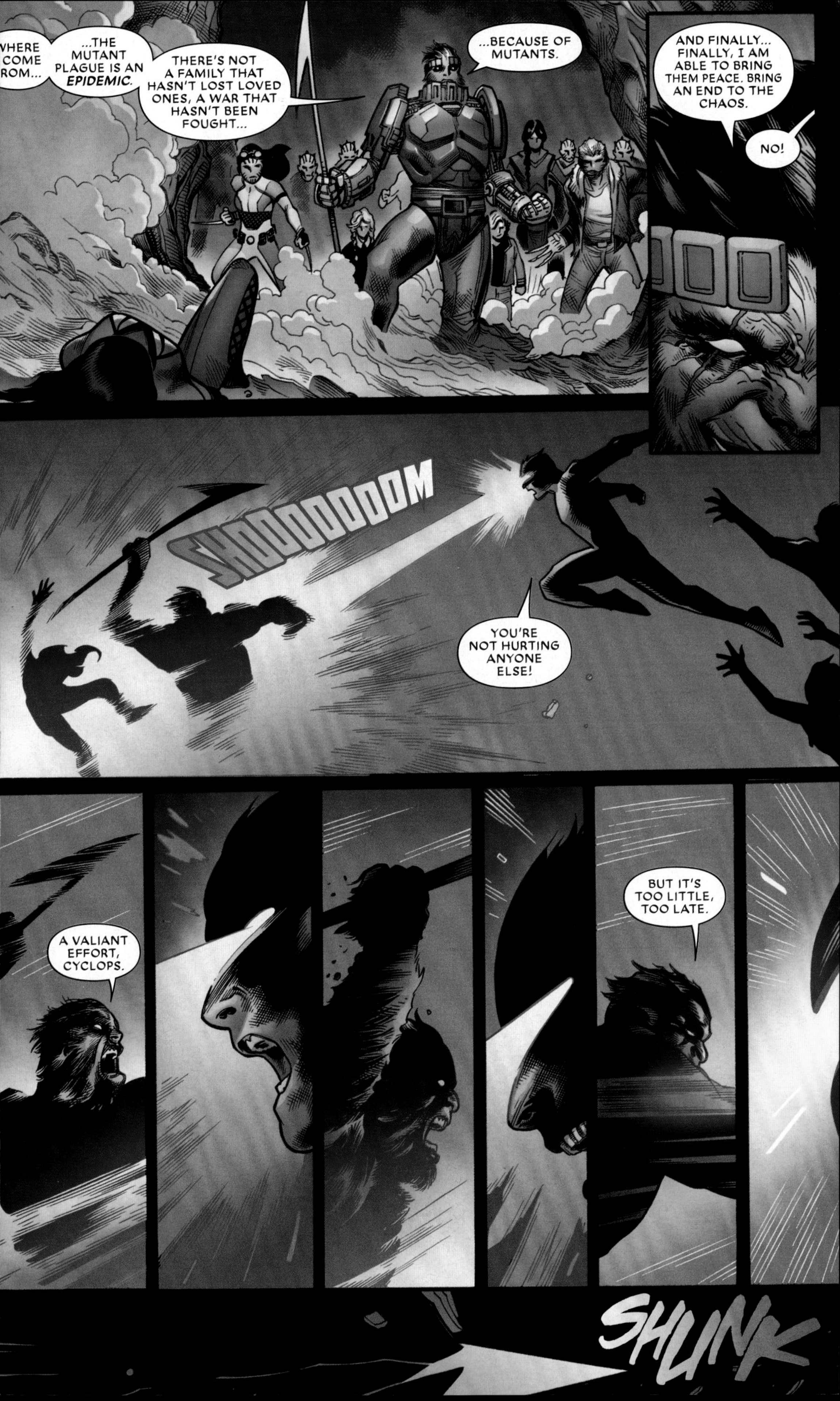

WHERE
COME
ROM...
...THE MUTANT PLAGUE IS AN EPIDEMIC.
THERE'S NOT A FAMILY THAT HASN'T LOST LOVED ONES, A WAR THAT HASN'T BEEN FOUGHT...
...BECAUSE OF MUTANTS.
AND FINALLY... FINALLY, I AM ABLE TO BRING THEM PEACE. BRING AN END TO THE CHAOS.
NO!
SHOOOOOOOOM
YOU'RE NOT HURTING ANYONE ELSE!
A VALIANT EFFORT, CYCLOPS.
BUT IT'S TOO LITTLE, TOO LATE.
SHUNK

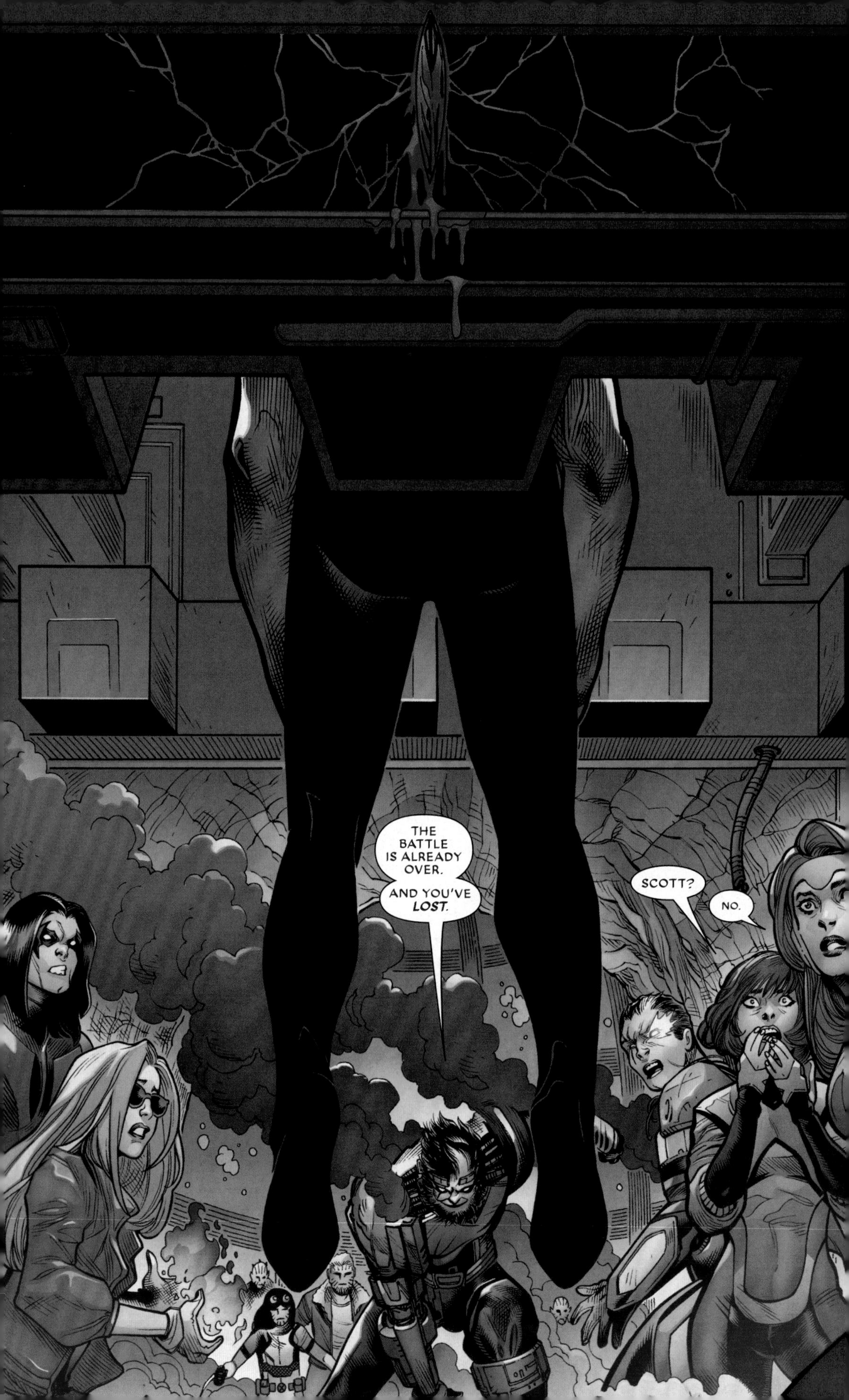
THE BATTLE IS ALREADY OVER.
AND YOU'VE *LOST*.
SCOTT?
NO.

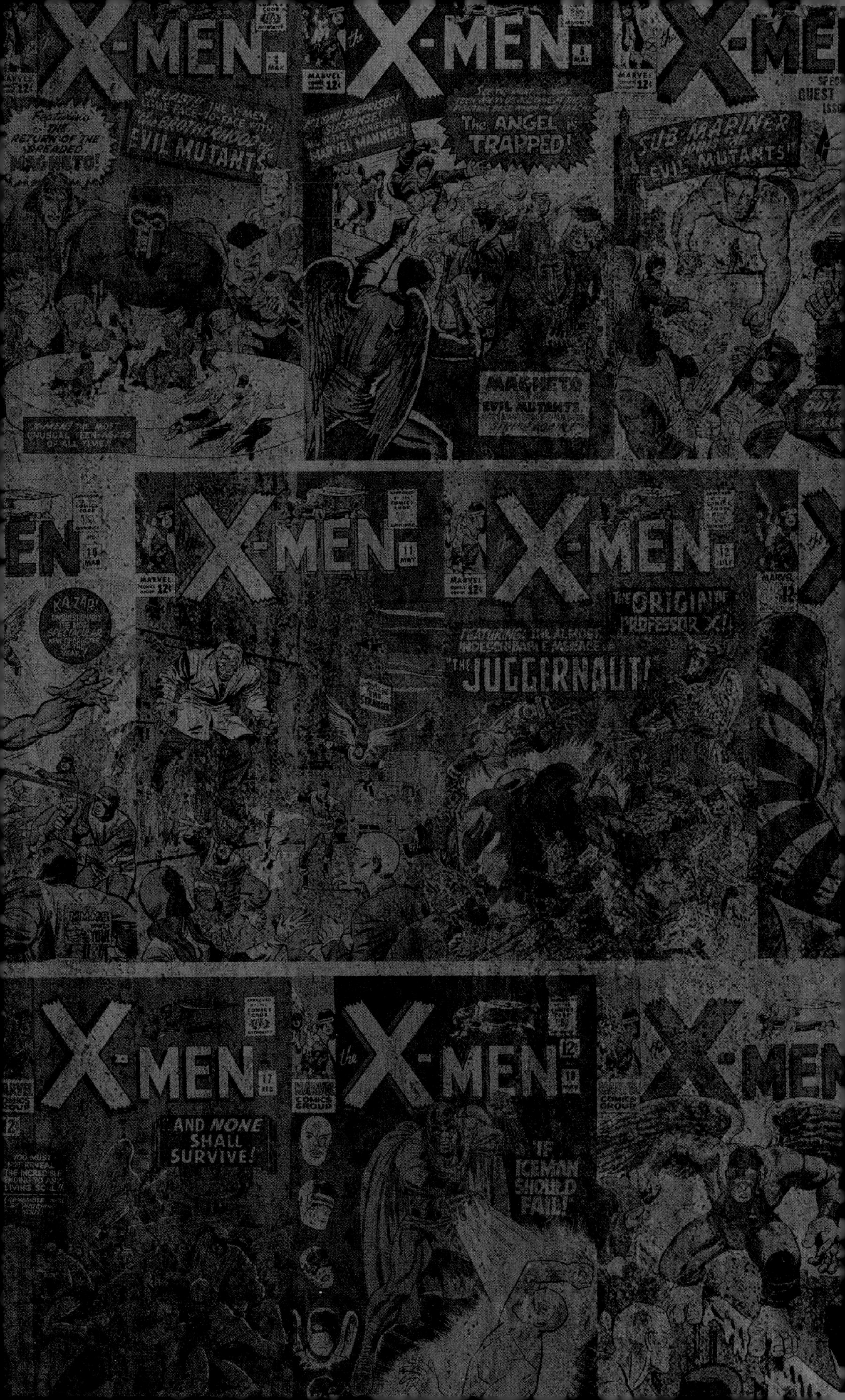

X-MEN
MARVEL 12¢
AT LAST!! THE X-MEN COME FACE-TO-FACE WITH the BROTHERHOOD of EVIL MUTANTS
THE RETURN OF THE DREADED MAGNETO!
X-MEN! THE MOST UNUSUAL TEEN-AGERS OF ALL TIME!!
X-MEN
SUSPENSE!
The ANGEL is TRAPPED!
MAGNETO
EVIL MUTANTS
X-MEN
SUB-MARINER
EVIL MUTANTS!
X-MEN
X-MEN
THE ORIGIN OF PROFESSOR X!
"THE JUGGERNAUT!"
X-MEN
...AND NONE SHALL SURVIVE!
X-MEN
"IF ICEMAN SHOULD FAIL!"
X-MEN

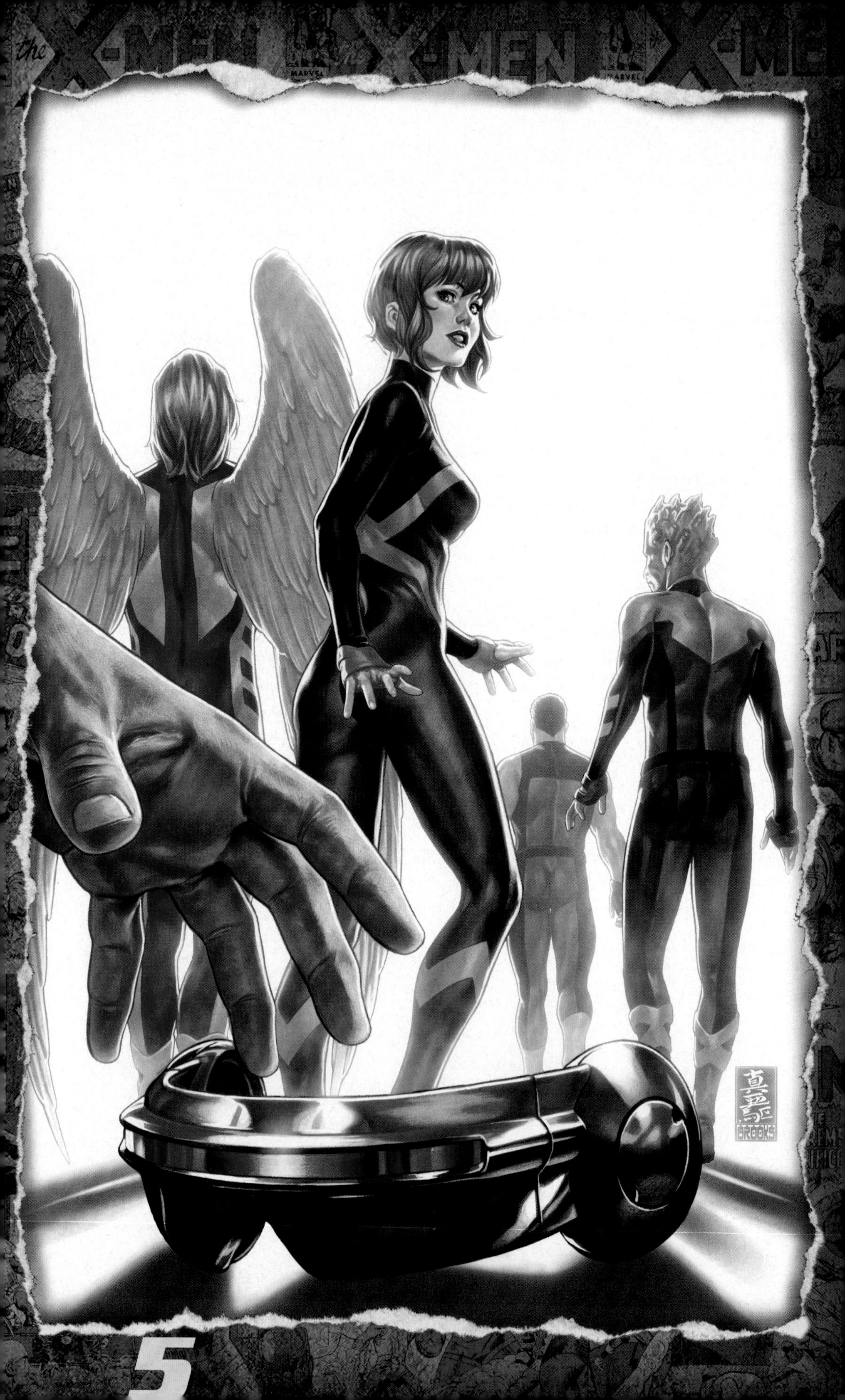
X-MEN
X-MEN
BROOKS
5

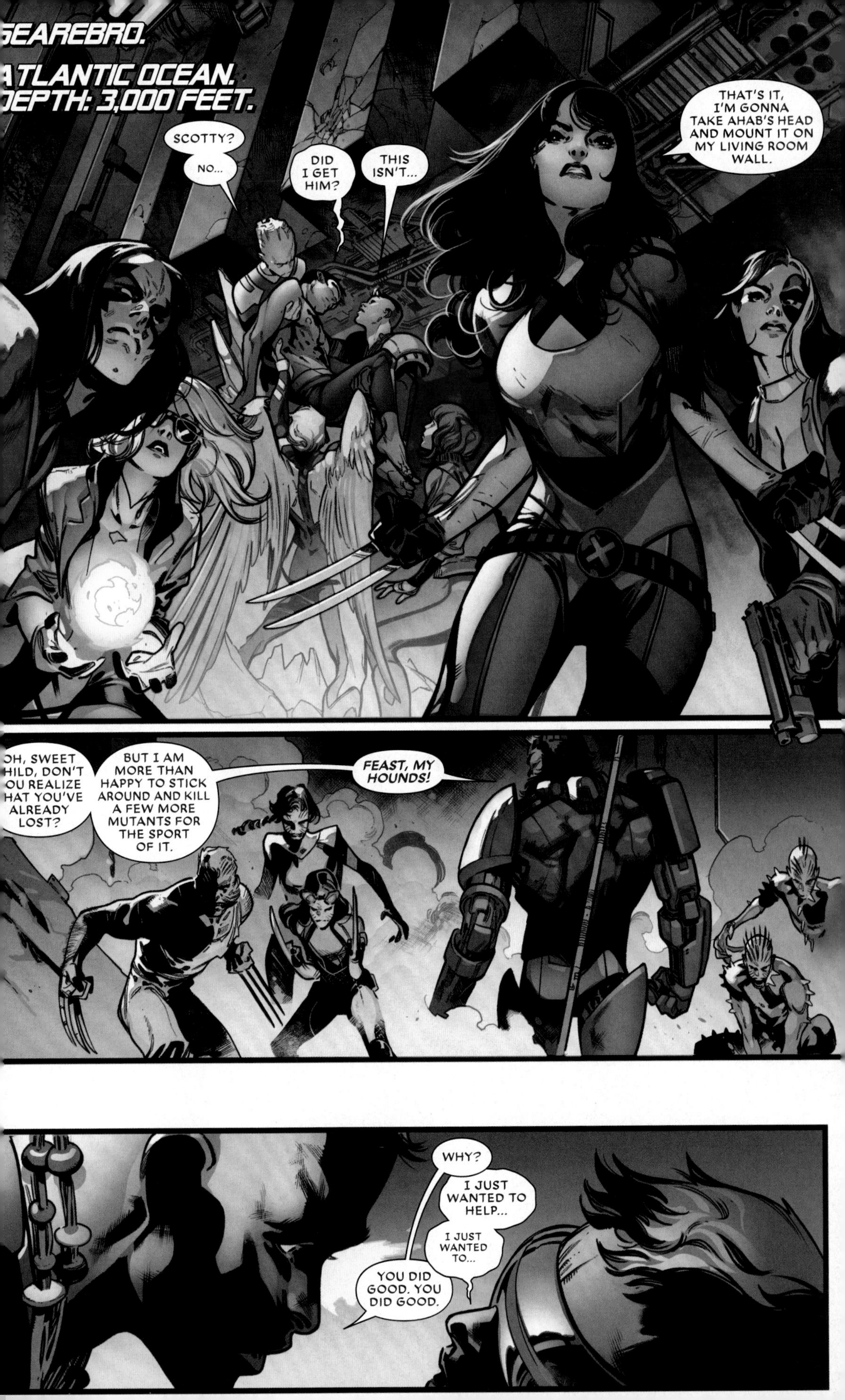
SEAREBRO.
ATLANTIC OCEAN.
DEPTH: 3,000 FEET.
SCOTTY?
NO...
DID I GET HIM?
THIS ISN'T...
THAT'S IT, I'M GONNA TAKE AHAB'S HEAD AND MOUNT IT ON MY LIVING ROOM WALL.
OH, SWEET HILD, DON'T OU REALIZE HAT YOU'VE ALREADY LOST?
BUT I AM MORE THAN HAPPY TO STICK AROUND AND KILL A FEW MORE MUTANTS FOR THE SPORT OF IT.
FEAST, MY HOUNDS!
WHY?
I JUST WANTED TO HELP...
I JUST WANTED TO...
YOU DID GOOD. YOU DID GOOD.

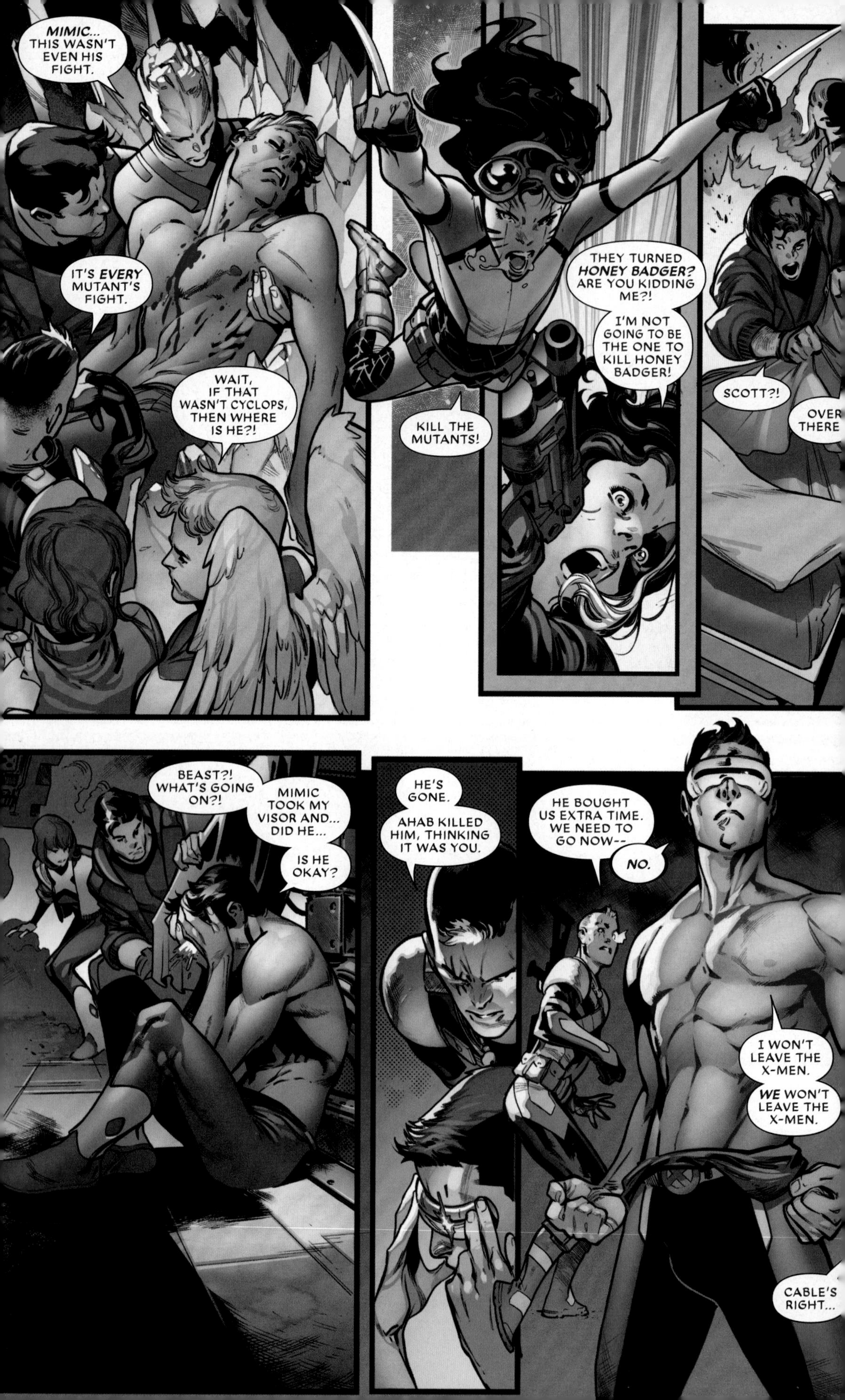
MIMIC... THIS WASN'T EVEN HIS FIGHT.
IT'S EVERY MUTANT'S FIGHT.
WAIT, IF THAT WASN'T CYCLOPS, THEN WHERE IS HE?!
KILL THE MUTANTS!
THEY TURNED HONEY BADGER? ARE YOU KIDDING ME?!
I'M NOT GOING TO BE THE ONE TO KILL HONEY BADGER!
SCOTT?!
OVER THERE
BEAST?! WHAT'S GOING ON?!
MIMIC TOOK MY VISOR AND... DID HE...
IS HE OKAY?
HE'S GONE.
AHAB KILLED HIM, THINKING IT WAS YOU.
HE BOUGHT US EXTRA TIME. WE NEED TO GO NOW--
NO.
I WON'T LEAVE THE X-MEN.
WE WON'T LEAVE THE X-MEN.
CABLE'S RIGHT...

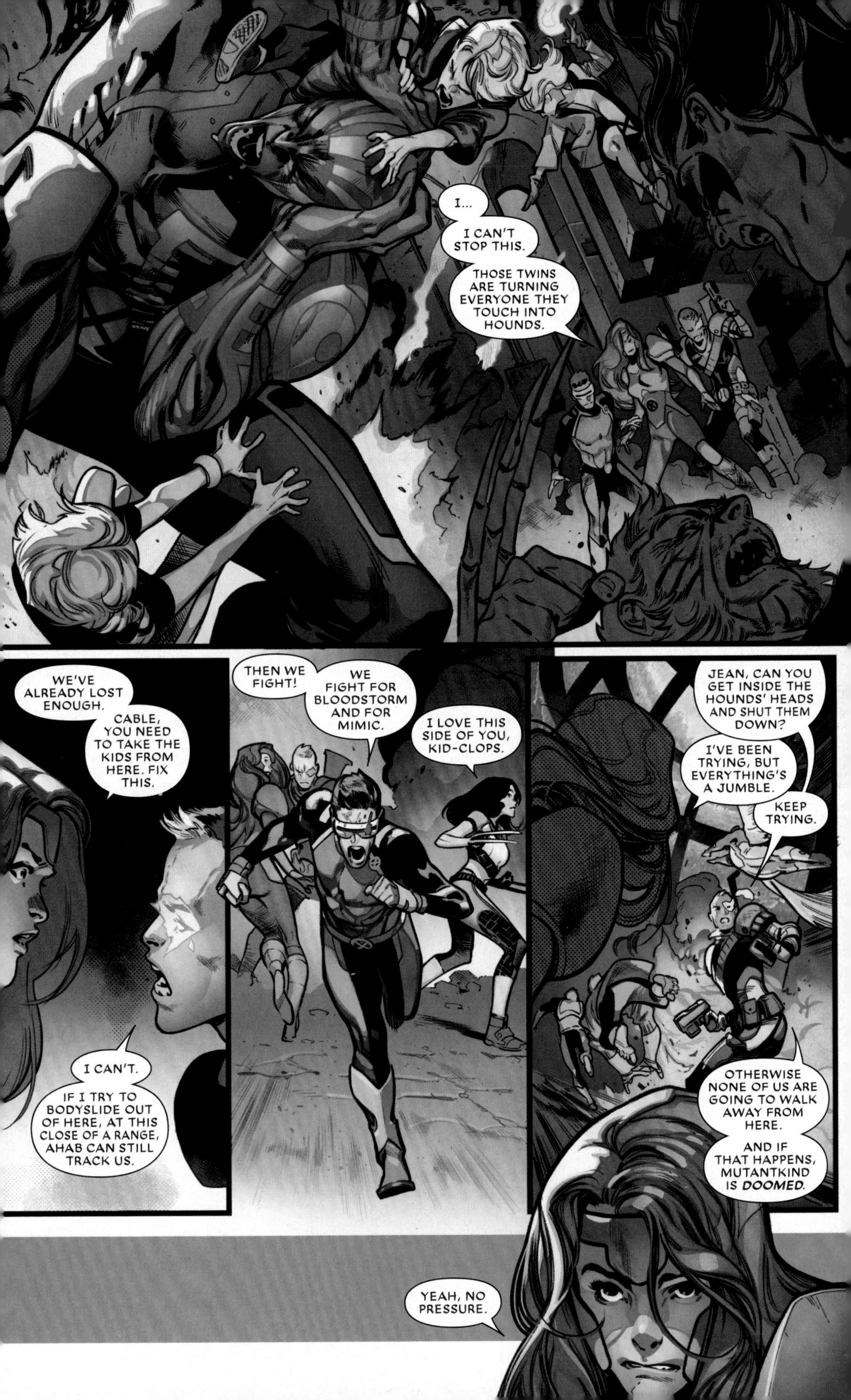
I...
I CAN'T STOP THIS.
THOSE TWINS ARE TURNING EVERYONE THEY TOUCH INTO HOUNDS.
WE'VE ALREADY LOST ENOUGH.
CABLE, YOU NEED TO TAKE THE KIDS FROM HERE. FIX THIS.
I CAN'T.
IF I TRY TO BODYSLIDE OUT OF HERE, AT THIS CLOSE OF A RANGE, AHAB CAN STILL TRACK US.
THEN WE FIGHT!
WE FIGHT FOR BLOODSTORM AND FOR MIMIC.
I LOVE THIS SIDE OF YOU, KID-CLOPS.
JEAN, CAN YOU GET INSIDE THE HOUNDS' HEADS AND SHUT THEM DOWN?
I'VE BEEN TRYING, BUT EVERYTHING'S A JUMBLE.
KEEP TRYING.
OTHERWISE NONE OF US ARE GOING TO WALK AWAY FROM HERE.
AND IF THAT HAPPENS, MUTANTKIND IS ***DOOMED.***
YEAH, NO PRESSURE.

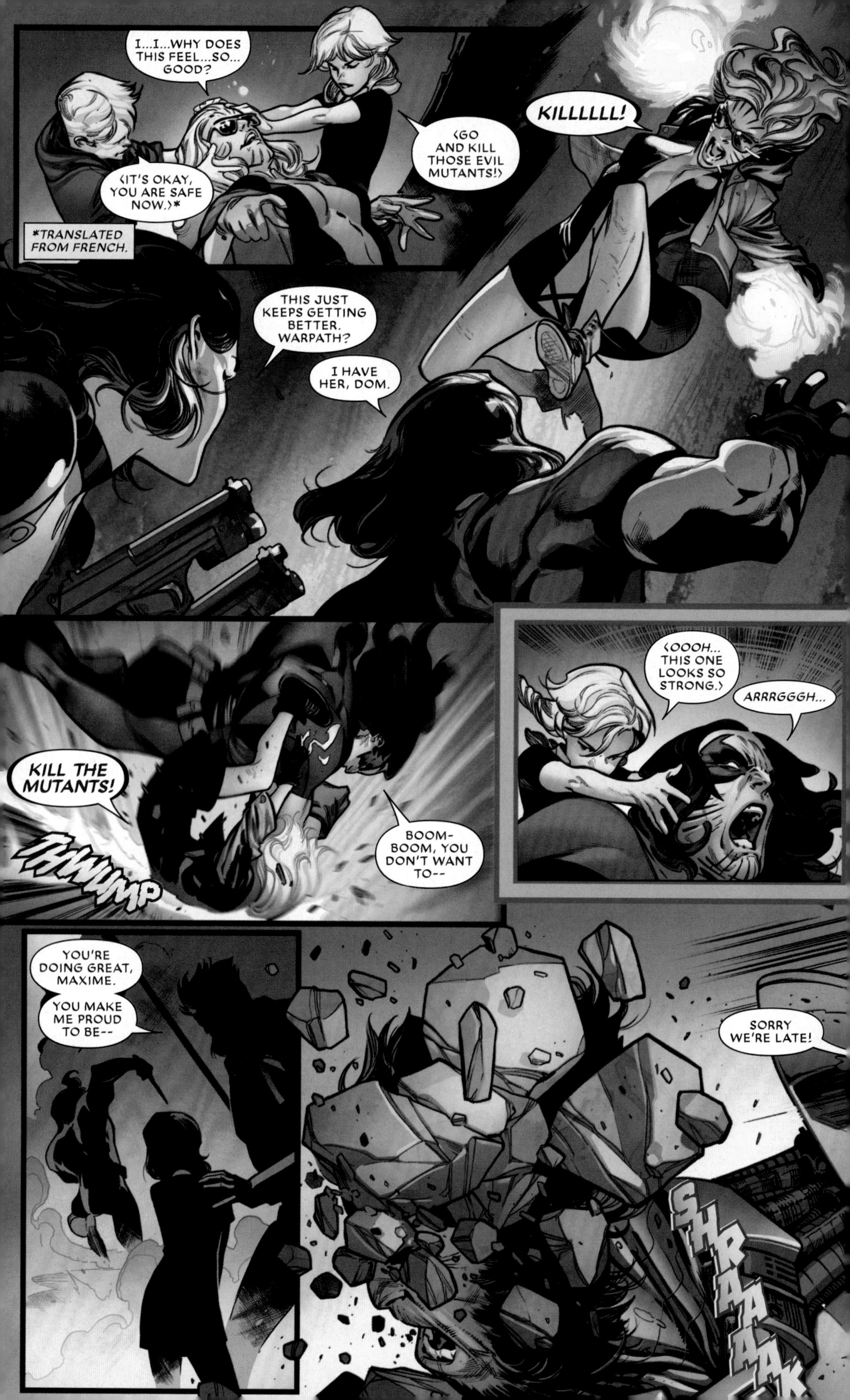
I...I...WHY DOES THIS FEEL...SO... GOOD?
‹IT'S OKAY, YOU ARE SAFE NOW.›*
‹GO AND KILL THOSE EVIL MUTANTS!›
*TRANSLATED FROM FRENCH.
KILLLLLL!
THIS JUST KEEPS GETTING BETTER. WARPATH?
I HAVE HER, DOM.
KILL THE MUTANTS!
THWUMP
BOOM-BOOM, YOU DON'T WANT TO--
‹OOOH... THIS ONE LOOKS SO STRONG.›
ARRRGGGH...
YOU'RE DOING GREAT, MAXIME.
YOU MAKE ME PROUD TO BE--
SORRY WE'RE LATE!
SHRAAAAK

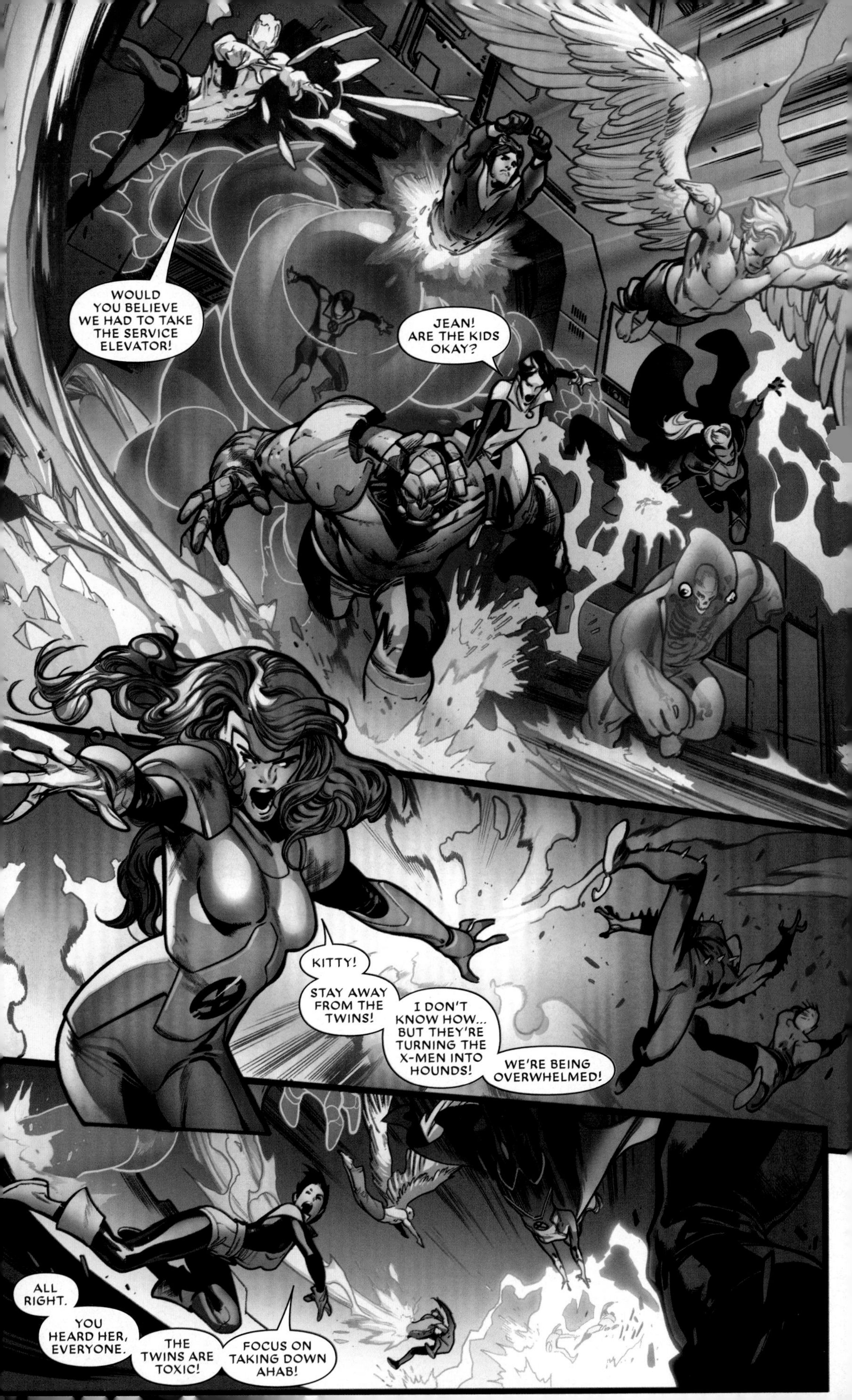
WOULD YOU BELIEVE WE HAD TO TAKE THE SERVICE ELEVATOR!
JEAN! ARE THE KIDS OKAY?
KITTY!
STAY AWAY FROM THE TWINS!
I DON'T KNOW HOW... BUT THEY'RE TURNING THE X-MEN INTO HOUNDS!
WE'RE BEING OVERWHELMED!
ALL RIGHT.
YOU HEARD HER, EVERYONE.
THE TWINS ARE TOXIC!
FOCUS ON TAKING DOWN AHAB!

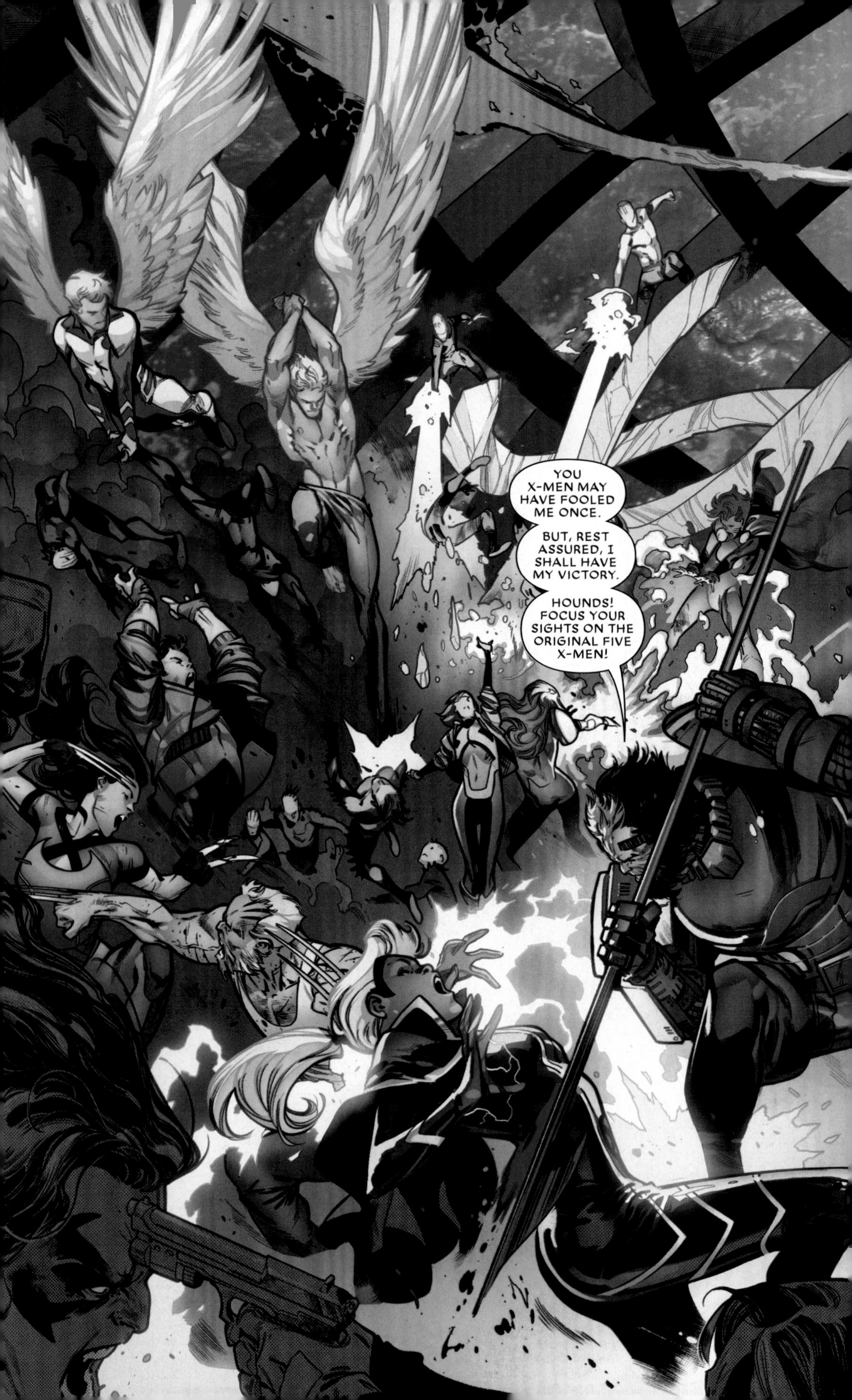
YOU X-MEN MAY HAVE FOOLED ME ONCE.
BUT, REST ASSURED, I SHALL HAVE MY VICTORY.
HOUNDS! FOCUS YOUR SIGHTS ON THE ORIGINAL FIVE X-MEN!

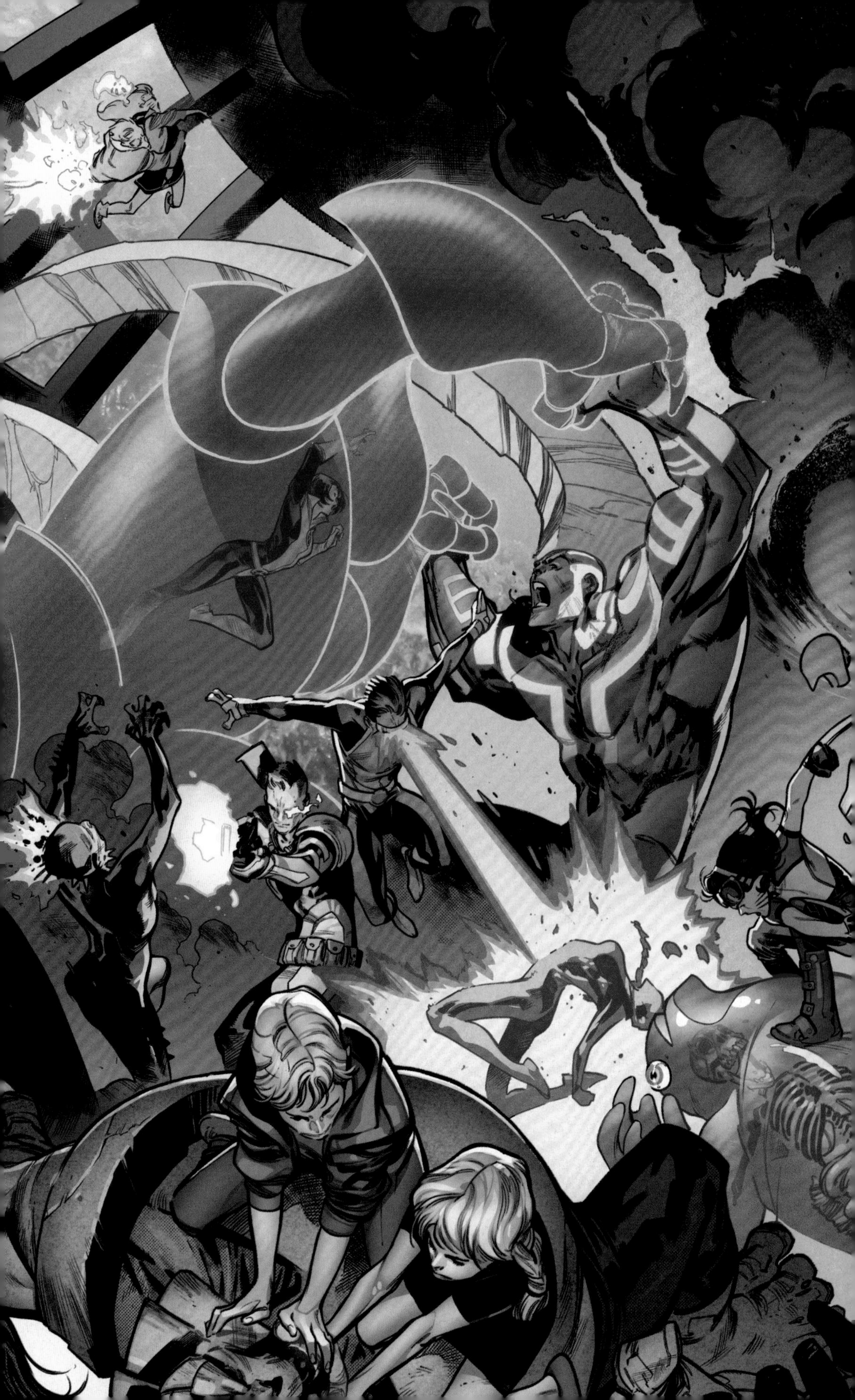

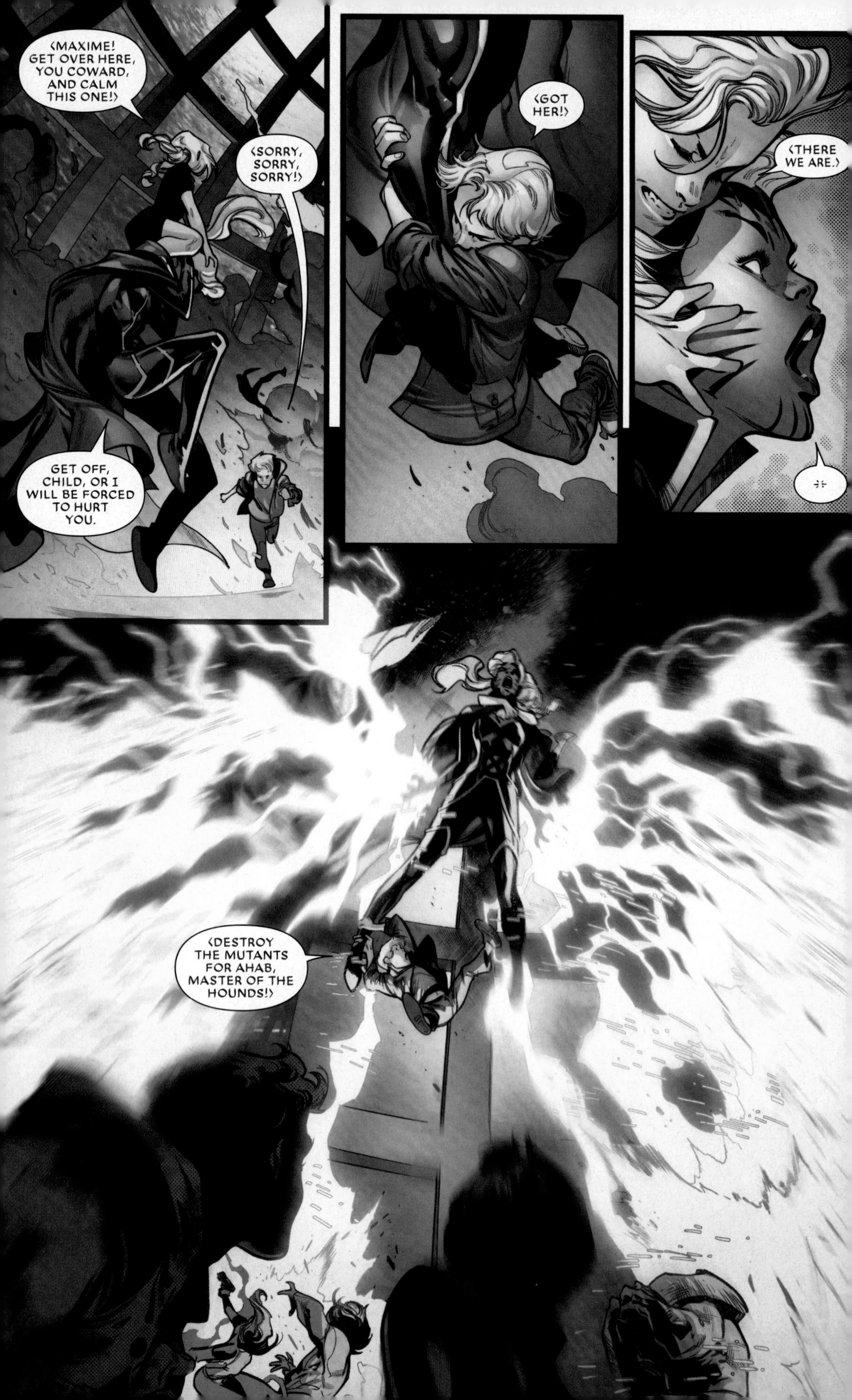
‹MAXIME! GET OVER HERE, YOU COWARD, AND CALM THIS ONE!›
‹SORRY, SORRY, SORRY!›
GET OFF, CHILD, OR I WILL BE FORCED TO HURT YOU.
‹GOT HER!›
‹THERE WE ARE.›
‹DESTROY THE MUTANTS FOR AHAB, MASTER OF THE HOUNDS!›

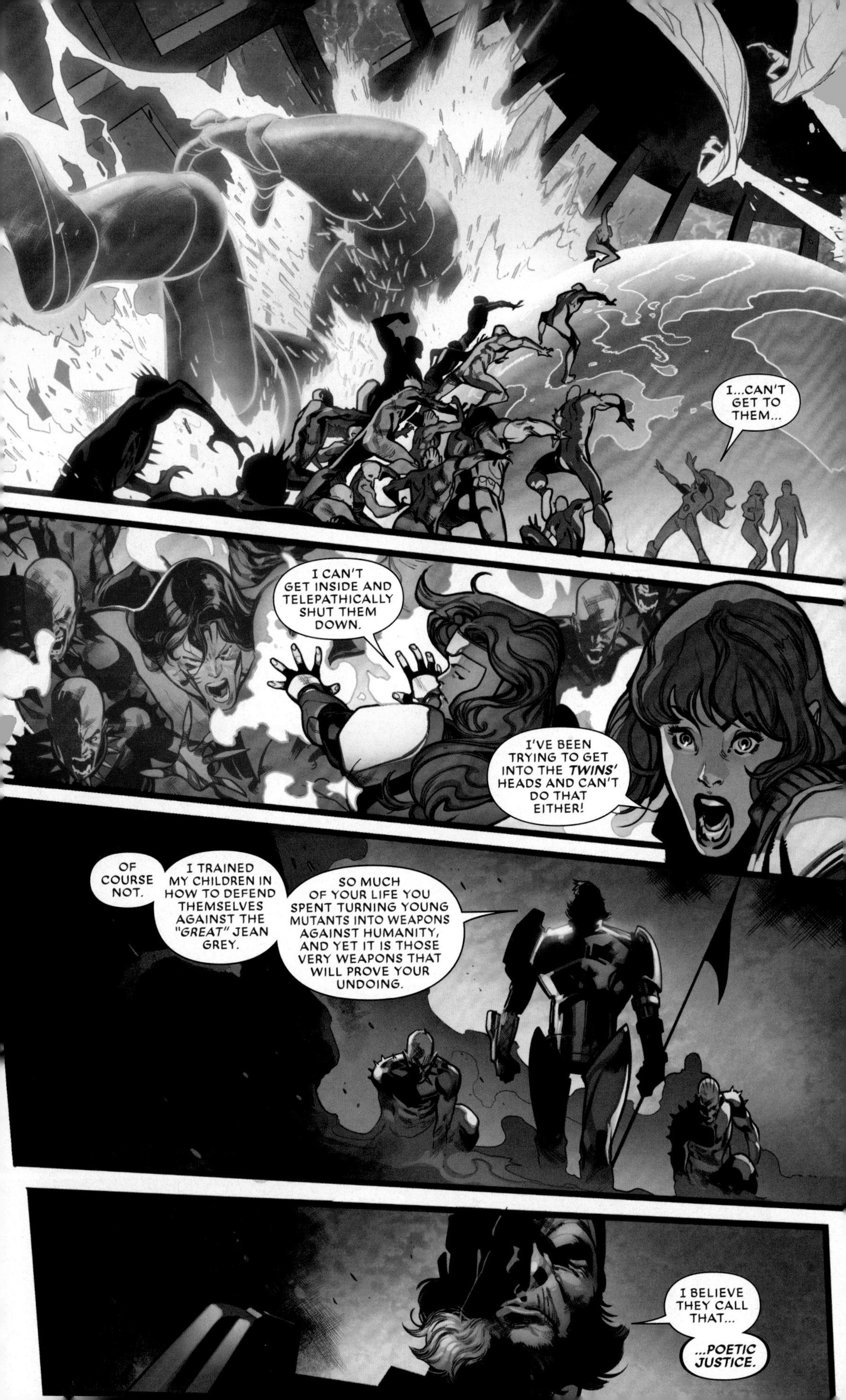
I...CAN'T GET TO THEM...
I CAN'T GET INSIDE AND TELEPATHICALLY SHUT THEM DOWN.
I'VE BEEN TRYING TO GET INTO THE TWINS' HEADS AND CAN'T DO THAT EITHER!
OF COURSE NOT.
I TRAINED MY CHILDREN IN HOW TO DEFEND THEMSELVES AGAINST THE "GREAT" JEAN GREY.
SO MUCH OF YOUR LIFE YOU SPENT TURNING YOUNG MUTANTS INTO WEAPONS AGAINST HUMANITY, AND YET IT IS THOSE VERY WEAPONS THAT WILL PROVE YOUR UNDOING.
I BELIEVE THEY CALL THAT...
...POETIC JUSTICE.

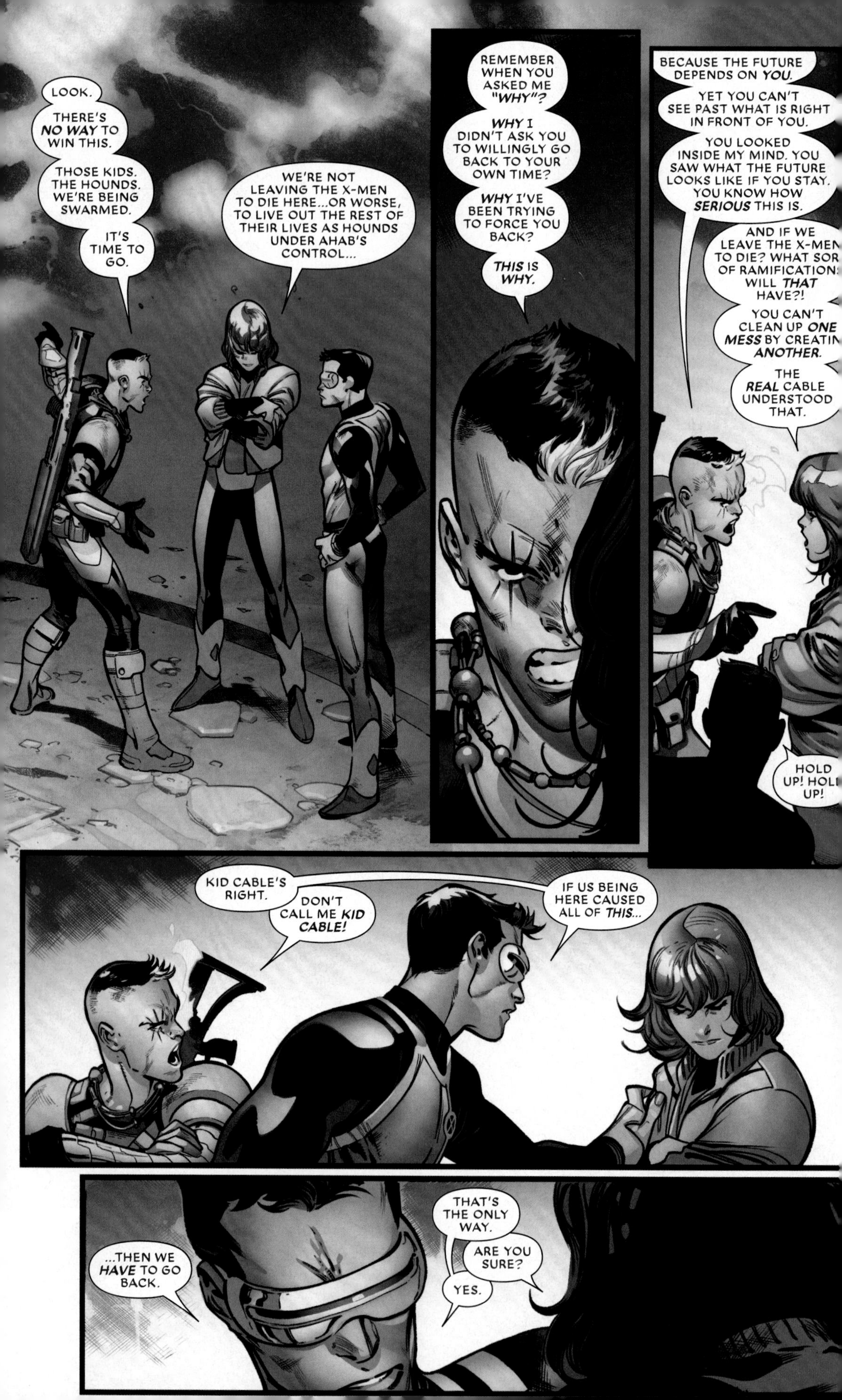
LOOK.
THERE'S NO WAY TO WIN THIS.
THOSE KIDS. THE HOUNDS. WE'RE BEING SWARMED.
IT'S TIME TO GO.
WE'RE NOT LEAVING THE X-MEN TO DIE HERE...OR WORSE, TO LIVE OUT THE REST OF THEIR LIVES AS HOUNDS UNDER AHAB'S CONTROL...
REMEMBER WHEN YOU ASKED ME "WHY"?
WHY I DIDN'T ASK YOU TO WILLINGLY GO BACK TO YOUR OWN TIME?
WHY I'VE BEEN TRYING TO FORCE YOU BACK?
THIS IS WHY.
BECAUSE THE FUTURE DEPENDS ON YOU.
YET YOU CAN'T SEE PAST WHAT IS RIGHT IN FRONT OF YOU.
YOU LOOKED INSIDE MY MIND. YOU SAW WHAT THE FUTURE LOOKS LIKE IF YOU STAY. YOU KNOW HOW SERIOUS THIS IS.
AND IF WE LEAVE THE X-MEN TO DIE? WHAT SOR OF RAMIFICATION WILL THAT HAVE?!
YOU CAN'T CLEAN UP ONE MESS BY CREATIN ANOTHER.
THE REAL CABLE UNDERSTOOD THAT.
HOLD UP! HOL UP!
KID CABLE'S RIGHT.
DON'T CALL ME KID CABLE!
IF US BEING HERE CAUSED ALL OF THIS...
...THEN WE HAVE TO GO BACK.
THAT'S THE ONLY WAY.
ARE YOU SURE?
YES.

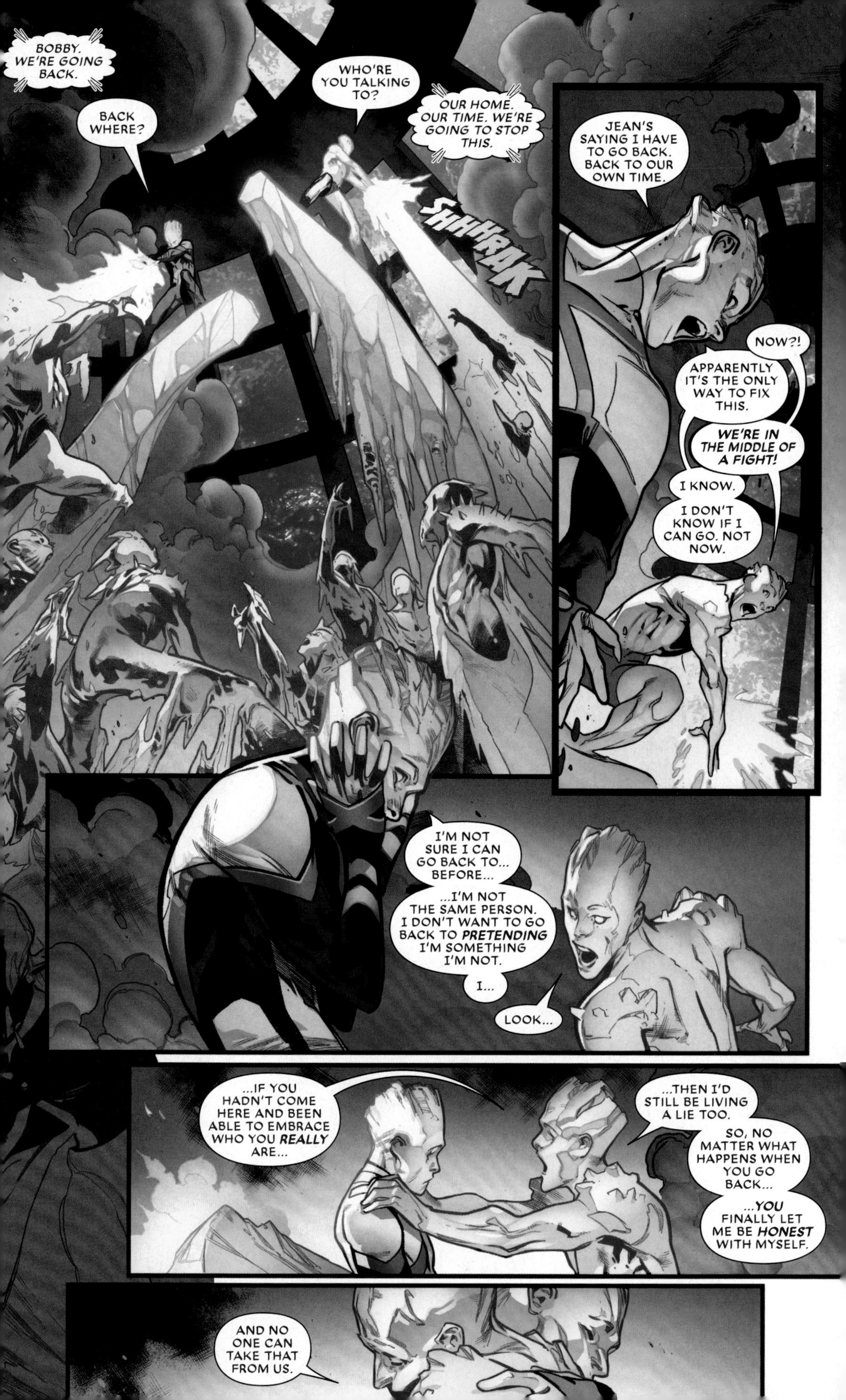
BOBBY. WE'RE GOING BACK.
BACK WHERE?
WHO'RE YOU TALKING TO?
OUR HOME. OUR TIME. WE'RE GOING TO STOP THIS.
SHHHRAK
JEAN'S SAYING I HAVE TO GO BACK. BACK TO OUR OWN TIME.
NOW?!
APPARENTLY IT'S THE ONLY WAY TO FIX THIS.
WE'RE IN THE MIDDLE OF A FIGHT!
I KNOW.
I DON'T KNOW IF I CAN GO. NOT NOW.
I'M NOT SURE I CAN GO BACK TO... BEFORE...
...I'M NOT THE SAME PERSON. I DON'T WANT TO GO BACK TO PRETENDING I'M SOMETHING I'M NOT.
I...
LOOK...
...IF YOU HADN'T COME HERE AND BEEN ABLE TO EMBRACE WHO YOU REALLY ARE...
...THEN I'D STILL BE LIVING A LIE TOO.
SO, NO MATTER WHAT HAPPENS WHEN YOU GO BACK...
...YOU FINALLY LET ME BE HONEST WITH MYSELF.
AND NO ONE CAN TAKE THAT FROM US.

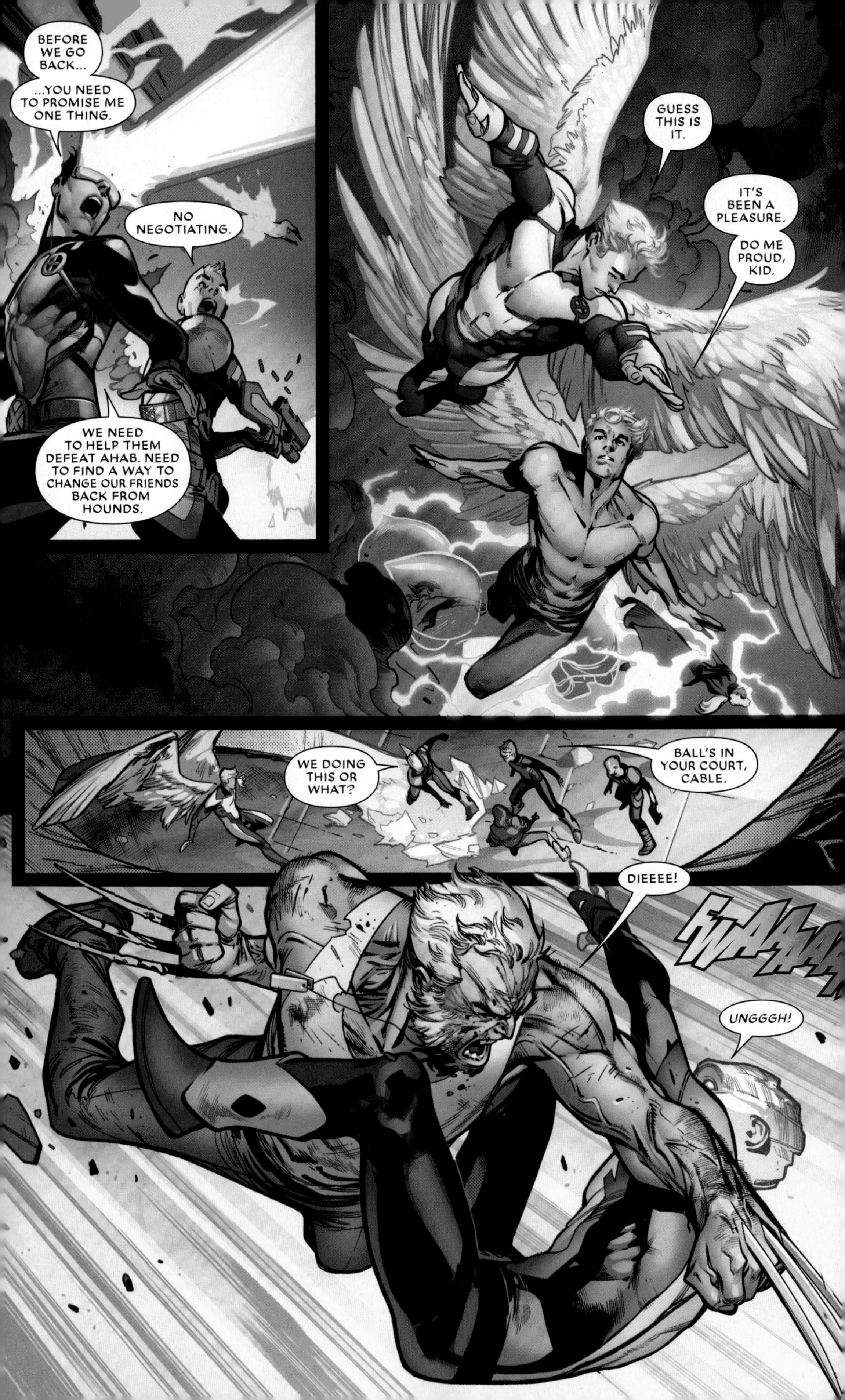
BEFORE WE GO BACK...
...YOU NEED TO PROMISE ME ONE THING.
NO NEGOTIATING.
WE NEED TO HELP THEM DEFEAT AHAB. NEED TO FIND A WAY TO CHANGE OUR FRIENDS BACK FROM HOUNDS.
GUESS THIS IS IT.
IT'S BEEN A PLEASURE.
DO ME PROUD, KID.
WE DOING THIS OR WHAT?
BALL'S IN YOUR COURT, CABLE.
DIEEEE!
UNGGGH!

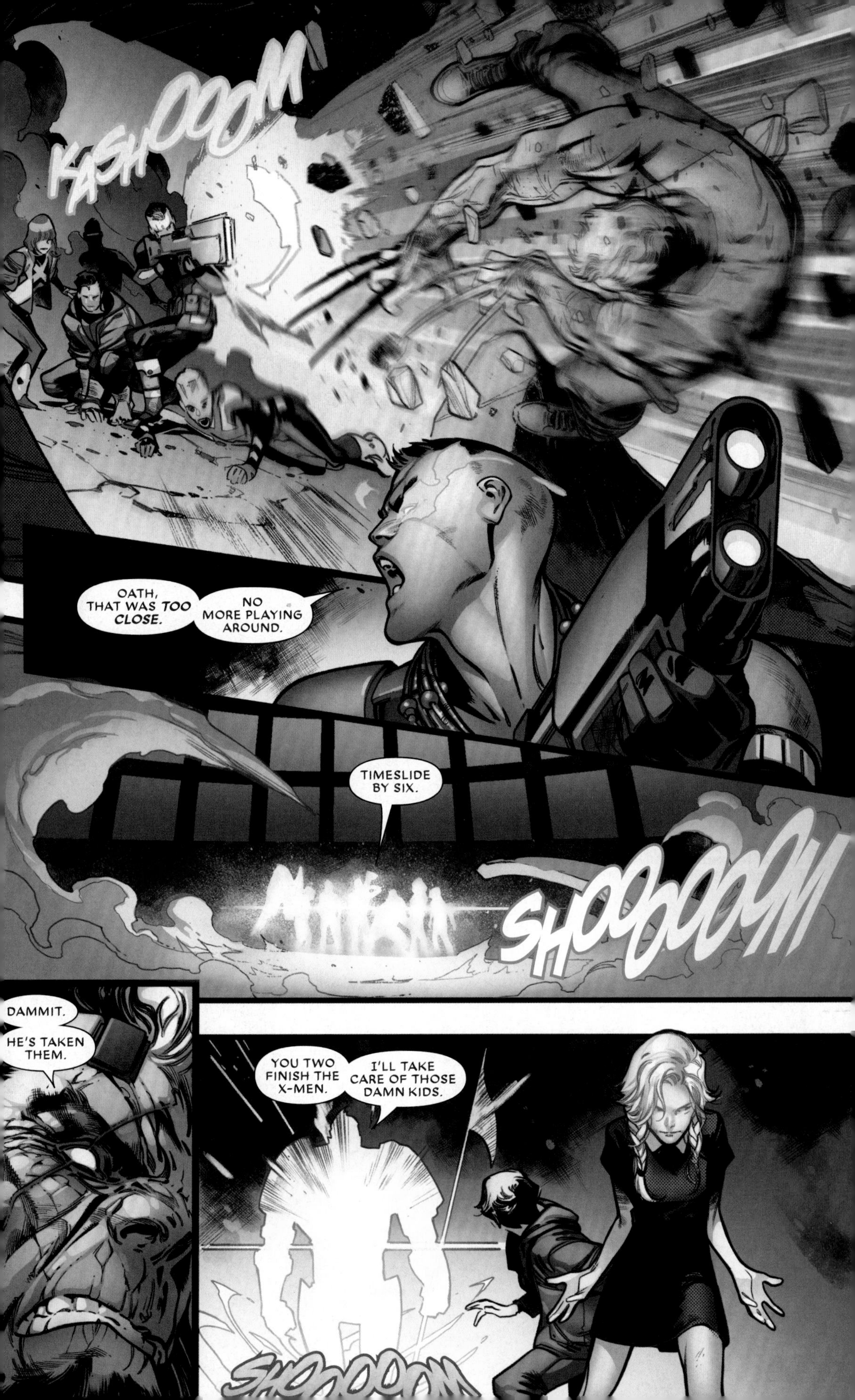
KASHOOOOM
OATH, THAT WAS TOO CLOSE.
NO MORE PLAYING AROUND.
TIMESLIDE BY SIX.
SHOOOOOOM
DAMMIT.
HE'S TAKEN THEM.
YOU TWO FINISH THE X-MEN.
I'LL TAKE CARE OF THOSE DAMN KIDS.
SHOOOOOOM

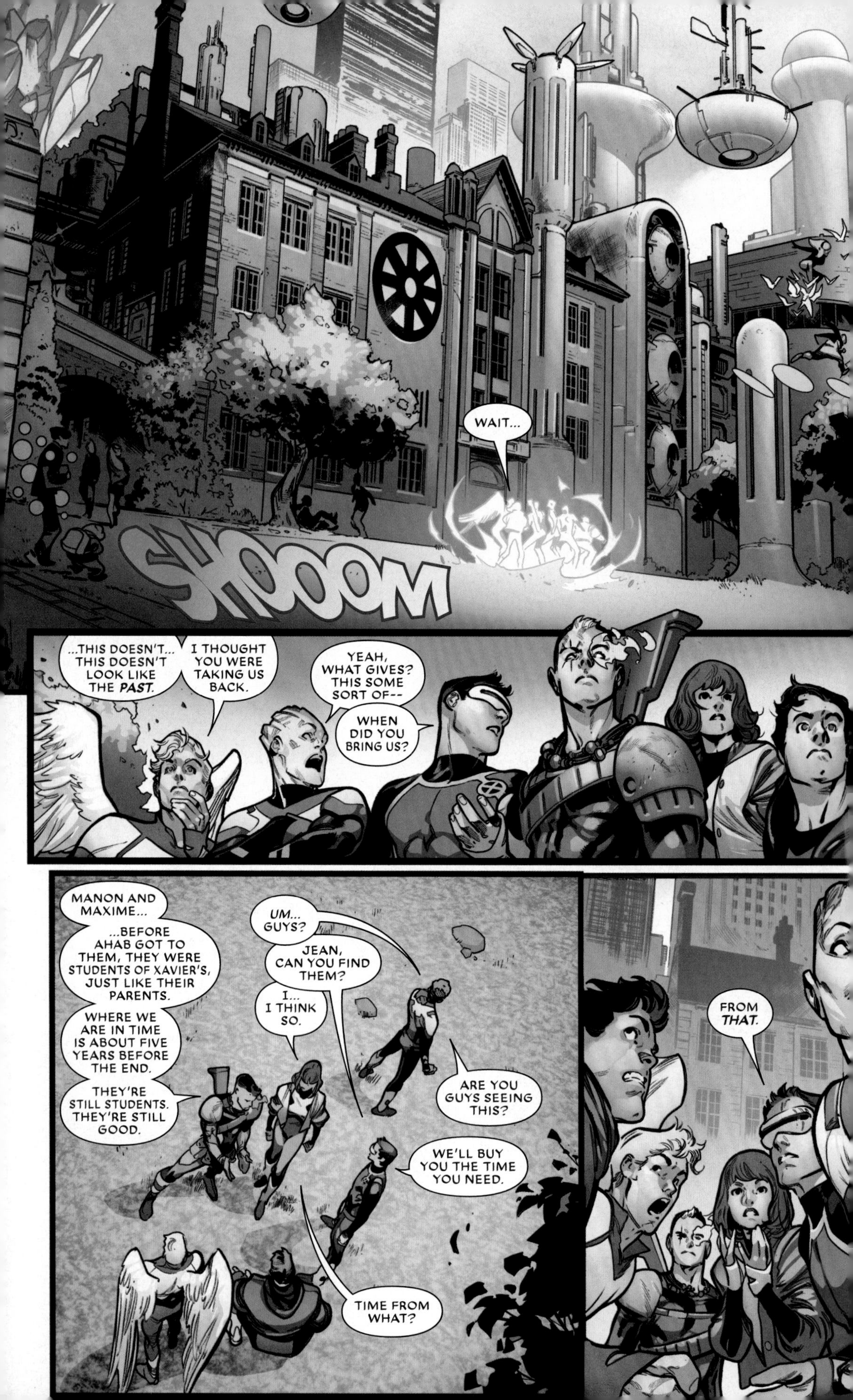
SHOOOM
WAIT...
...THIS DOESN'T... THIS DOESN'T LOOK LIKE THE *PAST*.
I THOUGHT YOU WERE TAKING US BACK.
YEAH, WHAT GIVES? THIS SOME SORT OF--
WHEN DID YOU BRING US?
MANON AND MAXIME...
...BEFORE AHAB GOT TO THEM, THEY WERE STUDENTS OF XAVIER'S, JUST LIKE THEIR PARENTS.
WHERE WE ARE IN TIME IS ABOUT FIVE YEARS BEFORE THE END.
THEY'RE STILL STUDENTS. THEY'RE STILL GOOD.
UM... GUYS?
JEAN, CAN YOU FIND THEM?
I... I THINK SO.
ARE YOU GUYS SEEING THIS?
WE'LL BUY YOU THE TIME YOU NEED.
TIME FROM WHAT?
FROM *THAT*.

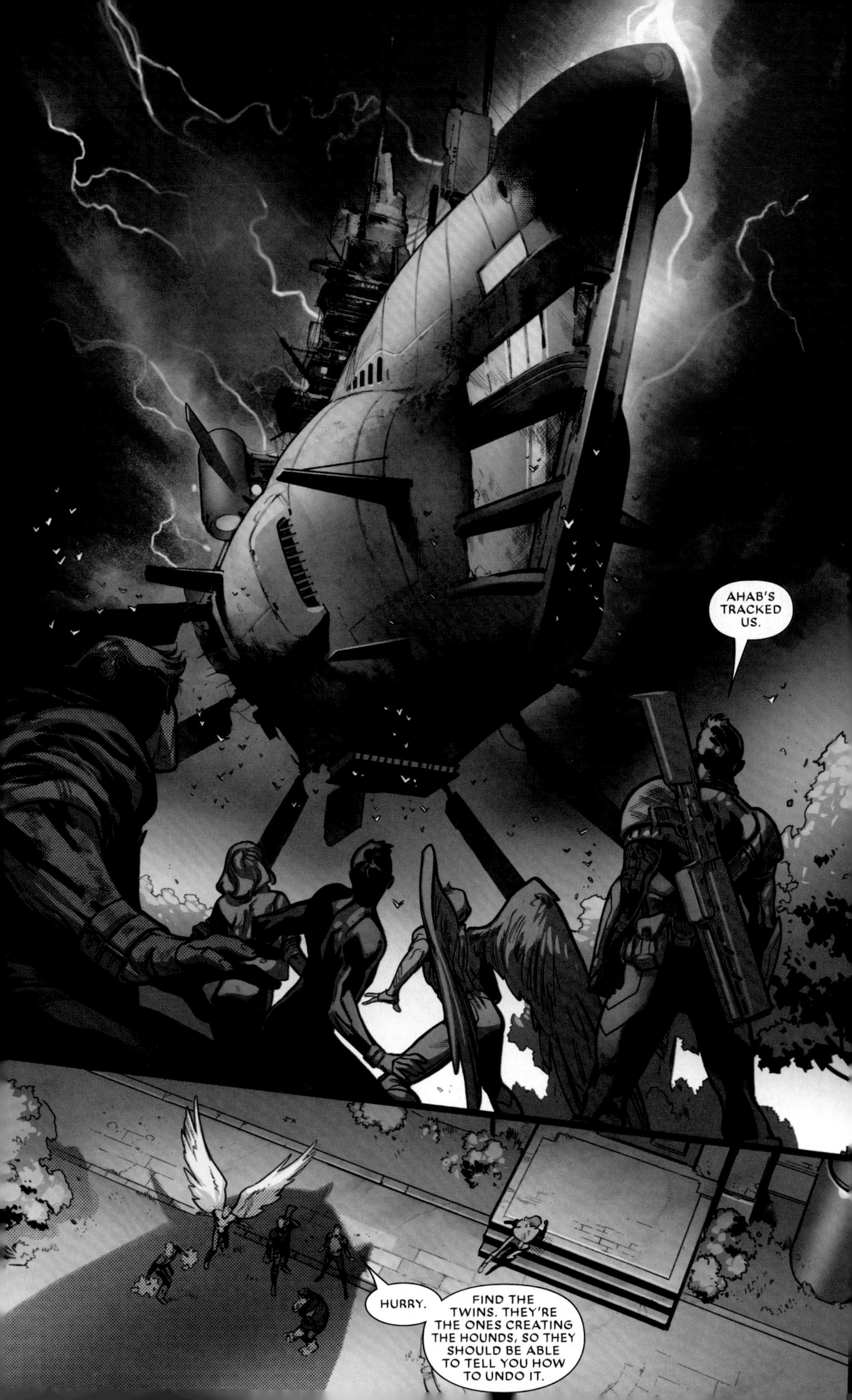
AHAB'S TRACKED US.
HURRY.
FIND THE TWINS. THEY'RE THE ONES CREATING THE HOUNDS, SO THEY SHOULD BE ABLE TO TELL YOU HOW TO UNDO IT.

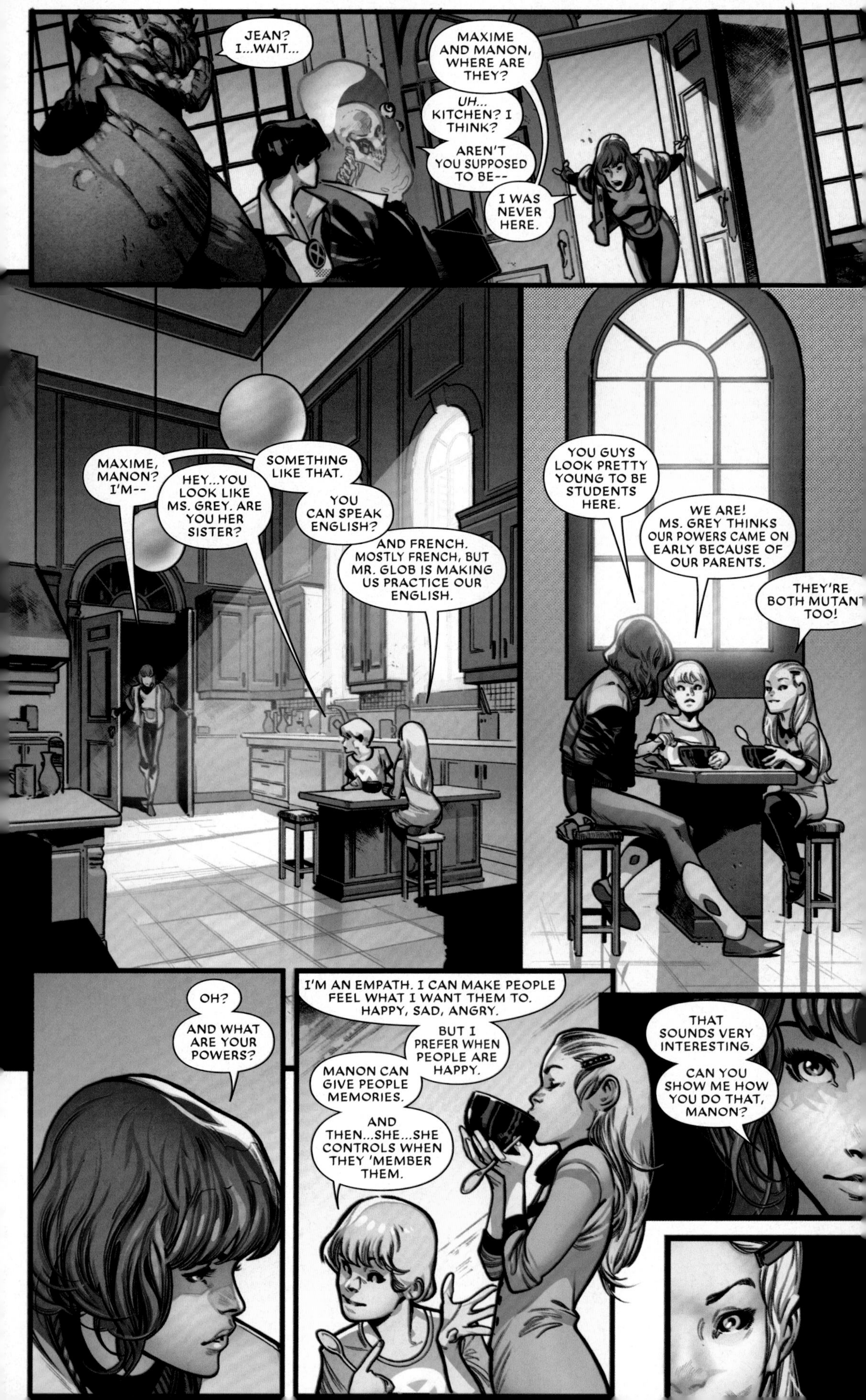
JEAN? I...WAIT...
MAXIME AND MANON, WHERE ARE THEY?
UH... KITCHEN? I THINK?
AREN'T YOU SUPPOSED TO BE--
I WAS NEVER HERE.
MAXIME, MANON? I'M--
HEY...YOU LOOK LIKE MS. GREY. ARE YOU HER SISTER?
SOMETHING LIKE THAT.
YOU CAN SPEAK ENGLISH?
AND FRENCH. MOSTLY FRENCH, BUT MR. GLOB IS MAKING US PRACTICE OUR ENGLISH.
YOU GUYS LOOK PRETTY YOUNG TO BE STUDENTS HERE.
WE ARE! MS. GREY THINKS OUR POWERS CAME ON EARLY BECAUSE OF OUR PARENTS.
THEY'RE BOTH MUTANT TOO!
OH?
AND WHAT ARE YOUR POWERS?
I'M AN EMPATH. I CAN MAKE PEOPLE FEEL WHAT I WANT THEM TO. HAPPY, SAD, ANGRY.
BUT I PREFER WHEN PEOPLE ARE HAPPY.
MANON CAN GIVE PEOPLE MEMORIES.
AND THEN...SHE...SHE CONTROLS WHEN THEY 'MEMBER THEM.
THAT SOUNDS VERY INTERESTING.
CAN YOU SHOW ME HOW YOU DO THAT, MANON?

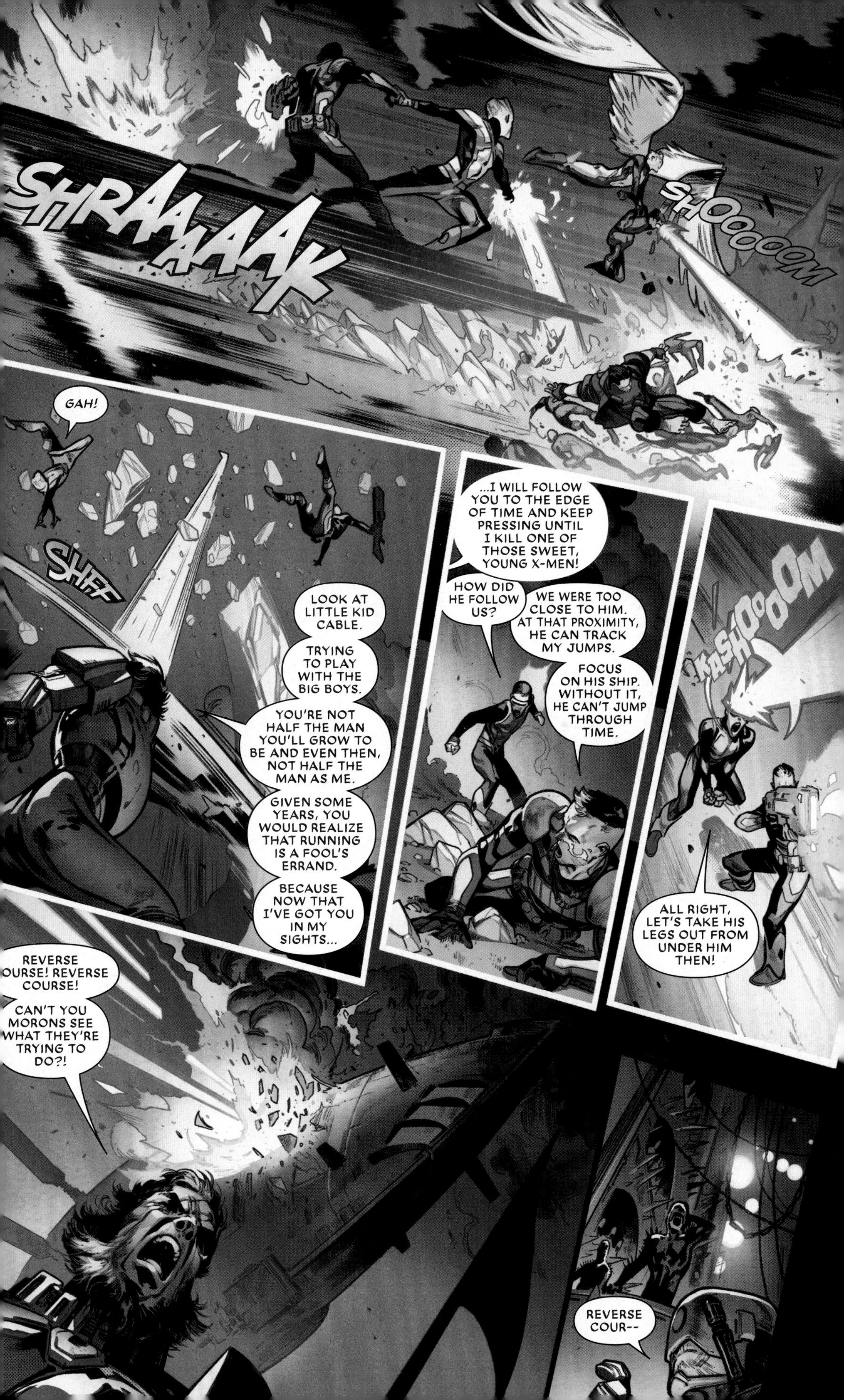
SHRAAAAAAK
SHOOOOOM
GAH!
SHFF
LOOK AT LITTLE KID CABLE.
TRYING TO PLAY WITH THE BIG BOYS.
YOU'RE NOT HALF THE MAN YOU'LL GROW TO BE AND EVEN THEN, NOT HALF THE MAN AS ME.
GIVEN SOME YEARS, YOU WOULD REALIZE THAT RUNNING IS A FOOL'S ERRAND.
BECAUSE NOW THAT I'VE GOT YOU IN MY SIGHTS...
...I WILL FOLLOW YOU TO THE EDGE OF TIME AND KEEP PRESSING UNTIL I KILL ONE OF THOSE SWEET, YOUNG X-MEN!
HOW DID HE FOLLOW US?
WE WERE TOO CLOSE TO HIM. AT THAT PROXIMITY, HE CAN TRACK MY JUMPS.
FOCUS ON HIS SHIP. WITHOUT IT, HE CAN'T JUMP THROUGH TIME.
KASHOOOOOM
ALL RIGHT, LET'S TAKE HIS LEGS OUT FROM UNDER HIM THEN!
OURSE! REVERSE COURSE!
CAN'T YOU MORONS SEE WHAT THEY'RE TRYING TO DO?!
REVERSE COUR--

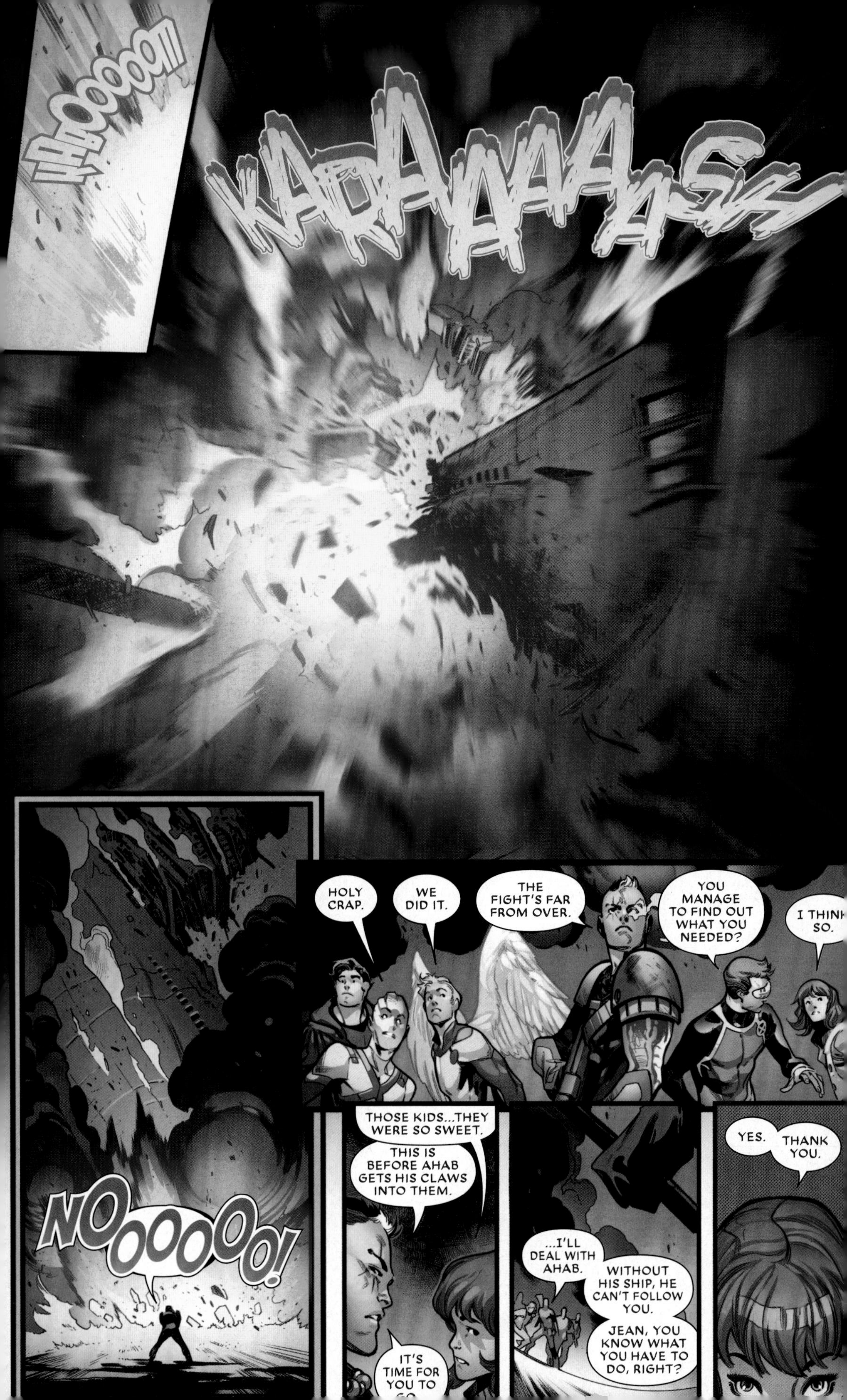
NOOOOOO!
HOLY CRAP.
WE DID IT.
THE FIGHT'S FAR FROM OVER.
YOU MANAGE TO FIND OUT WHAT YOU NEEDED?
I THINK SO.
THOSE KIDS...THEY WERE SO SWEET.
THIS IS BEFORE AHAB GETS HIS CLAWS INTO THEM.
IT'S TIME FOR YOU TO
...I'LL DEAL WITH AHAB.
WITHOUT HIS SHIP, HE CAN'T FOLLOW YOU.
JEAN, YOU KNOW WHAT YOU HAVE TO DO, RIGHT?
YES.
THANK YOU.

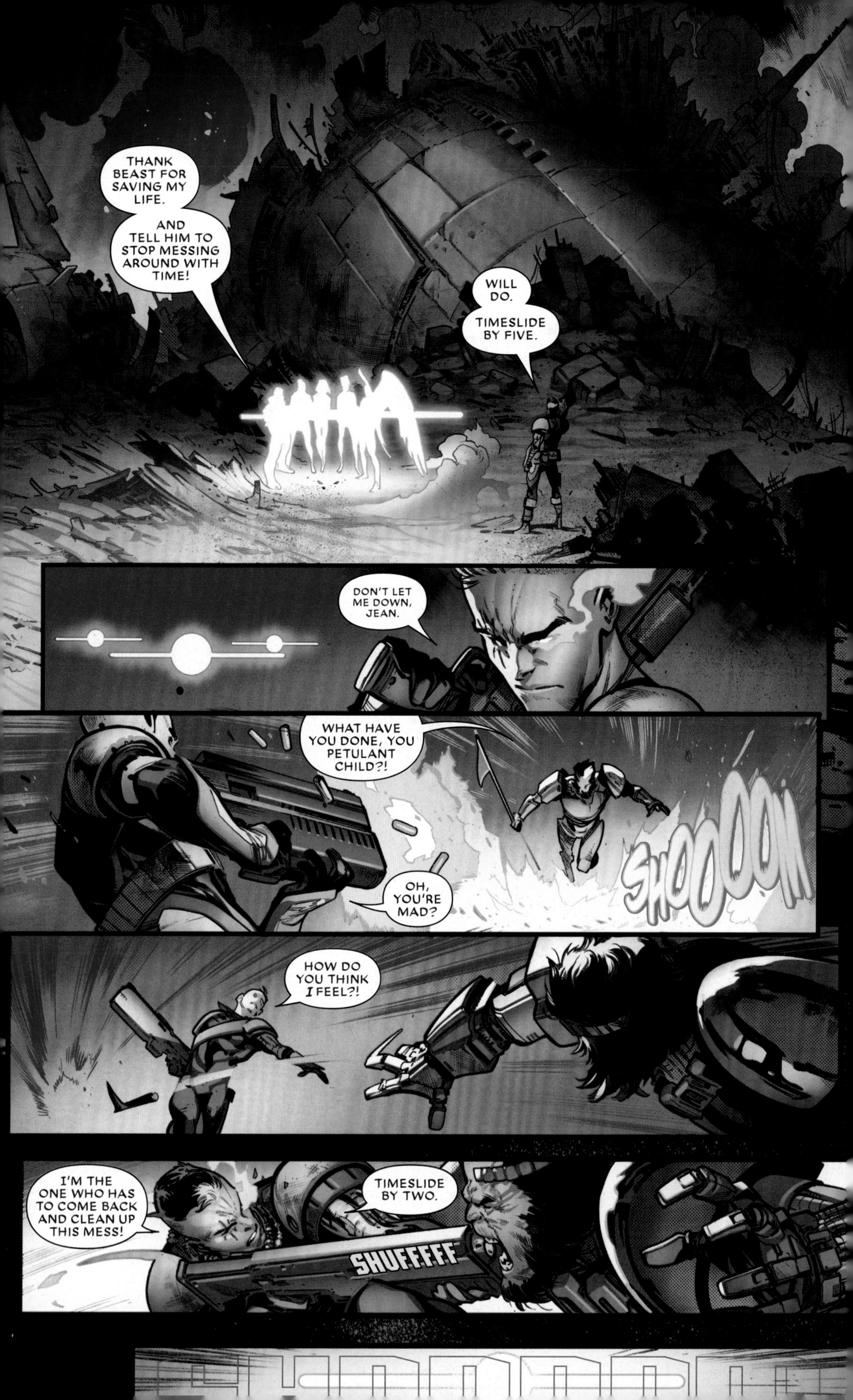
THANK BEAST FOR SAVING MY LIFE.
AND TELL HIM TO STOP MESSING AROUND WITH TIME!
WILL DO.
TIMESLIDE BY FIVE.
DON'T LET ME DOWN, JEAN.
WHAT HAVE YOU DONE, YOU PETULANT CHILD?!
SHOOOOM
OH, YOU'RE MAD?
HOW DO YOU THINK *I* FEEL?!
I'M THE ONE WHO HAS TO COME BACK AND CLEAN UP THIS MESS!
TIMESLIDE BY TWO.
SHUFFFFF

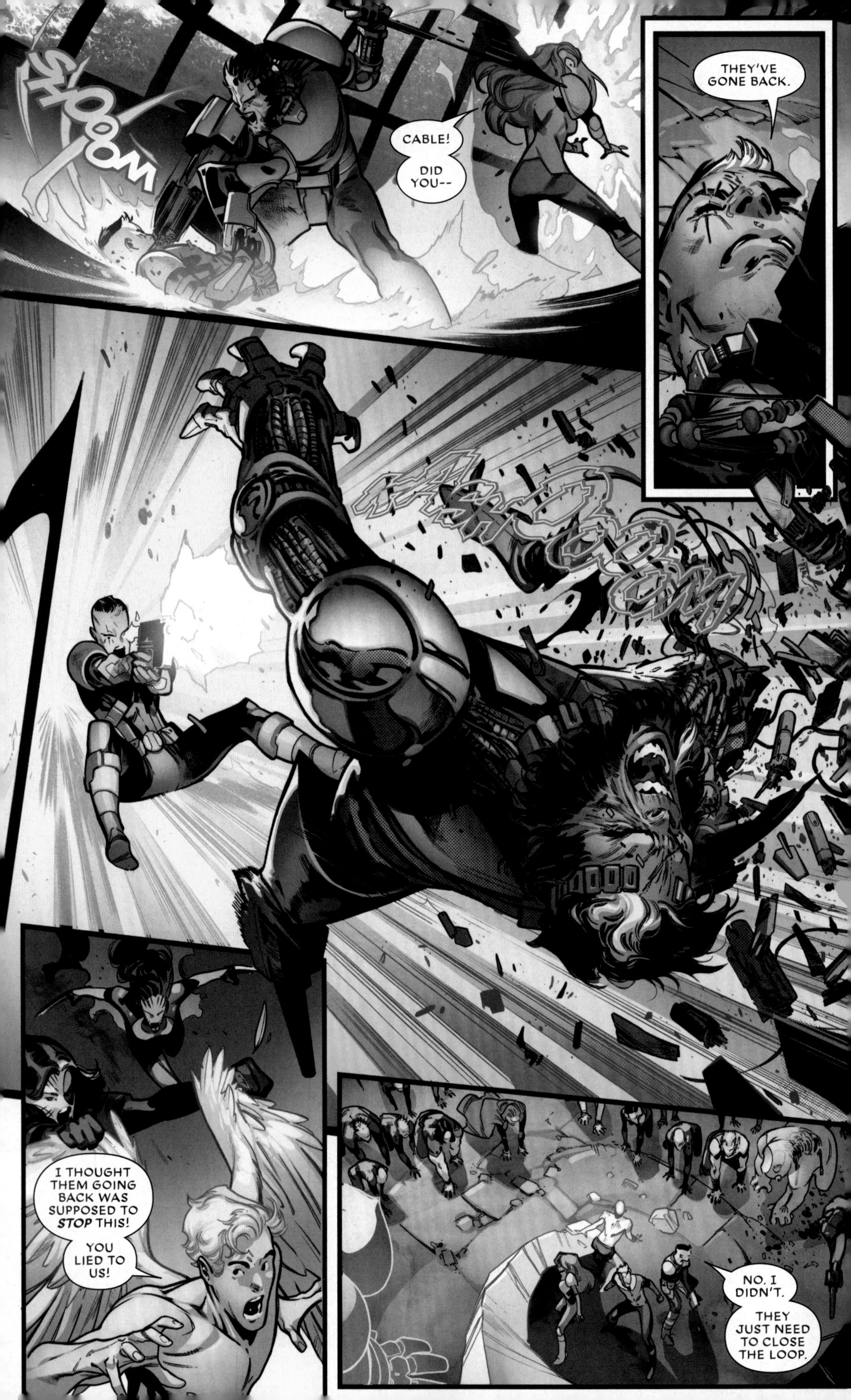
CABLE!
DID YOU--
THEY'VE GONE BACK.
I THOUGHT THEM GOING BACK WAS SUPPOSED TO *STOP* THIS!
YOU LIED TO US!
NO. I DIDN'T.
THEY JUST NEED TO CLOSE THE LOOP.

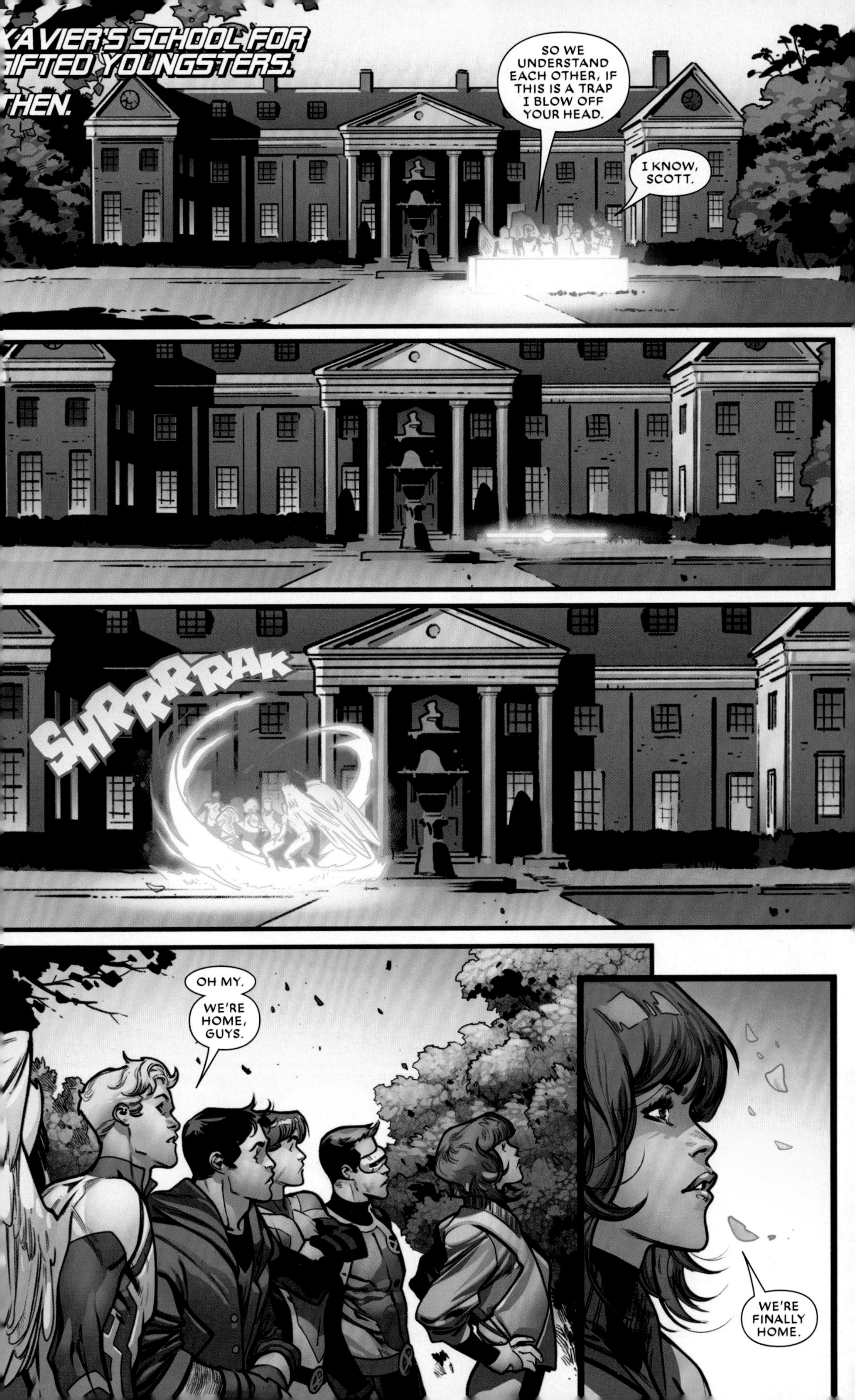
XAVIER'S SCHOOL FOR GIFTED YOUNGSTERS.
THEN.
SO WE UNDERSTAND EACH OTHER, IF THIS IS A TRAP I BLOW OFF YOUR HEAD.
I KNOW, SCOTT.
SHRRRRAK
OH MY.
WE'RE HOME, GUYS.
WE'RE FINALLY HOME.

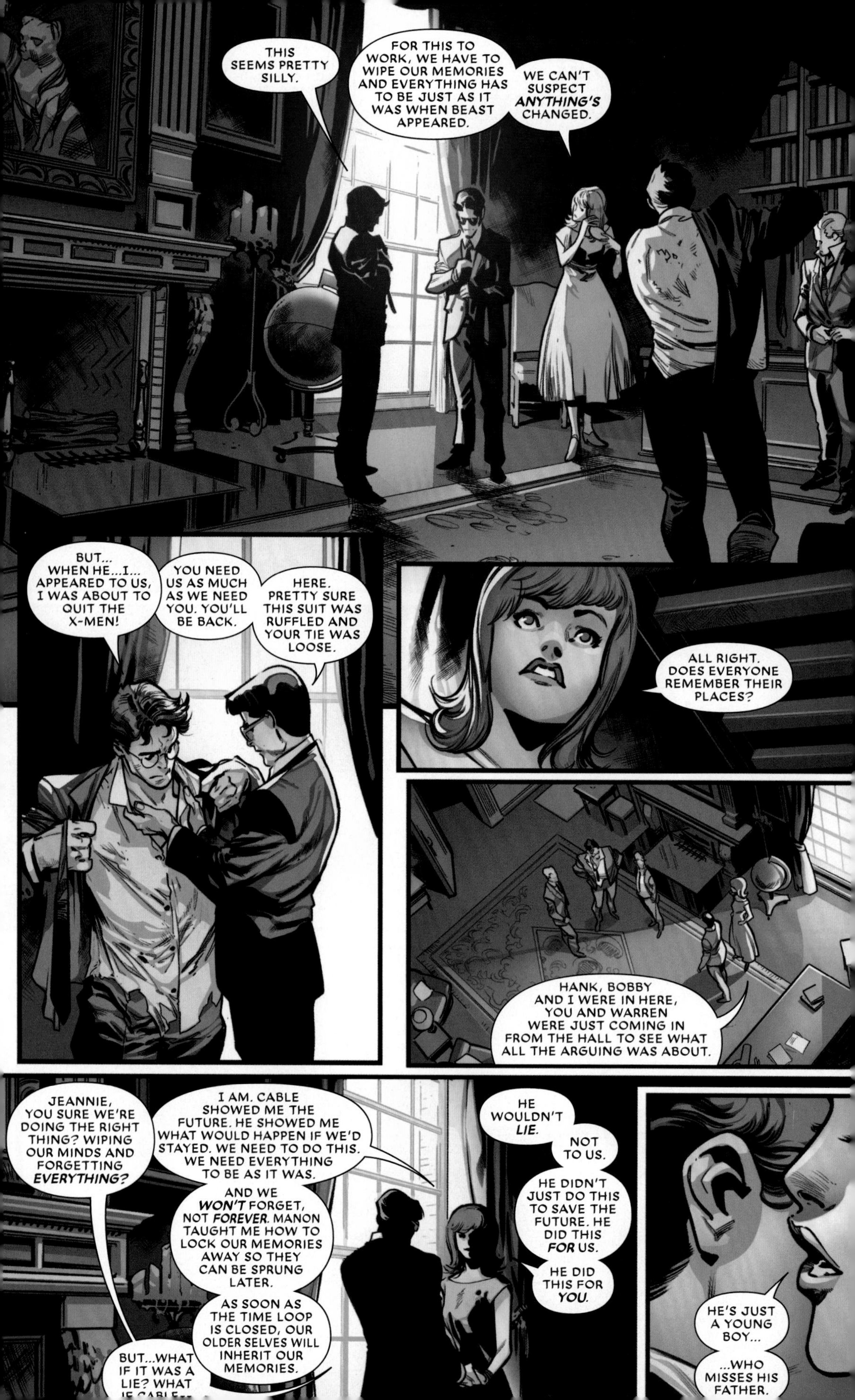
THIS SEEMS PRETTY SILLY.
FOR THIS TO WORK, WE HAVE TO WIPE OUR MEMORIES AND EVERYTHING HAS TO BE JUST AS IT WAS WHEN BEAST APPEARED.
WE CAN'T SUSPECT *ANYTHING'S* CHANGED.
BUT... WHEN HE...I... APPEARED TO US, I WAS ABOUT TO QUIT THE X-MEN!
YOU NEED US AS MUCH AS WE NEED YOU. YOU'LL BE BACK.
HERE. PRETTY SURE THIS SUIT WAS RUFFLED AND YOUR TIE WAS LOOSE.
ALL RIGHT. DOES EVERYONE REMEMBER THEIR PLACES?
HANK, BOBBY AND I WERE IN HERE, YOU AND WARREN WERE JUST COMING IN FROM THE HALL TO SEE WHAT ALL THE ARGUING WAS ABOUT.
JEANNIE, YOU SURE WE'RE DOING THE RIGHT THING? WIPING OUR MINDS AND FORGETTING *EVERYTHING?*
I AM. CABLE SHOWED ME THE FUTURE. HE SHOWED ME WHAT WOULD HAPPEN IF WE'D STAYED. WE NEED TO DO THIS. WE NEED EVERYTHING TO BE AS IT WAS.
AND WE *WON'T* FORGET, NOT *FOREVER*. MANON TAUGHT ME HOW TO LOCK OUR MEMORIES AWAY SO THEY CAN BE SPRUNG LATER.
AS SOON AS THE TIME LOOP IS CLOSED, OUR OLDER SELVES WILL INHERIT OUR MEMORIES.
BUT...WHAT IF IT WAS A LIE? WHAT
HE WOULDN'T *LIE*.
NOT TO US.
HE DIDN'T JUST DO THIS TO SAVE THE FUTURE. HE DID THIS *FOR* US.
HE DID THIS FOR *YOU*.
HE'S JUST A YOUNG BOY...
...WHO MISSES HIS FATHER.

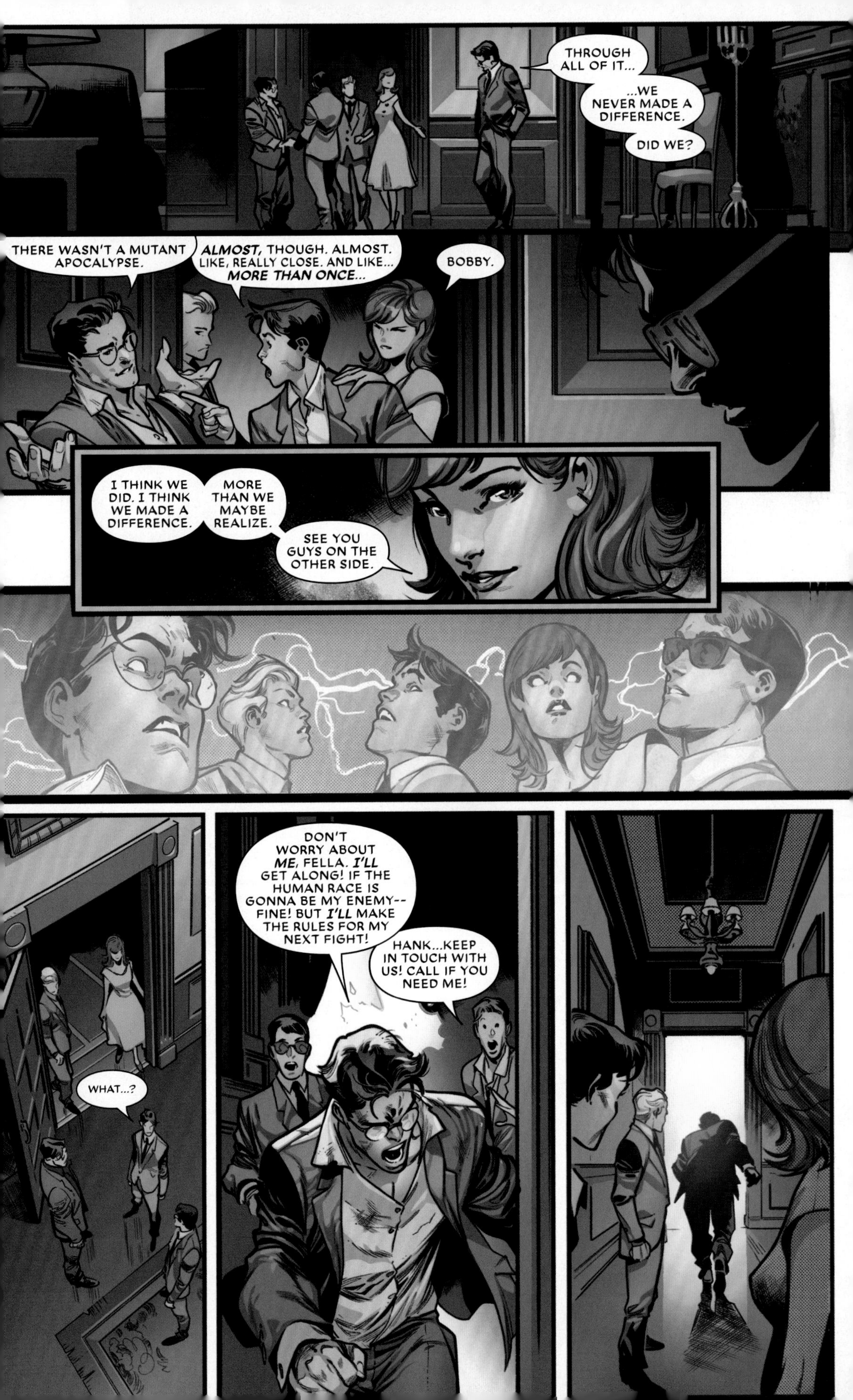
THROUGH ALL OF IT...
...WE NEVER MADE A DIFFERENCE.
DID WE?
THERE WASN'T A MUTANT APOCALYPSE.
*ALMOST,* THOUGH. ALMOST. LIKE, REALLY CLOSE. AND LIKE... *MORE THAN ONCE...*
BOBBY.
I THINK WE DID. I THINK WE MADE A DIFFERENCE.
MORE THAN WE MAYBE REALIZE.
SEE YOU GUYS ON THE OTHER SIDE.
WHAT...?
DON'T WORRY ABOUT *ME*, FELLA. *I'LL* GET ALONG! IF THE HUMAN RACE IS GONNA BE MY ENEMY-- FINE! BUT *I'LL* MAKE THE RULES FOR MY NEXT FIGHT!
HANK...KEEP IN TOUCH WITH US! CALL IF YOU NEED ME!

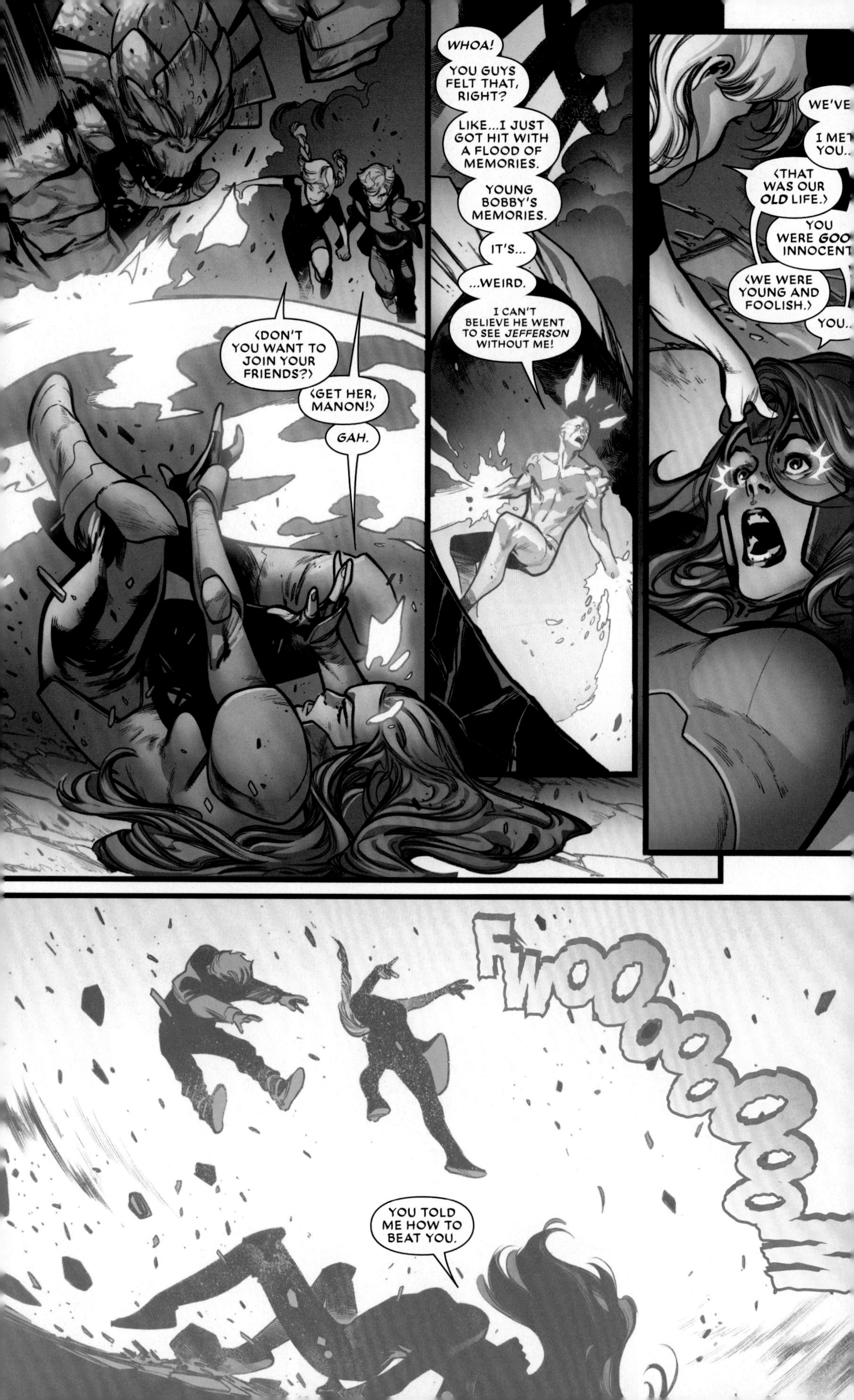
<DON'T YOU WANT TO JOIN YOUR FRIENDS?>
<GET HER, MANON!>
GAH.
WHOA!
YOU GUYS FELT THAT, RIGHT?
LIKE...I JUST GOT HIT WITH A FLOOD OF MEMORIES.
YOUNG BOBBY'S MEMORIES.
IT'S...
...WEIRD.
I CAN'T BELIEVE HE WENT TO SEE *JEFFERSON* WITHOUT ME!
WE'VE
I MET YOU...
<THAT WAS OUR **OLD** LIFE.>
YOU WERE
<WE WERE YOUNG AND FOOLISH.>
YOU...
FWOOOOOOOOM
YOU TOLD ME HOW TO BEAT YOU.

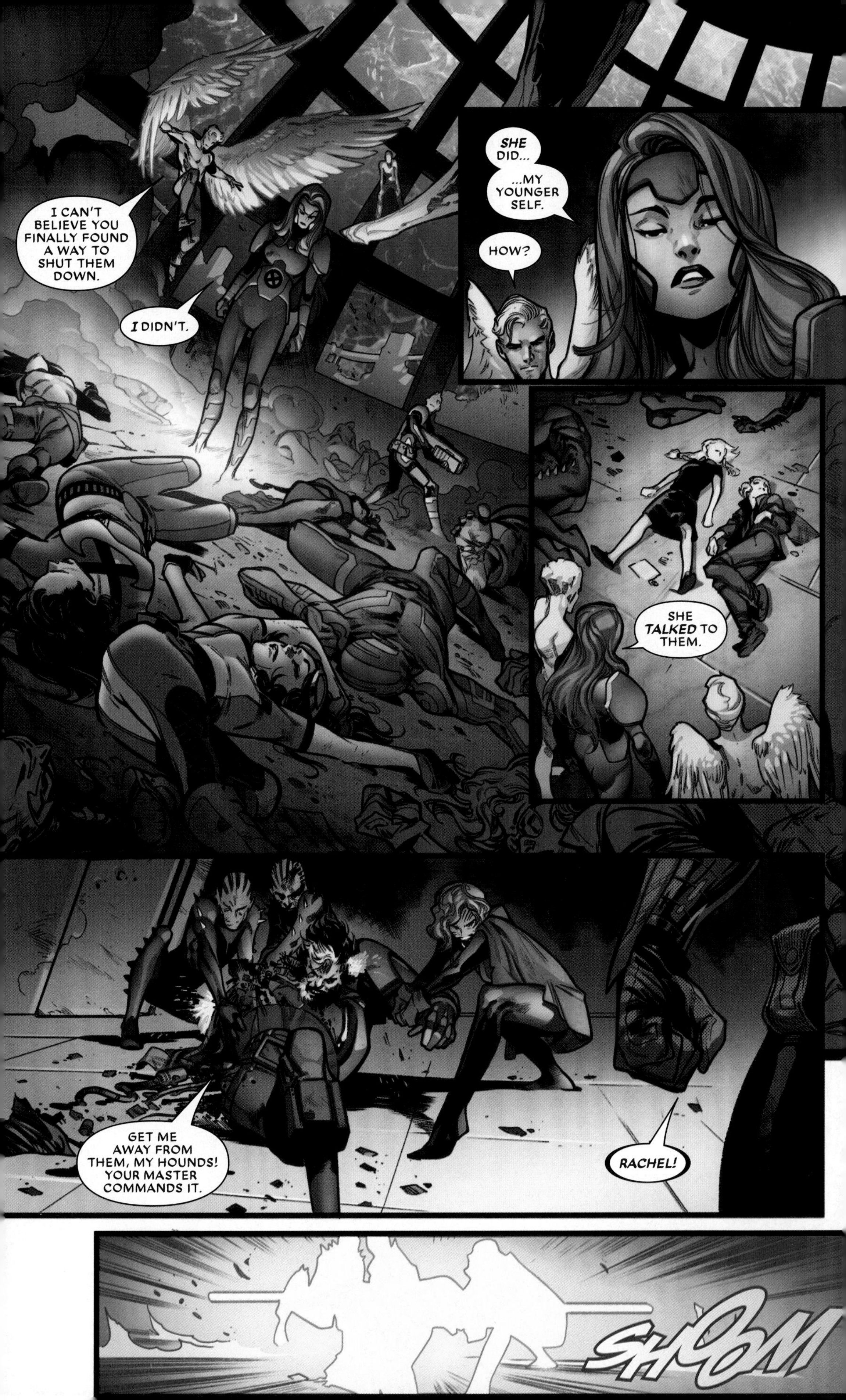
I CAN'T BELIEVE YOU FINALLY FOUND A WAY TO SHUT THEM DOWN.
*I* DIDN'T.
*SHE* DID...
...MY YOUNGER SELF.
HOW?
SHE *TALKED* TO THEM.
GET ME AWAY FROM THEM, MY HOUNDS! YOUR MASTER COMMANDS IT.
*RACHEL!*
SHOOM

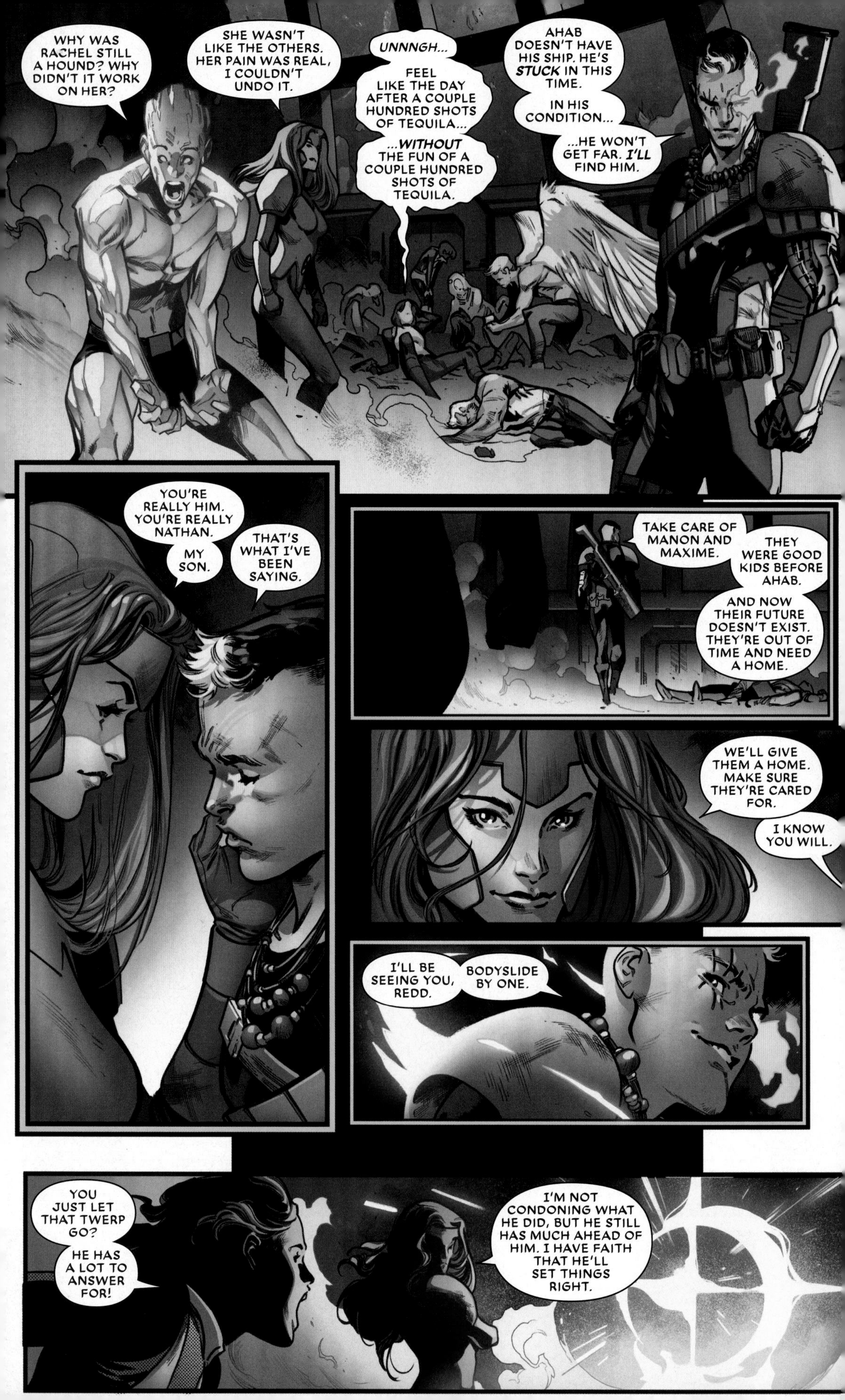
WHY WAS RACHEL STILL A HOUND? WHY DIDN'T IT WORK ON HER?
SHE WASN'T LIKE THE OTHERS. HER PAIN WAS REAL, I COULDN'T UNDO IT.
UNNNGH...
FEEL LIKE THE DAY AFTER A COUPLE HUNDRED SHOTS OF TEQUILA...
...WITHOUT THE FUN OF A COUPLE HUNDRED SHOTS OF TEQUILA.
AHAB DOESN'T HAVE HIS SHIP. HE'S STUCK IN THIS TIME.
IN HIS CONDITION...
...HE WON'T GET FAR. I'LL FIND HIM.
YOU'RE REALLY HIM. YOU'RE REALLY NATHAN.
MY SON.
THAT'S WHAT I'VE BEEN SAYING.
TAKE CARE OF MANON AND MAXIME.
THEY WERE GOOD KIDS BEFORE AHAB.
AND NOW THEIR FUTURE DOESN'T EXIST. THEY'RE OUT OF TIME AND NEED A HOME.
WE'LL GIVE THEM A HOME. MAKE SURE THEY'RE CARED FOR.
I KNOW YOU WILL.
I'LL BE SEEING YOU, REDD.
BODYSLIDE BY ONE.
YOU JUST LET THAT TWERP GO?
HE HAS A LOT TO ANSWER FOR!
I'M NOT CONDONING WHAT HE DID, BUT HE STILL HAS MUCH AHEAD OF HIM. I HAVE FAITH THAT HE'LL SET THINGS RIGHT.

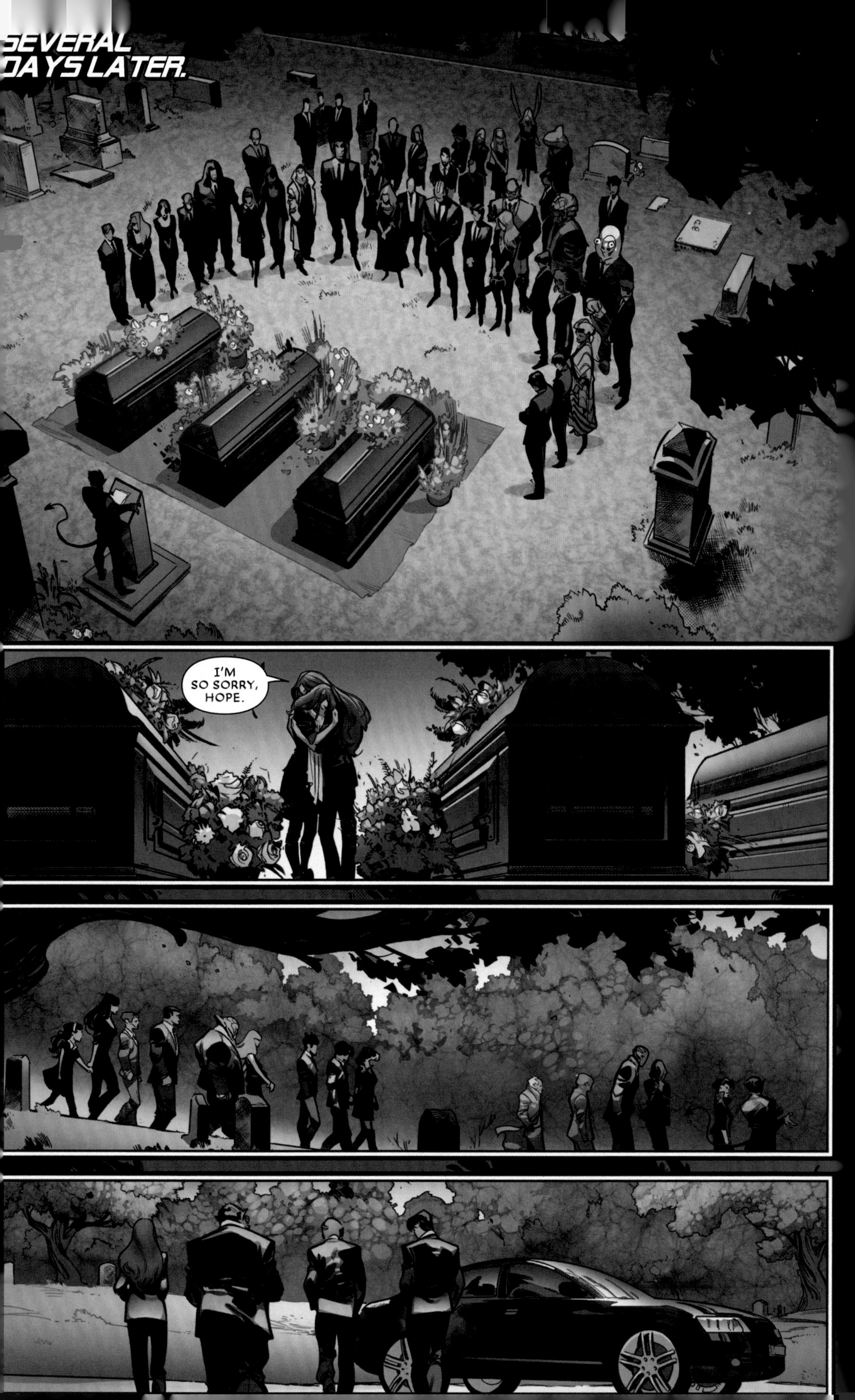
SEVERAL DAYS LATER.
I'M SO SORRY, HOPE.

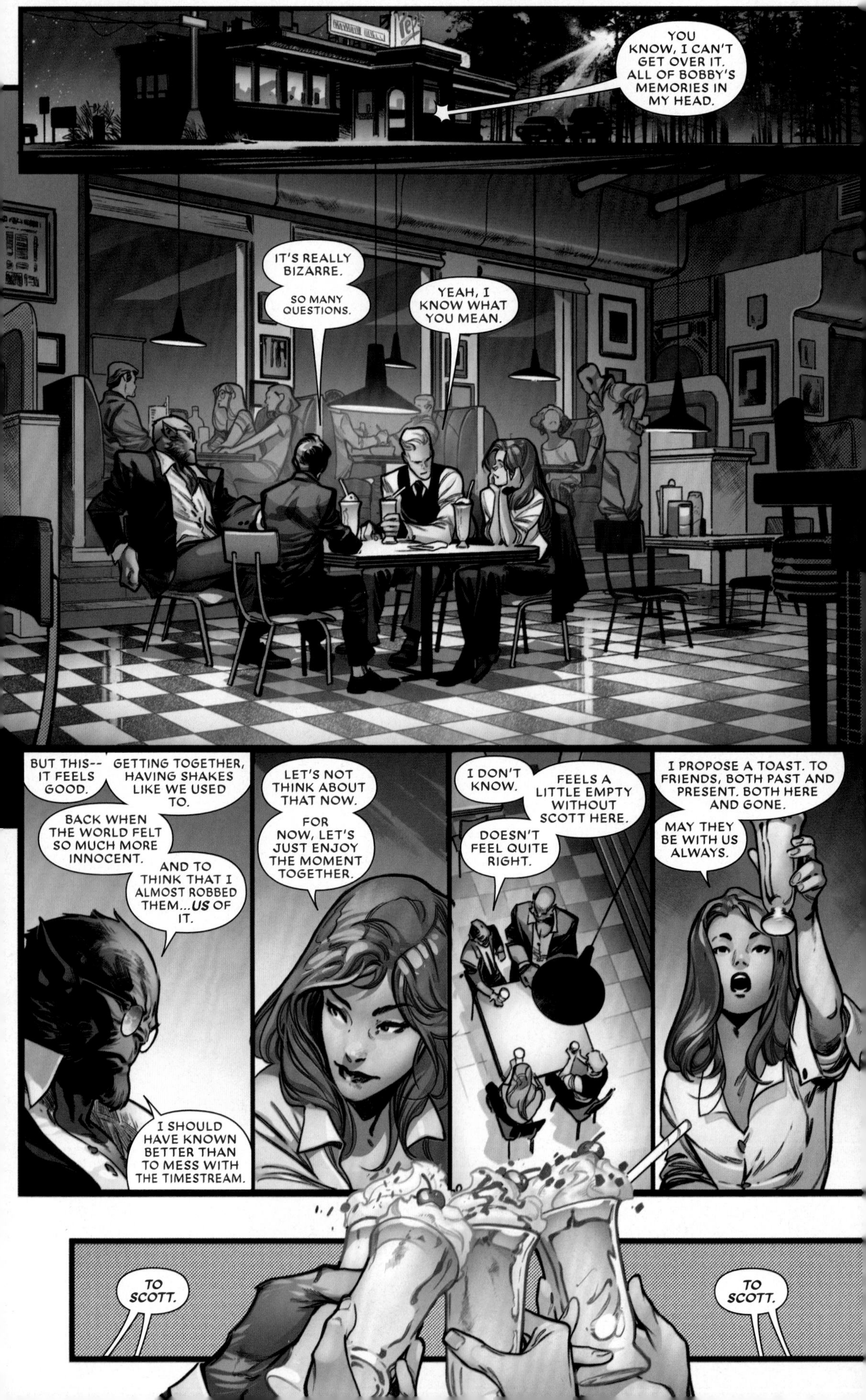

YOU KNOW, I CAN'T GET OVER IT. ALL OF BOBBY'S MEMORIES IN MY HEAD.
IT'S REALLY BIZARRE.
SO MANY QUESTIONS.
YEAH, I KNOW WHAT YOU MEAN.
BUT THIS-- IT FEELS GOOD.
GETTING TOGETHER, HAVING SHAKES LIKE WE USED TO.
BACK WHEN THE WORLD FELT SO MUCH MORE INNOCENT.
AND TO THINK THAT I ALMOST ROBBED THEM...US OF IT.
I SHOULD HAVE KNOWN BETTER THAN TO MESS WITH THE TIMESTREAM.
LET'S NOT THINK ABOUT THAT NOW.
FOR NOW, LET'S JUST ENJOY THE MOMENT TOGETHER.
I DON'T KNOW.
FEELS A LITTLE EMPTY WITHOUT SCOTT HERE.
DOESN'T FEEL QUITE RIGHT.
I PROPOSE A TOAST. TO FRIENDS, BOTH PAST AND PRESENT. BOTH HERE AND GONE.
MAY THEY BE WITH US ALWAYS.
TO SCOTT.
TO SCOTT.

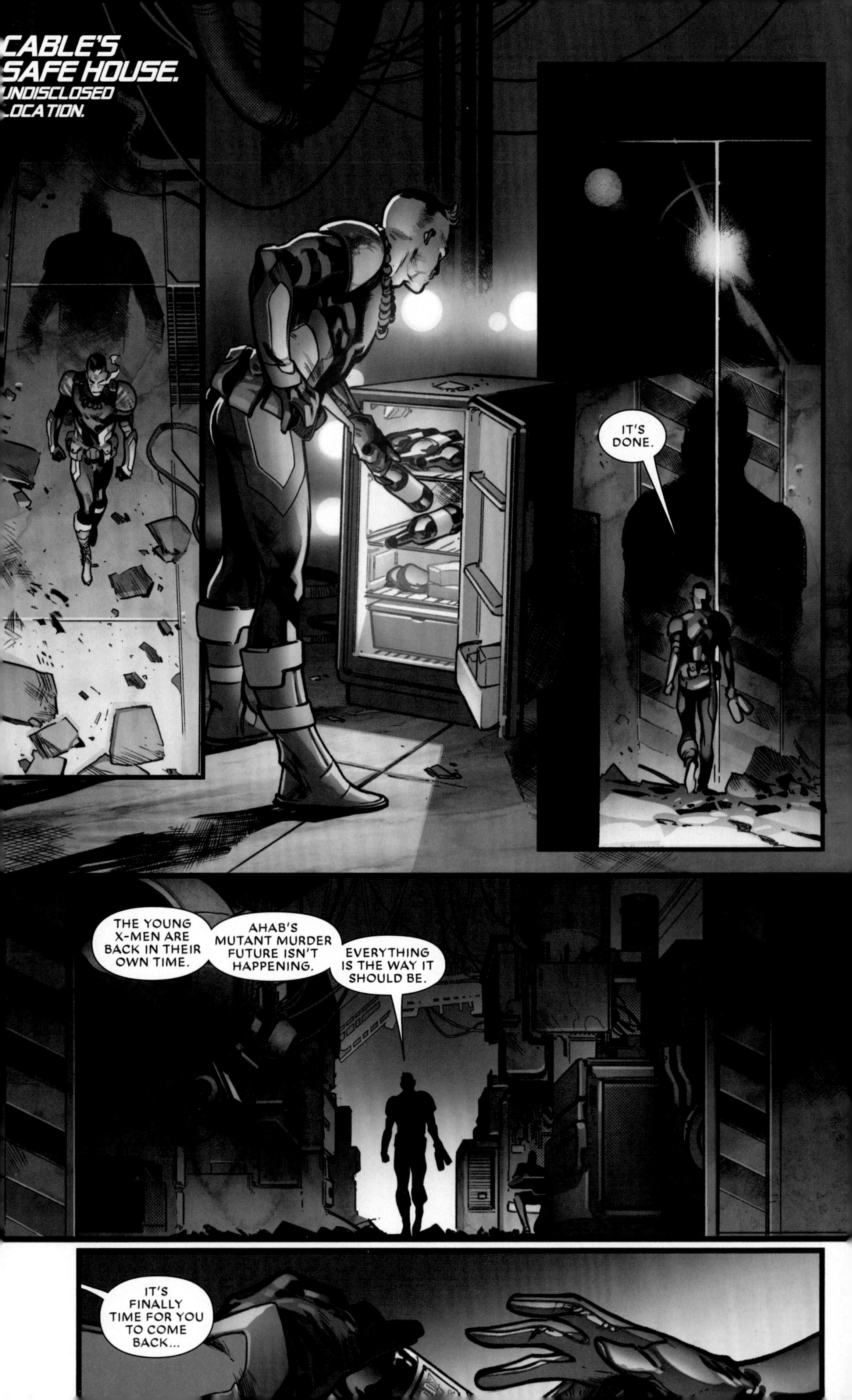
CABLE'S SAFE HOUSE. UNDISCLOSED LOCATION.
IT'S DONE.
THE YOUNG X-MEN ARE BACK IN THEIR OWN TIME.
AHAB'S MUTANT MURDER FUTURE ISN'T HAPPENING.
EVERYTHING IS THE WAY IT SHOULD BE.
IT'S FINALLY TIME FOR YOU TO COME BACK...

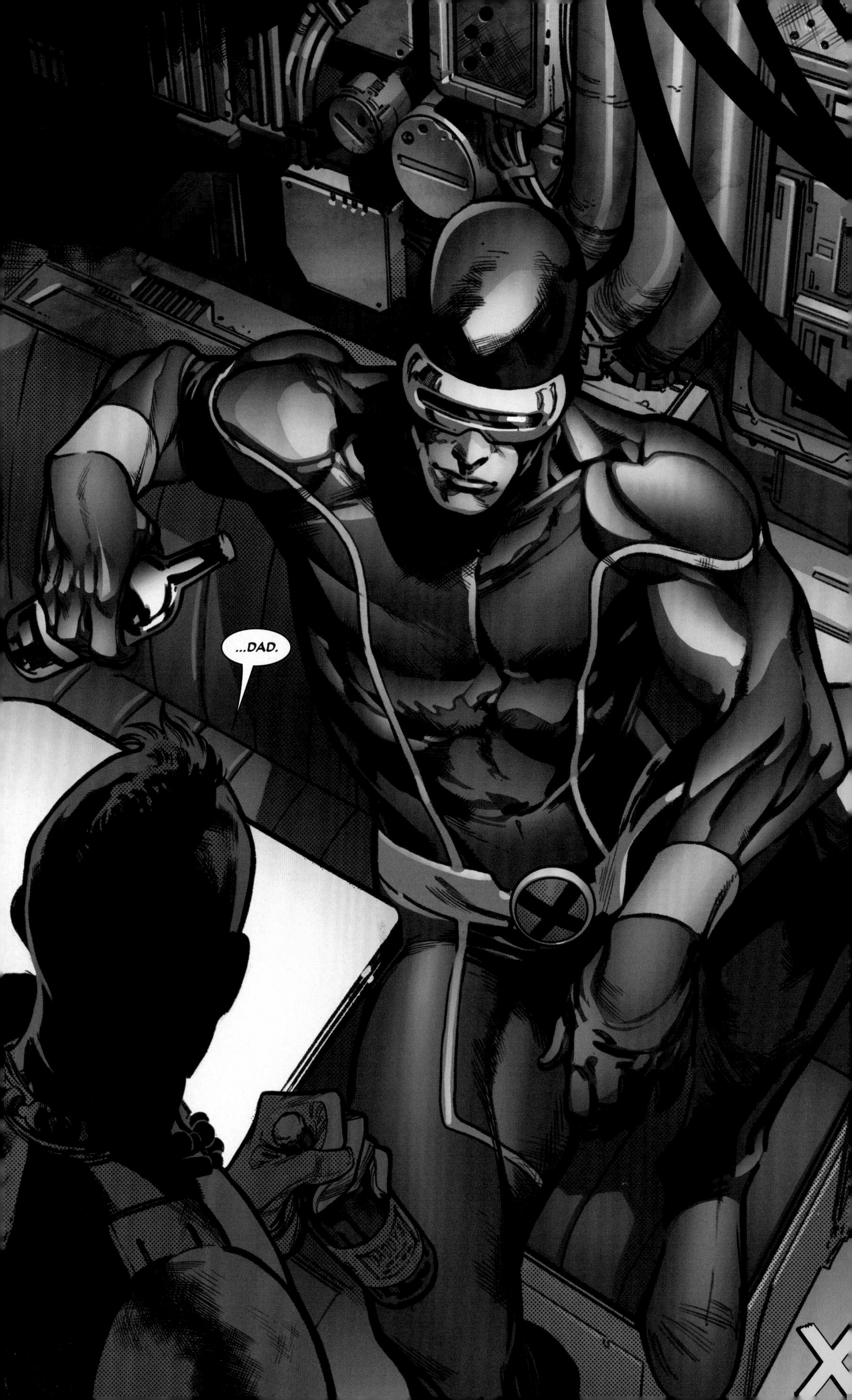
...DAD.

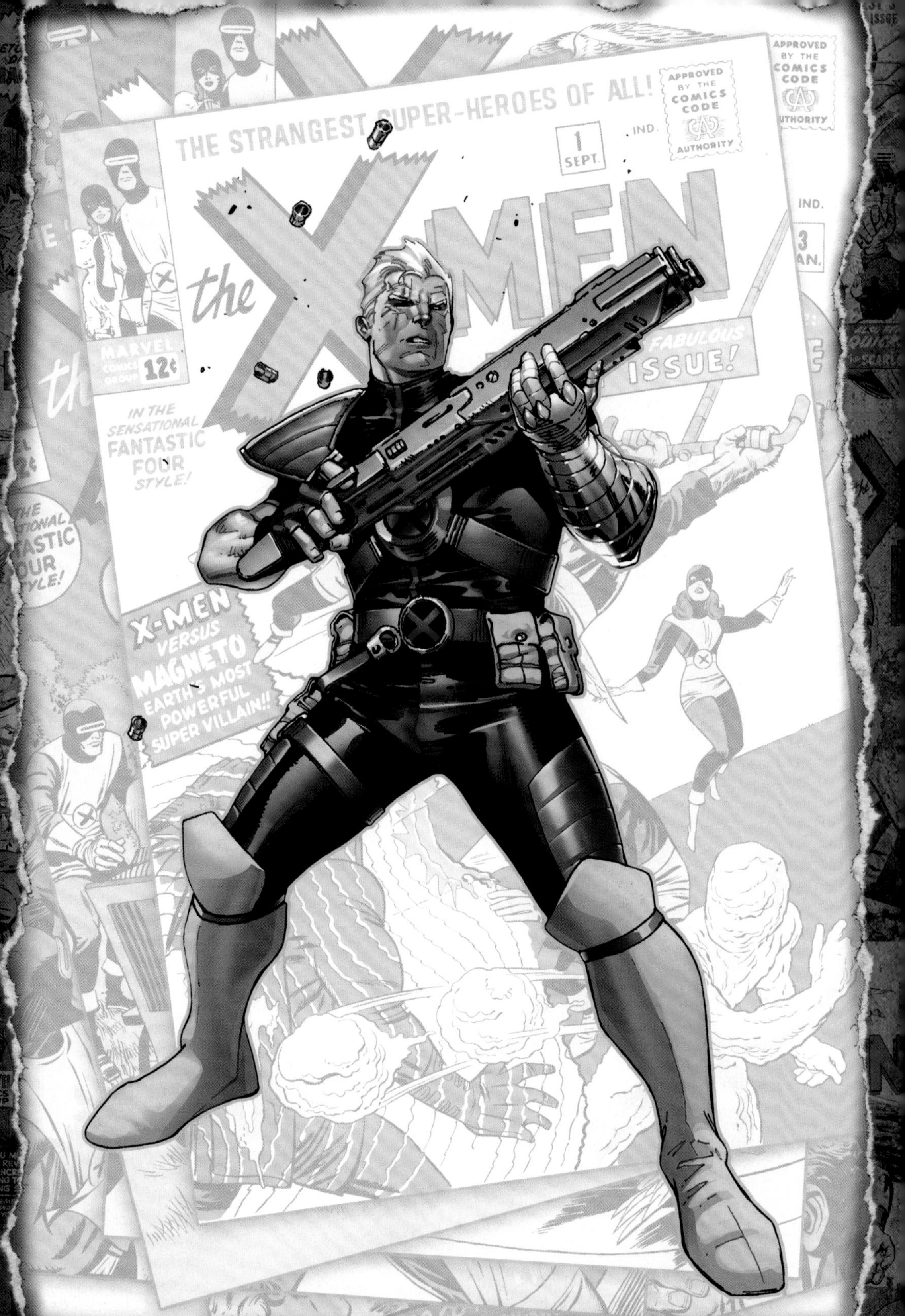
THE STRANGEST SUPER-HEROES OF ALL!
APPROVED BY THE COMICS CODE AUTHORITY
1 SEPT.
IND.
the X-MEN
MARVEL COMICS GROUP 12¢
IN THE SENSATIONAL FANTASTIC FOUR STYLE!
FABULOUS ISSUE!
X-MEN VERSUS MAGNETO EARTH'S MOST POWERFUL SUPER VILLAIN!!

#1 VARIANT ***Olivier Coipel***

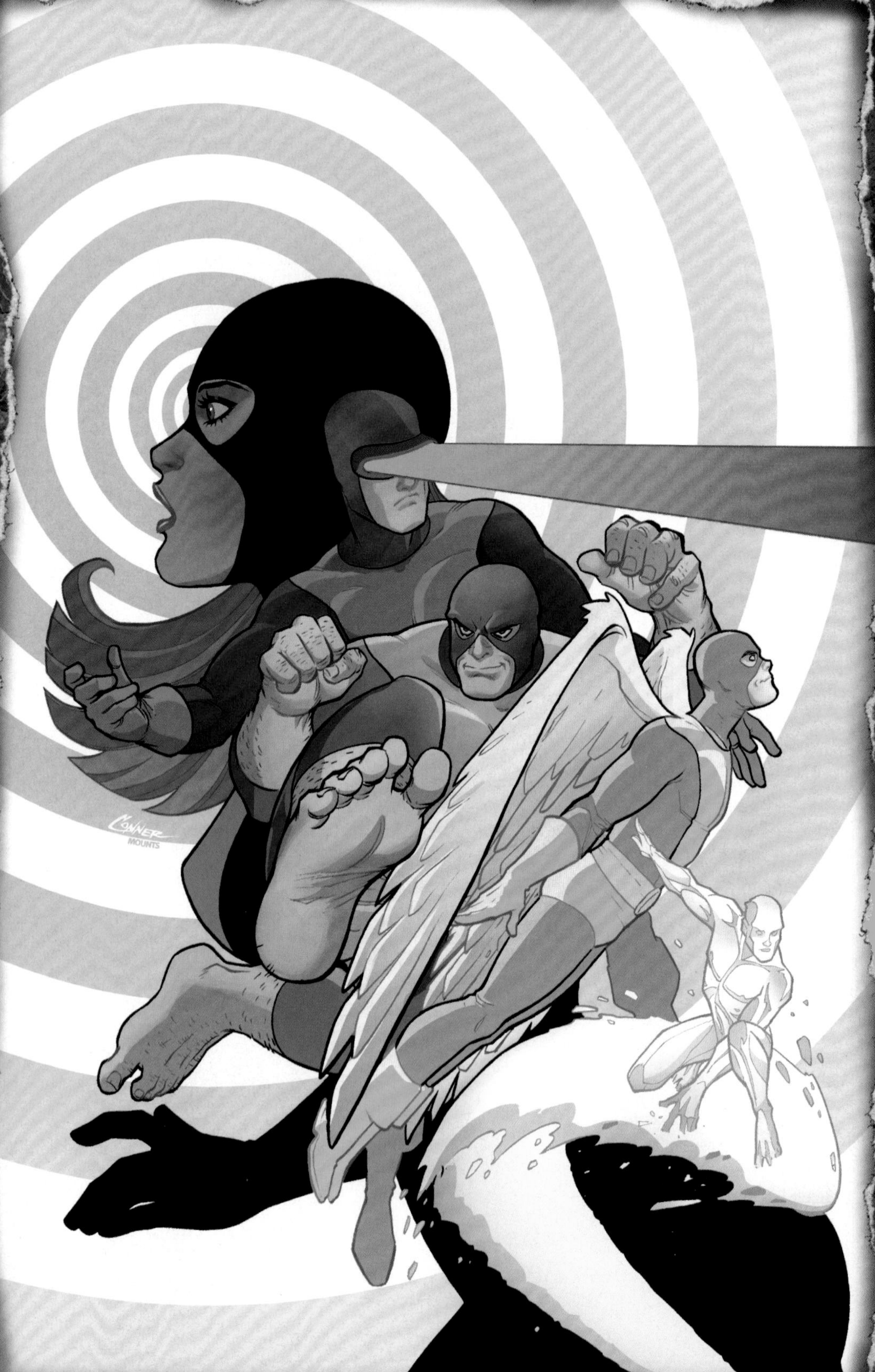
CONNER
MOUNTS

#1 VARIANT Amanda Conner & Paul Mounts

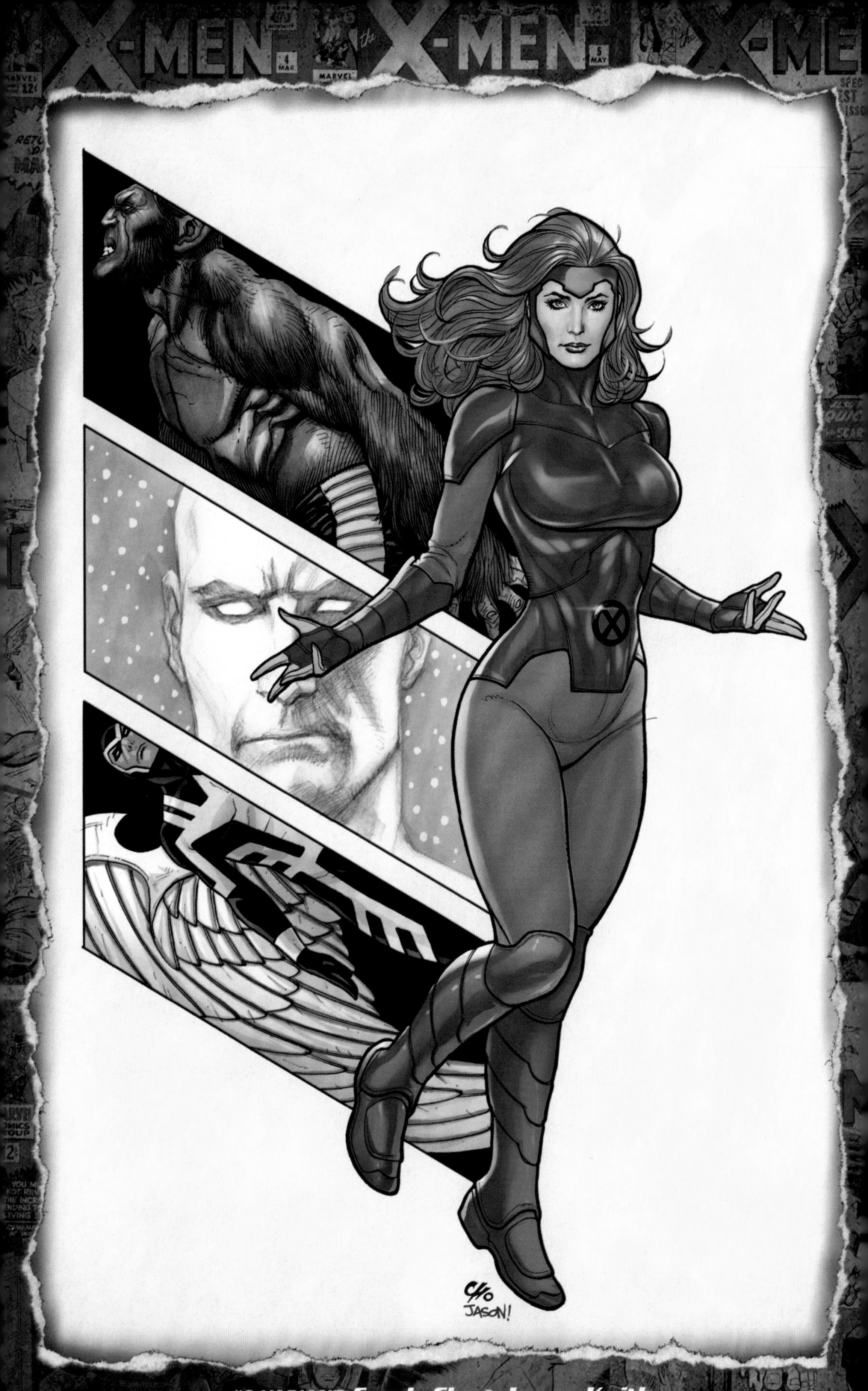
X-MEN
X-MEN
CHO
JASON!

#2 VARIANT **Frank Cho** & **Jason Keith**

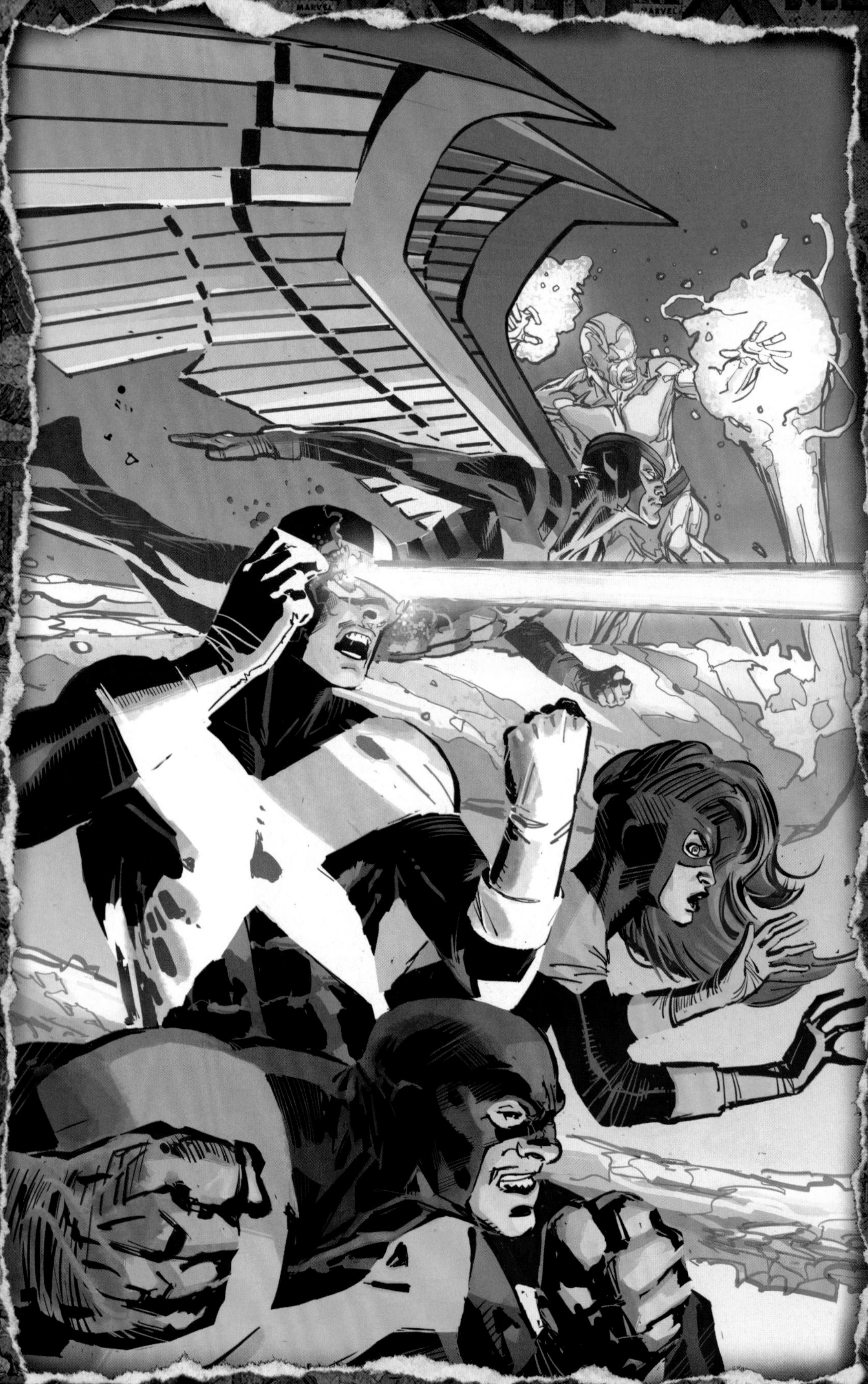

#3 VARIANT **Ron Garney** & **Matt Milla**

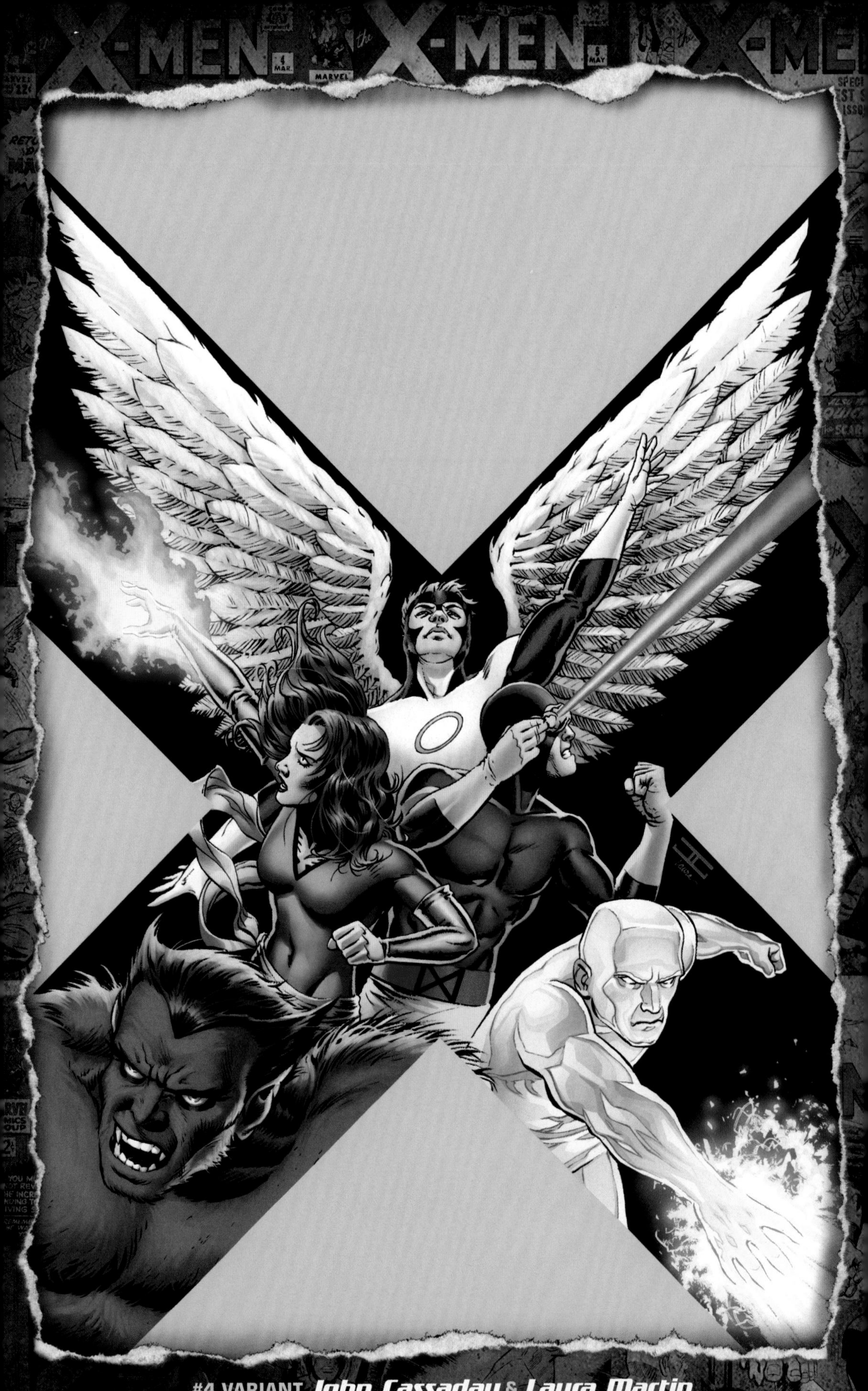
X-MEN
X-MEN
X-MEN

#4 VARIANT ***John Cassaday*** & ***Laura Martin***

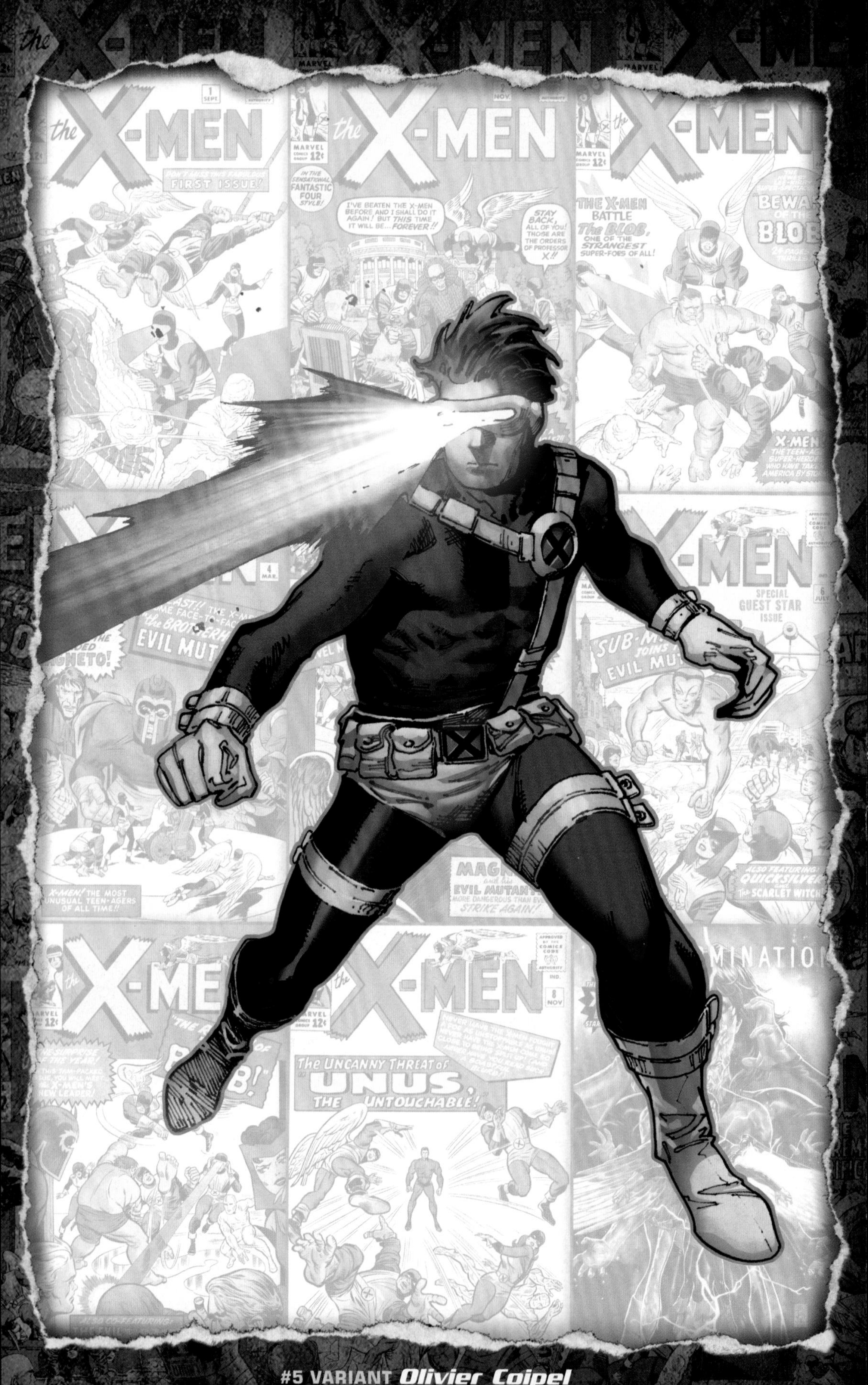
the X-MEN
the X-MEN
FIRST ISSUE!
I'VE BEATEN THE X-MEN BEFORE AND I SHALL DO IT AGAIN! BUT THIS TIME IT WILL BE... FOREVER!!
STAY BACK, ALL OF YOU! THOSE ARE THE ORDERS OF PROFESSOR X!!
IN THE SENSATIONAL FANTASTIC FOUR STYLE!
THE X-MEN BATTLE The BLOB, ONE OF THE STRANGEST SUPER-FOES OF ALL!
X-MEN
SPECIAL GUEST STAR ISSUE
EVIL MUT
X-MEN! THE MOST UNUSUAL TEEN-AGERS OF ALL TIME!!
ALSO FEATURING: QUICKSILVER and The SCARLET WITCH
The UNCANNY THREAT of "UNUS, THE UNTOUCHABLE!"

#5 VARIANT ***Olivier Coipel***

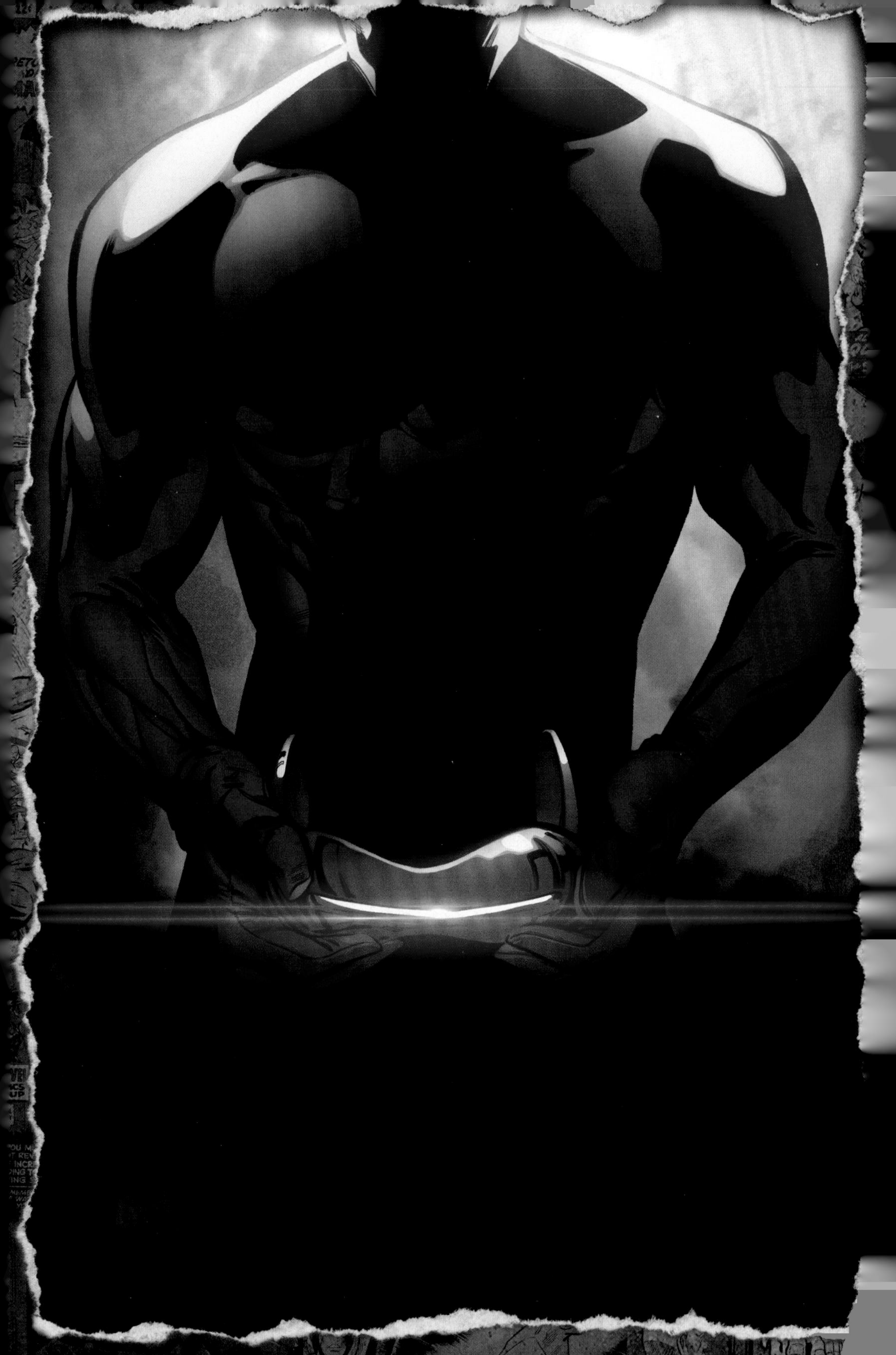

#5 VARIANT Pepe Larraz & Marte Gracia

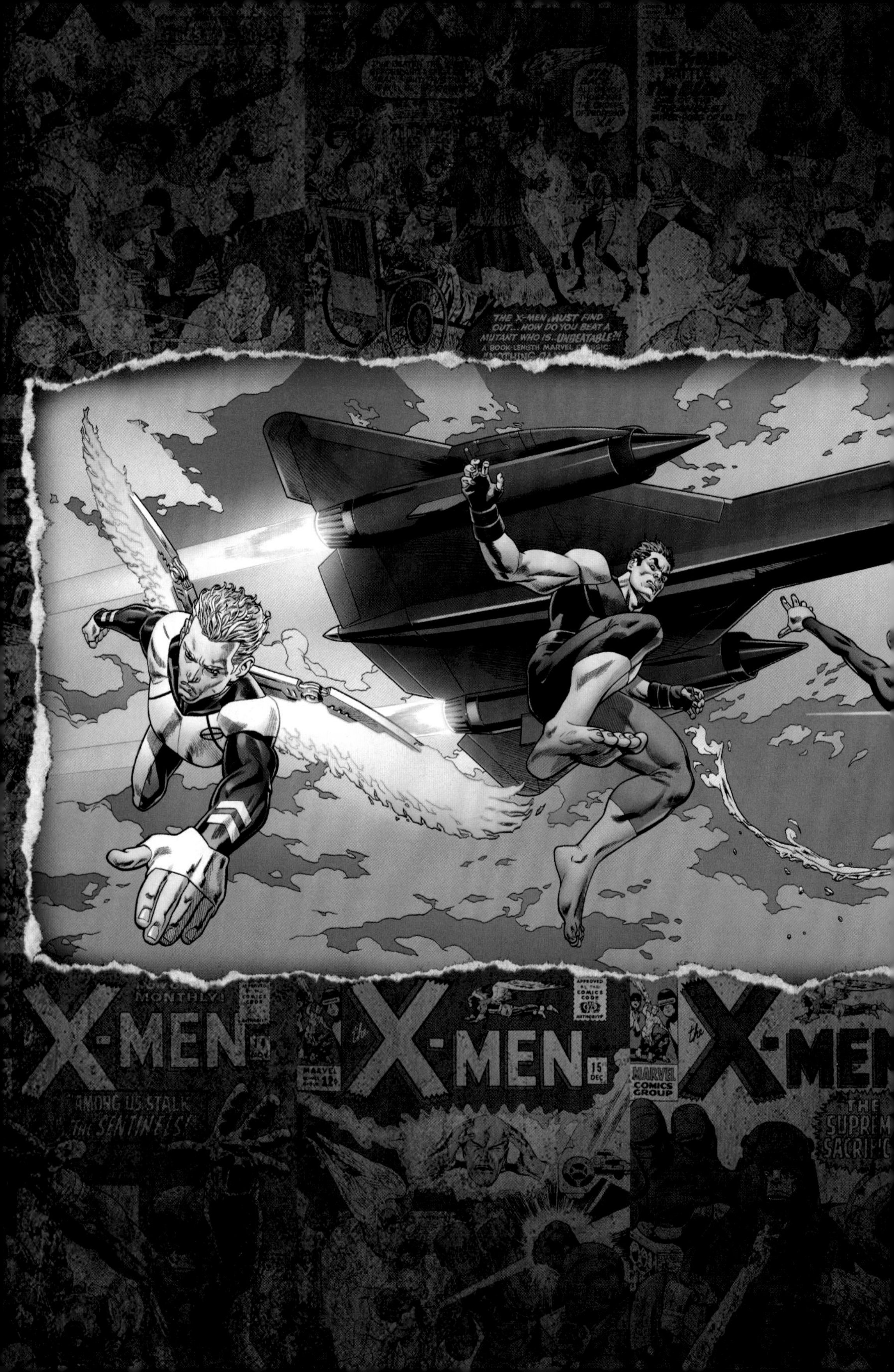
THE X-MEN MUST FIND OUT... HOW DO YOU BEAT A MUTANT WHO IS...UNBEATABLE?!
MONTHLY!
X-MEN
AMONG US STALK THE SENTINELS!
the X-MEN
APPROVED BY THE COMICS CODE AUTHORITY
15 DEC
MARVEL COMICS GROUP

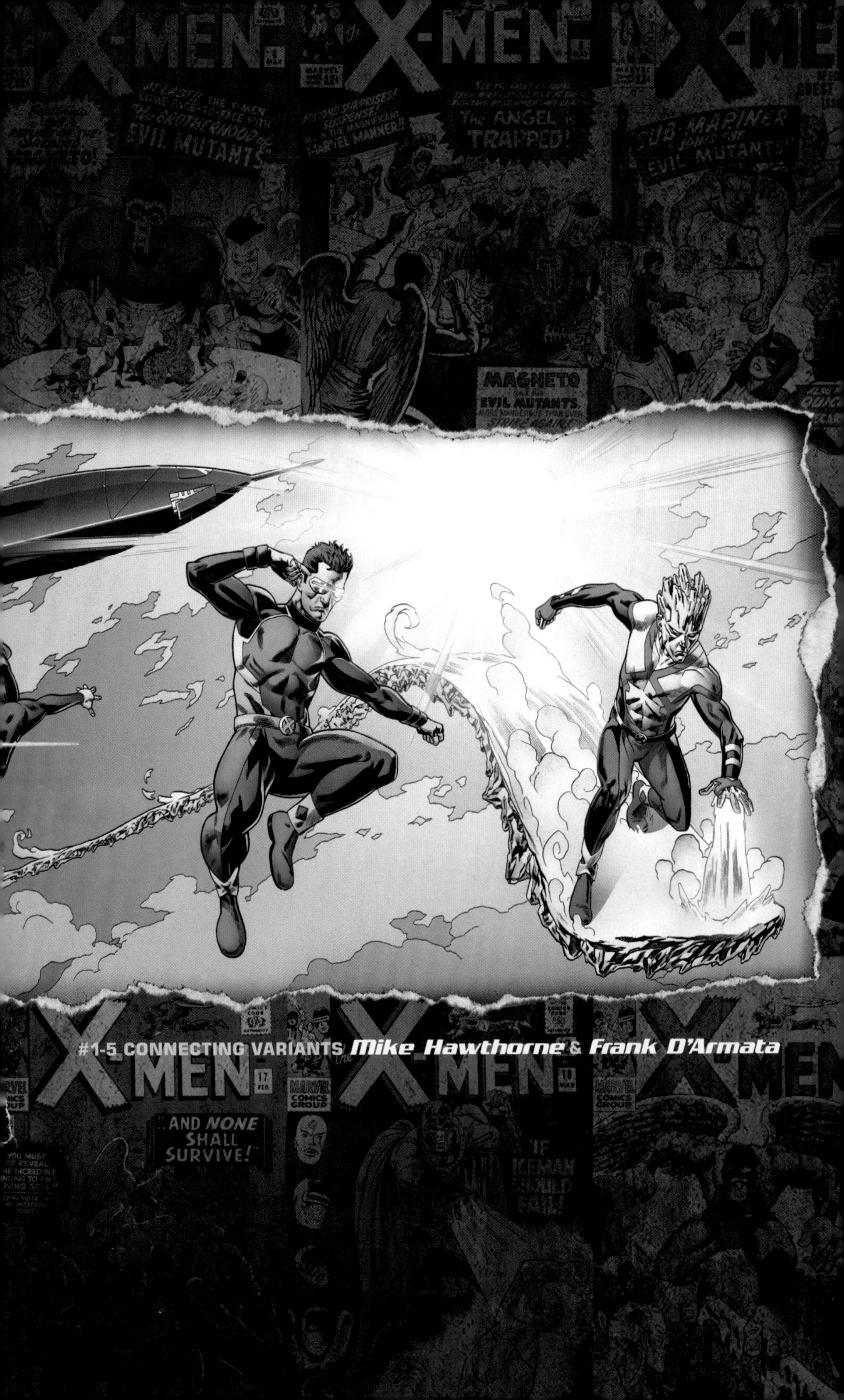
X-MEN
AT LAST!! THE X-MEN COME FACE-TO-FACE WITH The BROTHERHOOD of EVIL MUTANTS
ACTION!! SURPRISES! SUSPENSE! ALL IN THE MAGNIFICENT MARVEL MANNER!!
The ANGEL is TRAPPED!
SUB-MARINER JOINS THE EVIL MUTANTS!
MAGNETO AND HIS EVIL MUTANTS, MORE DANGEROUS THAN EVER, STRIKE AGAIN!
"...AND NONE SHALL SURVIVE!"
IF ICEMAN SHOULD FAIL!

#1-5 CONNECTING VARIANTS *Mike Hawthorne* & *Frank D'Armata*

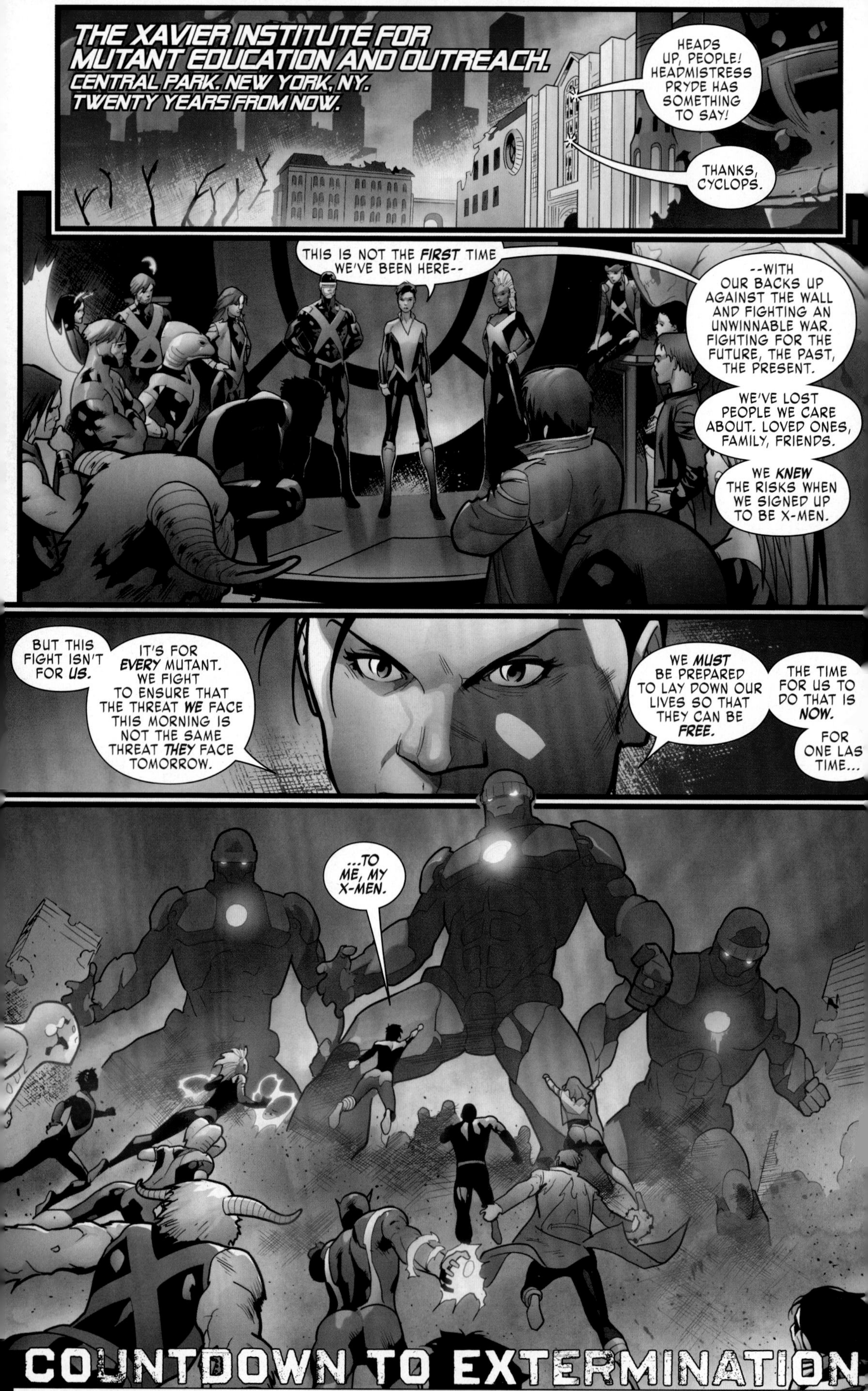
THE XAVIER INSTITUTE FOR MUTANT EDUCATION AND OUTREACH. CENTRAL PARK. NEW YORK, NY. TWENTY YEARS FROM NOW.
HEADS UP, PEOPLE! HEADMISTRESS PRYDE HAS SOMETHING TO SAY!
THANKS, CYCLOPS.
THIS IS NOT THE FIRST TIME WE'VE BEEN HERE--
--WITH OUR BACKS UP AGAINST THE WALL AND FIGHTING AN UNWINNABLE WAR. FIGHTING FOR THE FUTURE, THE PAST, THE PRESENT.
WE'VE LOST PEOPLE WE CARE ABOUT. LOVED ONES, FAMILY, FRIENDS.
WE KNEW THE RISKS WHEN WE SIGNED UP TO BE X-MEN.
BUT THIS FIGHT ISN'T FOR US.
IT'S FOR EVERY MUTANT. WE FIGHT TO ENSURE THAT THE THREAT WE FACE THIS MORNING IS NOT THE SAME THREAT THEY FACE TOMORROW.
WE MUST BE PREPARED TO LAY DOWN OUR LIVES SO THAT THEY CAN BE FREE.
THE TIME FOR US TO DO THAT IS NOW.
FOR ONE LAS TIME...
...TO ME, MY X-MEN.
COUNTDOWN TO EXTERMINATION

WRITER: ED BRISSON ARTIST: OSCAR BAZALDUA COLORIST: ERICK ARCINIEGA LETTERER: VC'S CORY PETIT ASSISTANT EDITOR: CHRIS ROBINSON EDITORS: DARREN SHAN & JORDAN D. WHITE

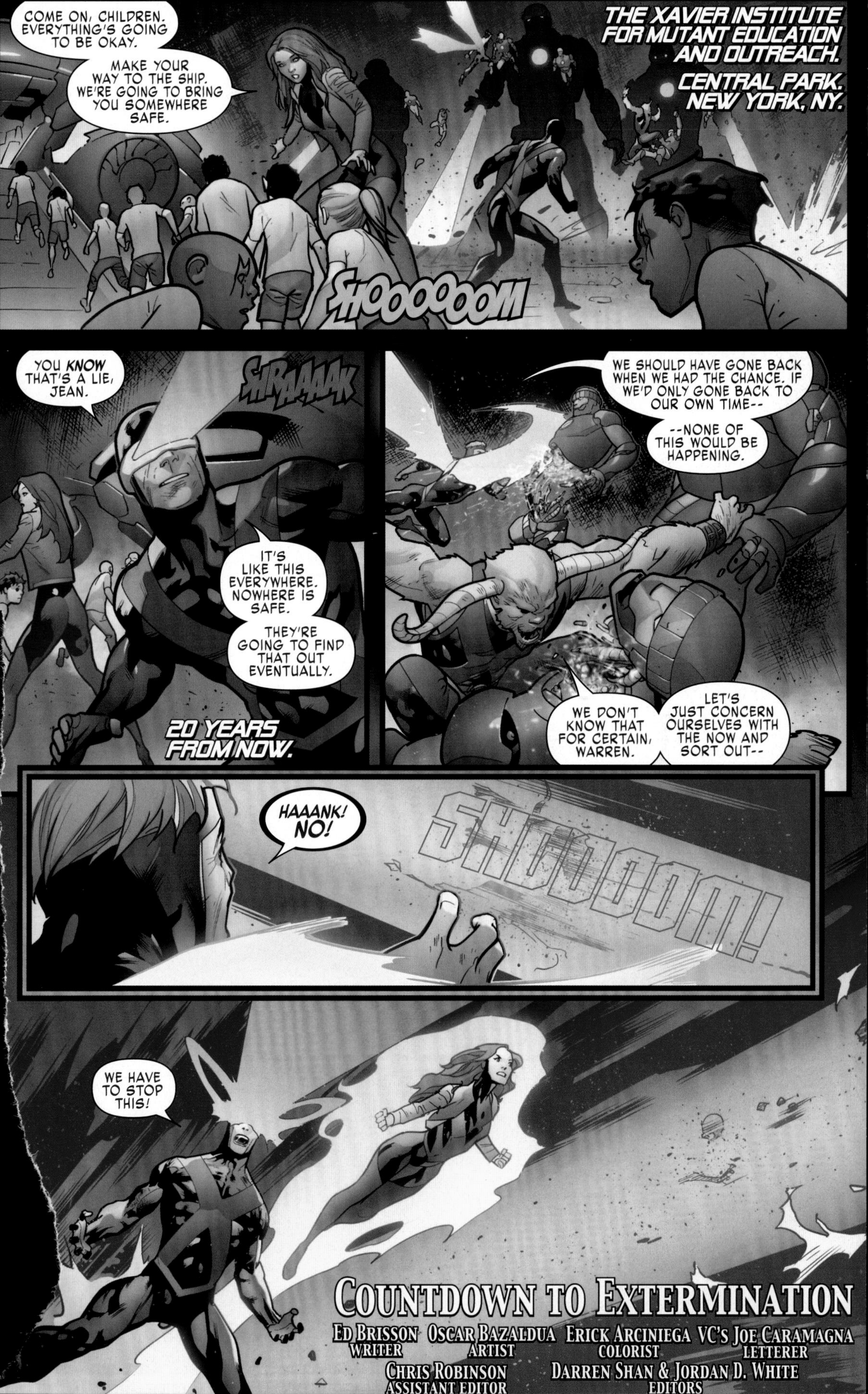
THE XAVIER INSTITUTE FOR MUTANT EDUCATION AND OUTREACH.
CENTRAL PARK. NEW YORK, NY.
COME ON, CHILDREN. EVERYTHING'S GOING TO BE OKAY.
MAKE YOUR WAY TO THE SHIP. WE'RE GOING TO BRING YOU SOMEWHERE SAFE.
SHOOOOOOM
SHRAAAAK
YOU KNOW THAT'S A LIE, JEAN.
IT'S LIKE THIS EVERYWHERE. NOWHERE IS SAFE.
THEY'RE GOING TO FIND THAT OUT EVENTUALLY.
20 YEARS FROM NOW.
WE SHOULD HAVE GONE BACK WHEN WE HAD THE CHANCE. IF WE'D ONLY GONE BACK TO OUR OWN TIME--
--NONE OF THIS WOULD BE HAPPENING.
WE DON'T KNOW THAT FOR CERTAIN, WARREN.
LET'S JUST CONCERN OURSELVES WITH THE NOW AND SORT OUT--
HAAANK! NO!
SHOOOOM!
WE HAVE TO STOP THIS!
COUNTDOWN TO EXTERMINATION
ED BRISSON WRITER
OSCAR BAZALDUA ARTIST
ERICK ARCINIEGA COLORIST
VC's JOE CARAMAGNA LETTERER
CHRIS ROBINSON ASSISTANT EDITOR
DARREN SHAN & JORDAN D. WHITE EDITORS

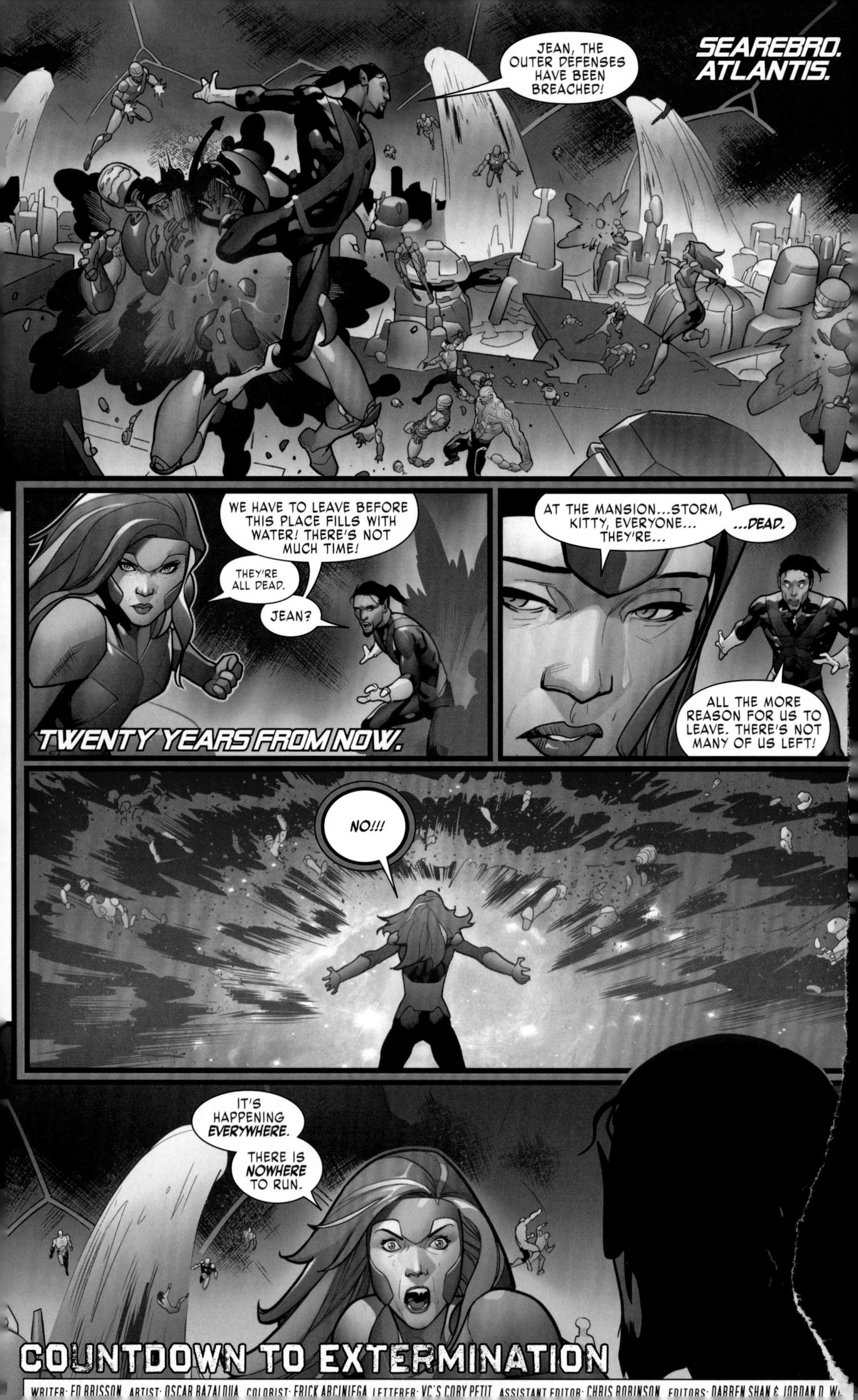

SEAREBRO. ATLANTIS.
JEAN, THE OUTER DEFENSES HAVE BEEN BREACHED!
WE HAVE TO LEAVE BEFORE THIS PLACE FILLS WITH WATER! THERE'S NOT MUCH TIME!
THEY'RE ALL DEAD.
JEAN?
TWENTY YEARS FROM NOW.
AT THE MANSION...STORM, KITTY, EVERYONE... THEY'RE...
...DEAD.
ALL THE MORE REASON FOR US TO LEAVE. THERE'S NOT MANY OF US LEFT!
NO!!!
IT'S HAPPENING EVERYWHERE.
THERE IS NOWHERE TO RUN.
COUNTDOWN TO EXTERMINATION
WRITER: ED BRISSON ARTIST: OSCAR BAZALDUA COLORIST: ERICK ARCINIEGA LETTERER: VC'S CORY PETIT ASSISTANT EDITOR: CHRIS ROBINSON EDITORS: DARREN SHAN & JORDAN D. W

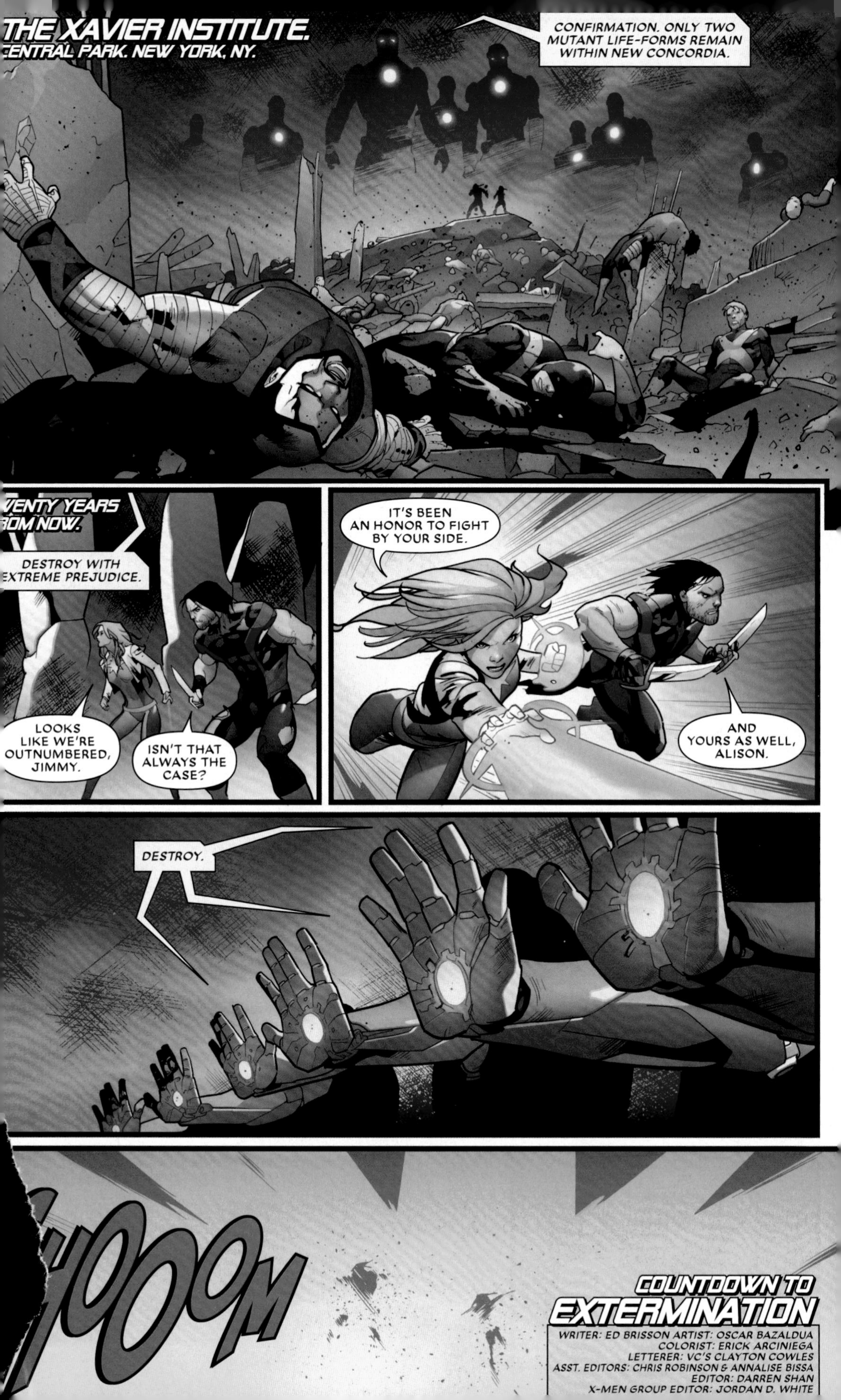
THE XAVIER INSTITUTE.
ENTRAL PARK. NEW YORK, NY.
CONFIRMATION. ONLY TWO MUTANT LIFE-FORMS REMAIN WITHIN NEW CONCORDIA.
VENTY YEARS
ROM NOW.
DESTROY WITH EXTREME PREJUDICE.
LOOKS LIKE WE'RE OUTNUMBERED, JIMMY.
ISN'T THAT ALWAYS THE CASE?
IT'S BEEN AN HONOR TO FIGHT BY YOUR SIDE.
AND YOURS AS WELL, ALISON.
DESTROY.
HOOOM
COUNTDOWN TO EXTERMINATION
WRITER: ED BRISSON ARTIST: OSCAR BAZALDUA
COLORIST: ERICK ARCINIEGA
LETTERER: VC'S CLAYTON COWLES
ASST. EDITORS: CHRIS ROBINSON & ANNALISE BISSA
EDITOR: DARREN SHAN
X-MEN GROUP EDITOR: JORDAN D. WHITE

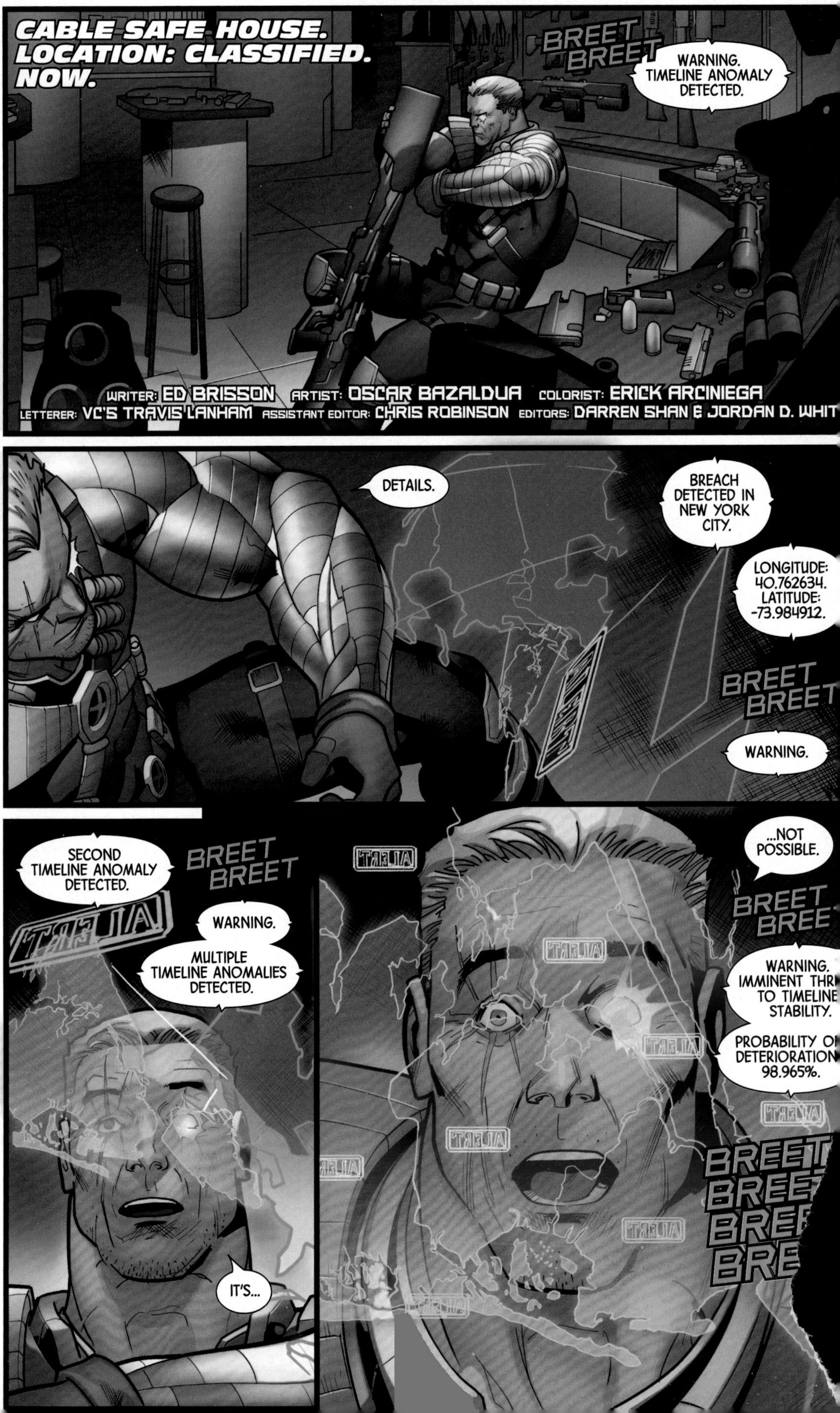
CABLE SAFE HOUSE. LOCATION: CLASSIFIED. NOW.
BREET BREET
WARNING. TIMELINE ANOMALY DETECTED.
WRITER: ED BRISSON ARTIST: OSCAR BAZALDUA COLORIST: ERICK ARCINIEGA
LETTERER: VC'S TRAVIS LANHAM ASSISTANT EDITOR: CHRIS ROBINSON EDITORS: DARREN SHAN & JORDAN D. WHIT
DETAILS.
BREACH DETECTED IN NEW YORK CITY.
LONGITUDE: 40.762634. LATITUDE: -73.984912.
BREET BREET
WARNING.
SECOND TIMELINE ANOMALY DETECTED.
BREET BREET
ALERT
WARNING.
MULTIPLE TIMELINE ANOMALIES DETECTED.
IT'S...
...NOT POSSIBLE.
BREET BREE
WARNING. IMMINENT THR TO TIMELINE STABILITY.
PROBABILITY OI DETERIORATION 98.965%.